The Logic of Fantasy

THE LOGIC OF
FANTASY

H. G. WELLS and SCIENCE FICTION

John Huntington

New York
Columbia University Press
1982

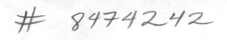
Library of Congress Cataloging in Publication Data

Huntington, John.
The logic of fantasy.

Includes bibliographical references and
index.
1. Wells, H. G. (Herbert George), 1866–1946
—Criticism and interpretation.   2. Science in
literature.   3. Science fiction—History and
criticism.   I. Title.
PR5778.S35H8 1982   823'.912   82-4593
ISBN 0-231-05378-9   AACR2

Columbia University Press
New York   Guildford, Surrey

Clothbound editions of Columbia University Press books are Smyth-sewn
and printed on permanent and durable acid-free paper.

To the memory of my father,
John Willard Huntington,
who first taught me to value the
"experimental inconsistency of an enquiring man."

Contents

Preface

V. S. PRITCHETT observed that "there are always fistfights and fires in the early Wells. Above all, there are fires."[1] This remark must have touched something central to what we conceive as typically Wellsian, for it has been often quoted or alluded to by later critics. Pritchett links this imagery to "the Wellsian optimism" and to what he calls Wells's "ruthlessness." To be sure, those qualities exist in Wells. But the images and acts that Pritchett isolates function in a particular way in Wells: they are not emblems of a philosophy, and they are never unqualified. In the larger economy of Wells's imaginative operations the fires and the fistfights are gestures toward intellectual balance. In themselves the images are violent, but either they oppose a calm that needs disruption, or they contain within themselves elements that counter their own potential violence—a fire goes out; a blow is deflected. These images do not form a part of the utopian totalitarianism or regimentation that is sometimes attributed to Wells; they participate in a daring intellectual order achieved by extravagant imaginative gestures that offset gestures in the opposite direction. Like a clown on a high wire, Wells combines wildness and balance; he looks as if he were about to tumble to one side or another, but at the last moment, by a lunge that itself may look like a fall, he holds the wire. His is an art that while treading a straight line yokes opposites on either side of that line.

Such high wire antics are attractive in themselves, but in Wells they have the additional virtue of being motions in a cognitive activity. The balance in disarray that Wells achieves in his early fiction has an intellectual quality; it marks a dialectical exploration of the area he has charted. Here the high wire simile may be too frivolous, for in Wells's fiction the lungings are those of rational consciousness feeling out the possibilities of the intellectual space. Though extravagant and inconclusive, such intellectual movement and balance is a way of thinking.

Wells's scientific romances constitute both an important experiment in and a central model for such thought. By studying the way Wells's imagination works in his fiction we can get a clearer idea of what problems and issues have to be treated if we are to think about the possibilities of British civilization at the beginning of this century. And by comparing the logic of his scientific romances with that of other Wells works and with science fiction by other writers, we can begin to explain the possibilities and failures of the form in general.

To understand the value of Wells's accomplishment, we must get beyond the easy praise that is sometimes accorded science fiction. At its simplest the party line goes that SF is prophetic. Jules Verne's complaint in 1903 that Wells was not dealing in real technological possibilities set up a criterion for the form that misses the point.[2] Aside from some close "hits"—Verne sends Captain Barbican around the moon from a hill near Tampa—the specific predictions of SF are generally trivial. And even if they were more significant, such prophecies are undependable: for every trip originating in Florida there are hundreds from such places as Kent (Wells) or Pikes Peak (Heinlein), and only hindsight reveals which were prophetic and which merely "imaginative." And if Verne gets Florida right, the rest of the story has still no particular relevance to the shape of things to come. The social ideas are quaintly antique, and even the technology, for all its realism, brings a smile: Verne shoots his astronauts from a cannon; the team travels with "a ten gallon demijohn of Gibson's old Monogram" and a pair of friendly dogs; no one bothers to plan a return until the projectile is on its way.[3] More modern fancies contain a similar mixture of the pleasant, true, and absurd. I do not mean at all to claim that such literature is useless for such mixtures, but surely whatever prophetic value it has is minimal.

A more satisfying description of the form's distinctiveness argues that SF exercises the reader's imagination by breaking down old assumptions and habits of seeing and by offering new possibilities. Thus, though the vision may not be of what will actually happen, by helping the reader enact a restructuring of conventional presumptions SF opens the way for true innovation and change. The enthusiasts speak of "the sense of wonder," and though the phrase is vague and ambiguous, often only an advertising catchphrase, it is nevertheless a stab in the direction of describing a special quality. But the enthusiasts' dream of a literature is betrayed by most of the actual production. The popular SF of "the golden age," which is supposed to stimulate its readership to imagine change, tells us little and asks little of us. It is basically a conservative popular art form which, as I have elsewhere argued,[4] reconciles freedom and necessity in order to console its addicted readership.

Once we have seen through the claims of popular SF, however, we become aware that the important questions have yet to be confronted. By proving that a certain literature is unprepared to think about the future, we merely sidestep the disturbing and important question, how can any literature think about the future? Darko Suvin's definition of SF as the "literature of cognitive estrangement" is a useful move toward answering this question.[5] Suvin gives a rigorous meaning to the vague sense of wonder, though in doing so he also, necessarily, ends up restricting the field severely. The works that the sense-of-wonder school tends most to admire—American pulp SF in particular—Suvin finds trivial, and many of the works that Suvin finds most central to the form the popularists find boring. At the core of this disagreement lies a political debate about the nature and necessity of change. Yet the two schools do find common ground in Wells. Here, all agree, is a literature both of "wonder" and of "cognitive estrangement."

Wells's scientific romances define a new form and have remained a popular model as the form evolved. In the early days of SF magazines Wells's stories were frequently reprinted.[6] But what the example of Wells represented remains unclear. Suvin has begun to clarify the relationship between Wells and modern SF by analyzing *The Time Machine* as a "structural model" for one sort of SF. He derives from Wells's novella the rule that "the principle of a Wellsian structure of science fiction is mutation of scientific into aesthetic cognition."[7] That is a useful start; it posits a special kind of thought and distinguishes it from scientific thought, thus placing the form in the literary realm where it belongs while at the same time acknowledging its special connection to other ways of thinking. What needs further analysis is the nature and structure of that "aesthetic cognition."

For the study of Wells's "aesthetic cognition" *The Time Machine* is central, but in isolation it is a misleading model: it is untypically programmatic and is more carefully rationalized and explained than is common for Wells. *The Time Machine* is best viewed as the quintessence of a larger project, the whole body of early romances and stories which constitutes a coherent imaginative whole. This corpus is an extraordinary creation, focused on crucial issues of civilization and its future, to a surprising degree deeply systematic, but ultimately uncommitted, free from the need to prove anything, true to the problems it can discover rather than to their solution.

Before we can analyze this accomplishment, we need to understand some of the contradictions in Wells's own sense of his mission. We can see his own confidence that he is up to something important and his confusion about what it is in the way he tries to describe his achievement in a letter to his friend Arnold Bennett in 1902. He is offering Bennett advice on an article the latter is writing, and he indignantly puts his work apart from and above the kind of adventure Jules Verne had written:

> There's a quality in the worst of my so-called "pseudo-scientific"—(imbecile adjective) stuff that the American [critic] doesn't master which differentiates it from Jules Verne, e.g. just as Swift is differentiated from fantasia—isn't there? There is something other than either story writing or artistic merit which has emerged through the series of my books, something one might regard as a new system of ideas—"thought." It's in *Anticipations* especially Ch IX and it's in my Royal Institution Lecture and it's also in *The First Men in the Moon* and *The Invisible Man* and Chaffery's chapter in *Love and Mr. L[ewisham]*. That's as much as I can say to you in this matter if we talked all day.[8]

This is a curious list. The frustration Wells expresses in the last sentence of the quotation may derive from his having mistaken some broad thematic similarities for a "system of ideas." We might note, for instance, that there is a recurrent "ruthlessness" of the sort Pritchett points to in all these works. But no sooner have we noted that identity than we have also to remark that the ruthlessness is treated in very different ways. Griffin in *The Invisible Man* and the New Man in *Anticipations* are daring and solitary, but Griffin is a monster in a fiction while the New Man is the projected hero of what Wells claims is a real future. Griffin is the object of criticism; the New Man the object of praise.

In my first chapter I will begin to clarify the bases of this confusion by distinguishing between two ways of thought that Wells employs, what he would later categorize as "undirected thought" and "directed thought." If "directed thought" strives toward a method of achieving solutions to consciously posed problems, "undirected thought" disclaims conclusions; it meditates on the sources of difficulty and conflict. In blunt terms, Wells's career is a movement from the "undirected thought" of the scientific romances toward the "directed thought" of his later work, both fiction and nonfiction.

"Directed thought" is an accomplishment of a high order, to be sure, yet it is only within the inconclusive ironic universe of undirected thought that Wells can do justice to one of the great puzzles of the late Victorian era, the conflict between evolution and ethics. In this first chapter, after explicating the broad structural distinctions to be observed in Wells's works, we will survey the evolution-ethics debate in Darwin and T. H. Huxley in order to establish the base of the logical system by which Wells will be able to explore the central contradictions of his civilization. The dilemma of evolution and ethics will serve as both a structural and as a thematic core for the whole book, and we will learn to distinguish works and writers according to how they treat it.

Chapters 2 through 5 explicate this system by a detailed analysis of Wells's early fiction. Chapter 2 analyzes the short stories and *The Wonderful Visit* to display the simple logical devices that structure Wells's early fiction and to show how such fiction can be said to "think." Chapter 3 studies one work, *The Time Machine*, as a distilled essence of the whole system. Chapter 4 traces how broad thematic problems of civilization, especially problems posed by aliens and by domination, are formulated and explored throughout the body of the early work. Though this chapter refers to the whole of Wells's early work, it focuses on two novels, *The Island of Doctor Moreau* and *The War of the Worlds*, as the most extensive and complex meditations on the evolutionary and ethical puzzle. Chapter 5 examines two works, "A Story of the Days to Come" and *The First Men in the Moon*, which attain a totally balanced rendering of the contradictions that occupy Wells and thereby represent a crisis of the system.

Chapter 6 charts the ways Wells tries to convert his undirected thought into directed thought and to resolve some of the puzzles he has so accurately rendered in his early fiction. Because they fail to remain true to the difficulties and the logic that give the earlier fiction its clarity and integrity, the works we will be studying here may appear as a decline. But they also mark a necessary advance. As Wells begins to write for change, to advocate and to predict forms and inventions, he becomes more politically specific and he recedes into the issues of his own time. If, thanks to our experience of the twentieth century we may tend to view Wells's cheerful and rational arguments in these works as dated, naive, at times innocently dangerous, nevertheless, we have to admire Wells's attempt to go beyond merely understanding the dilemmas of civilization and to advocate solutions. After all, he might have retired to a supercilious and ironic distance and, safe in his popularity, enjoyed the fatal unfolding of disaster. Wells's humane intelligence inspired him to political advocacy which, as it sacrifices the more general and universal for the historically specific, also assumes responsibility for its world.

What emerges through the course of the examination of Wells's logic and his movement from undirected to directed thought is the isolation and definition of a special form of thought which in the final chapter I will call *anti-utopian*. I have intentionally refrained from applying such a title to this form throughout the main part of the book for two reasons. First, I do not want to posit the form; I want to derive it from the analysis of Wells's own development of it and his consequent abandonment of it. Second, once we understand the form, anti-utopia seems an apt name for it, but until we achieve that understanding, the name, because it loosely suggests a pessimistic and conservative political stance which I do not want to include in my meaning, may be more misleading than helpful. In this last chapter we are in a position to define *anti-utopia* and to demonstrate it to be significantly different from *dystopia* on the basis of its different logical mode. Though my focus will remain on Wells, I have also in this chapter looked to Zamyatin, Orwell, Bradbury, and Huxley in order to trace some broader possibilities and limits of the anti-utopian and dystopian modes.

Throughout the book I aim to understand how this anti-utopian thought works, not by developing a theoretical justification for it, but by the practical critical activity of watching it in action, of studying the texts closely and examining the ways they set up and treat opposition. But it would be naive to believe that the procedures of reading that I am employing are self-evident. Certainly Wells's texts do not inevitably attract such methods; if they did this study would have been made decades ago. Even such a practical study as this must acknowledge certain methodological influences, in this case structuralist (especially Lévi-Strauss) and to a lesser extent Marxist (especially Lukács) theories, two schools that emphasize the importance of thinking by opposition and contradiction. The debts, however, are to general ways of thinking rather than to single insights. The charts and diagrams that at one stage of the writing littered the manuscript have been translated back into prose. My goal has been to avoid the esoteric, to be as clear as I can about subjects and as simple as I can with methods that tend to lure their students and practitioners into obscurity and entangle them in complexity.

Since my attention to contradiction has a superficial resemblance to the championing of "the Baroque" by the proponents of "Geistes-geschichte," let me here disclaim any close connection. René Wellek's essay, "The Parallelism between Literature and the Arts" has to my mind completely exposed the obfuscation and subjective delusion that often mar the method of "Geistesgeschichte."[9] But in addition to this disavowal of descent, let me also point out that I am making none of the historical or cultural claims that traditionally go along with proving that a writer is "baroque" or "classical." I am interested in the logical implications of fictional forms, and though I may find one logical structure more intellectually provocative than another, my sub-ject, Wells himself, used any number of forms. Thus, even if I wanted to, I could not claim that a single style of dealing with contradiction is particularly English, or scientific, or Victorian, or even "postmodern."

I cannot, nor do I want to, deny my debt to some values we associate with the New Criticism. I remember certain essays from *The Well Wrought Urn* and certain classes, especially with Reuben Brower and his disciples, as my first inklings that literary criticism not only could do something different from philosophy and history but could be intellectually valuable and rigorous. If I look back and sometimes won-der at the easy assumption that one can simply "read," I also bridle at the claims of some recent critics to have overthrown the naive New Critics. I do not propose to engage in a debate about theory here. Suffice it for me to acknowledge the broad shoulders on which I stand even as I reach out to other critical traditions.

Finally, a study such as this one, whatever its claims to originality, is inevitably deeply indebted to previous scholars. My argument takes off from the basic work of Bergonzi, Philmus, Hillegas, Parrinder, and others.[10] Wells has not been the center of interpretative controversy, and I do not intend to make him such a center. My goal is not to replace or dispute previous criticism, but to renew inquiry and thought into some simple and basic questions that have always been implicit in the praise of Wells and of SF but which have not yet been studied for themselves.[11]

Acknowledgments

I wish to thank the Rutgers University Research Board for a summer grant during the tenure of which I began this book, and the Graduate College of the University of Illinois at Chicago for grants for the summers of 1977 and 1979.

Versions of chapters 2 and 7 have appeared in *Science-Fiction Studies*, and a sketch of the method and argument of the whole book appeared as an essay, "H. G. Wells," in Patrick Parrinder, ed., *Science Fiction: A Critical Guide* (London: Longman, 1979).

I can no longer disentangle the specific contributions of my family, friends, colleagues, teachers, and students. I hope they will take occasion to remind me what I owe them. For wonderful discussions, not just about Wells, but about art, literature, and politics that have deeply shaped this book, I thank especially Clark Hulse, Mary Huntington, William Keach, Kenneth Lewes, Barry Qualls, John Richetti, and Ellen Stone. Richard Newton singlehandedly renewed my interest in science fiction. David Hemmendinger has spent many hours patiently helping me understand science and philosophy. Judy Gardiner, Chris Messenger, and Virginia Wexman have given me the kind of honest and helpful readings and advice that can come only from true friends.

The Logic of Fantasy

CHAPTER 1

The Logic of Evolution and Ethics

W HEN we read Wells now, more than thirty years after his death and more than eighty-five years after his first works appeared, we get a picture of him and of his importance that is somewhat different from that experienced by his contemporaries. Alive, Wells was an immense personality, an actor on the historical stage who so occupied his audience's attention with his presence and was so adept at responding to the immediate issues of the times that the more meditative questions of his many undertakings seldom could receive much considered thought.[1] To praise him was to choose a program; to condemn him was to enter into polemical opposition. Books and essays that were enormously important in their time—for instance the essays around the First World War or even *The Outline of History*—now appear dated and naive. And works that Wells's contemporaries, and often even Wells himself, tended to ignore in the rush of history, now begin to take on a significance that they could never have had in their own time.[2] Wells's importance as a thinker is different now from what it was when he was alive and active.

A major source of confusion for our present understanding of Wells's importance is that Wells himself thought about the future in two very different ways. If before 1900 he tended to think ironically and to put much of his most adventuresome imaginative energy into writing fantasies, after 1900 he paid increasing attention to developing modes of forecasting. We can depict that difference loosely as one between fiction and nonfiction, or at a more precise level as the difference between the scientific romance and the future forecast. Though that dichotomy has a certain obvious truth as it stands, it explains little. There are, after all, fictions that we now see as future forecasts and forecasts that time has revealed to be fictions. To understand both

Wells's intellectual accomplishment and his confusion we need to explore the structure and possibility of the two modes more carefully.

The split between forecast and fantasy represents a distinction between two kinds of thought process which late in his career Wells would neatly define as that between "directed thought," which enters philosophy with Plato and defines the scientific aspect of modern civilization, and "undirected thought," which is basic to primitive, nontechnological civilization.[3] "Undirected thought" is "imaginative play" checked by experience and thus close to but different from mere dreaming. "Directed thought" is purposeful and conscious; it arrives at conclusions; it leads to actions and exclusions:

> This change-over from a mental life that was merely experience checked imagining to an analytical mental life aiming at new and better Knowledge and leading on to planned and directed effort, is still in progress. It is the greatest change in the methods and nature of conscious life that has ever occurred. It is still only partly achieved. Over a large range of his interests man has still to acquire the habit of thinking with self-control and precision.[4]

This praise of directed thought is, in effect, praise of a myth of scientific method.[5] It is also praise of the kind of thinking Wells began to engage in at the turn of the century in *Anticipations.*

Wells himself saw his movement toward directed thought as an advance, but it is debatable whether the evolution was altogether fortunate. The problem with directed thought, whatever its stimulation and interest, is that it strives to reduce complexity. It generates results, but at a sacrifice. Insofar as it constitutes a genuine category of thought, its quality depends, not on the sensitivity, accuracy, intricacy, or truth of the process of thought, but on the validity and usefulness of the conclusions. One can catalogue and evaluate such thought according to its "ideas." Directed thought lends itself to practical evaluation: at its purest it is either right or wrong, productive or dead-ended. But, attractive as that clarity may be, it seldom can account for the richness and the ambiguity that characterize history itself. Directed thought is valuable in the laboratory and the boardroom, but it is a severely flawed technique in less controlled situations.

The sacrifices directed thought can entail are extravagantly demonstrated in Wells's last work, *Mind at the End of Its Tether* (1945).[6] Here for the last time Wells plays the prophet and predicts disaster. He asserts that in the last "weeks and months" the situation of "self-conscious existence" has changed and "the end of everything we call life is close at hand and cannot be evaded." It is the "irrationality" of this new age, the failure of the "congruences with mind" of the "secular process," that has convinced him of the disaster to come:

> Our universe is not merely bankrupt; there remains no dividend at all; it has not simply liquidated; it is going clean out of existence, leaving not a wrack behind. The attempt to trace a pattern of any sort is absolutely futile. (p. 77)

We sense this prose straining to say something precise and conclusive about the future. Despite the vagueness of his evidence, Wells here strives to picture a single and inevitable shape: disaster and ruin.

Single-minded as the assertion may be, it is expressed in a prediction that is absolutely vague. Is Wells talking about the end of high capitalist civilization? The end of the West? The end of industrial technology? The end of humanity? The end of the earth? The end of the universe? Perhaps it is only the end of H. G. Wells that he is perceiving when he talks of "the end of everything we call life." He further confuses the prediction by an occasional rhetorical understatement that makes the apocalyptic postures seem absurdly excessive: "something is happening so that life will never be *quite* the same again" (p. 69, Wells's emphasis). But then within two paragraphs he is saying, "The writer is convinced that there is no way out or round or through the impasse. It is the end." In this last work Wells strives for a conclusive and direct statement and, ironically, generates a meaningless ambiguity.

Contrast with this confused prediction of disaster a celebrated paragraph from Wells's first important published work, "The Rediscovery of the Unique" (1891). The universe, he here asserts, is composed of completely unique units; even atoms, if studied closely enough, will be seen to be each different from any other. The classifications of science are, therefore, artificial falsifications, and all perceptions of order are illusions:

> Science is a match that man has just got alight. He thought he was in a room—in moments of devotion, a temple—and that his light would be reflected from and display walls inscribed with wonderful secrets and pillars carved with philosophical systems wrought into harmony. It is a curious sensation, now that the preliminary splutter is over and the flame burns up clear, to see his hands lit and just a glimpse of himself and the patch he stands on visible, and around him, in place of all that human comfort and beauty he anticipated—darkness still.[7]

The difference between this passage and the argument of *Mind at the End of Its Tether* lies, not in their messages—both despair of pattern—but in the difference between a mode of thought that develops an abstract, rigid, and unintentionally ambiguous conclusion and one which builds an image which, while its allegory is debatable, holds together in complex balance a whole range of contradictory thoughts. If the darkness here represents disillusionment and incomprehension, the clear burning match and the illumined hands represent a genuine achievement. If the author can scoff at some of the expectations—a temple, indeed!—he also partakes in the disappointment. And if he is perhaps skeptical about further discoveries of temples and pillars, he nevertheless withholds the conclusion and allows the double possibilities of the present vision, the small light burning clear in the enveloping darkness, to suffice and carry the meaning.

In the directed thought of *Mind at the End of Its Tether*, we see the stiffness of a mind trying to bring an intuition down to a single conclusion; in the more undirected mode of "The Rediscovery of the Unique" we see the mind enjoying the complexity and contradictory attitudes implicit in the subject. Here he is not trying to reduce it to a single conclusion or result. Both passages have their ambiguities, but those of the late work are evasive and rhetorical, the consequences of a desperate attempt to convince the reader of a single truth, while those of the early work are intrinsic to the subject and reflect a complex balance of hope and skepticism. If *Mind at the End of its Tether* seeks a single conclusion, "The Rediscovery of the Unique" delights in the process of thought itself.

The two modes of thought lead to different ways of thinking about the future. Directed thought, based on the model of positivist science, seeks unitary answers about the future, what can be called "forecasts." Undirected thought abjures such solutions; it wanders in the maze of balances and conflicts that compose history. If the former will be judged on the accuracy of its predictions, the latter will be judged on the aesthetic pattern it achieves, on the moral complexity it encompasses.

Wells makes his clearest statement of his faith that directed thought can usefully forecast the future in "The Discovery of the Future" (1902), the Royal Institution lecture he refers to in the latter to Arnold Bennett we looked at in the Preface. Wells's main axiom is that "in absolute fact the future is just as fixed and determinate, just as settled and inevitable, just as possible a matter of knowledge as the past."[8] Wells's model for thinking about the future here is the science of geology which has been able to reason backwards to events and times of which we have no witness or verbal report:

> If it has been possible for men by picking out a number of suggestive and significant looking things in the present, by comparing them, criticising them, and discussing them, with a perpetual insistence upon "Why?" without any guiding tradition, and indeed in the teeth of established beliefs, to construct the amazing searchlight of inference into the remoter past, is it really, after all, such an extravagant and hopeless thing to suggest that by seeking for operating causes instead of for fossils, and by criticising them as persistently and thoroughly as the geological record has been criticised, it may be possible to throw a searchlight of inference forward instead of backward, and to attain to a knowledge of coming things as clear, as universally convincing, and infinitely more important to mankind than the clear vision of the past that geology has opened to us during the nineteenth century? (pp. 372–73)

The consideration of large numbers of individuals together, Wells argues, should simplify the project, for on the analogy of a heap of sand, "the whole may be simpler than its component parts" (p. 377). As he must if he is going to maintain the analogy with the sand pile, Wells emphatically rejects any belief in the power of "great Men" to shape history.[9]

"The Discovery of the Future" represents a special moment of assurance and clarity for Wells, but we should note that even at this moment of confident revelation Wells introduces ambiguities that deprive such directed thought of its conclusive power. He undermines the scientific aspect of forecasting the future by declaring that he sees a "purpose" in the sandheap of history. After listing possible catastrophes that might simply annihilate humanity and terminate history (cosmic collisions, new pestilences, new predators, sheer entropy), Wells declares, "I do not believe in these things because I have come to believe in certain other things—in the coherency and purpose in the world and in the greatness of human destiny" (p. 386).[10] Such a faith becomes the basis for excluding any future which, however scientifically plausible, the author would rather not contemplate.

This trust in "destiny" severely flaws the predictive enterprise; Wells, in spite of his claim to a naturalist method, shows up here as a rather naive historicist. If naturalism assumes that the present dynamic of society, like the shape of the sandheap, is universal, historicism believes that in order to comprehend history one must respect the uniqueness of each historical moment and see the way the stage under study will change, the way it aligns with the "process of history." According to historicism, the historian does not imitate the physical or natural scientist; he develops a special science, that of history itself, in order to understand the process of social change. Wells's positivist naturalism, according to this view, would mistake a surface sequence of events as the movement of history; the demographic, economic, and technological changes that so concern Wells are merely the symptoms of the "historical process," and until one understands the underlying process one cannot make satisfactory sense of the surface phenomena. But to argue this will be to argue against scientific prediction of the sort Wells proposes. As Karl Popper proves, the historicist undertakings, whether Wells's vague trust in "coherence" and "destiny" or the more elaborate historicisms of Plato, Marx, or even National Socialism, fail themselves to offer any scientific method.[11] In effect, if we accept any sort of historicism, we must give up altogether the hope of trustworthy prediction on the pattern of the natural sciences. To put it another way, Wells's belief in "purpose" and "destiny" renders irrelevant the "scientific" mode of understanding he is in the act of proposing. Scientific prediction has become mere superstition.

The compromises in the presentation of the case for scientific prediction, like the ambiguity of *Mind at the End of Its Tether,* are signs of the inadequacy of directed thought to deal with history. We might further note that by its own criteria of useful results and practical conclusions, the record of Wells's directed thought about the future, while it has some stimulating prospects, is finally unimpressive. We need only point to the failures of his prophesies in the early twenties of a World State and a Universal Religion. And if failure of a forecast were enough to disprove the method, we could drop the topic right here; certainly forecasting itself would be in poor repute. But no prophet seems much daunted by his or her predecessors' failures. The method which Wells here fathered lives on, even thrives. It is not our purpose here to examine in detail its possibilities or deficits; later, in chapter 6, we will examine some of the logical problems that arise when Wells attempts to practice the method. Let it here suffice to observe that the method exists and that it represents a way of thought antithetical to the undirected, aesthetic mode of most of Wells's early fiction.

The difference between the earlier undirected mode and the later directed mode can be clearly seen if we look at the essay, "Zoological Retrogression," published a decade before "The Discovery of the Future." In place of the assured vision of linear cause and effect that he projects in "The Discovery of the Future," here Wells draws our attention to the way opposites balance. He sets out to counter the optimists who interpret evolutionary theory as describing the past as a "great scroll of nature [that] has been steadily unfolding to reveal a constantly richer harmony of forms and successively higher grades of being," and who look to the future for more of the same.[12] The problem with this kind of argument, Wells says, is not that the prediction itself is necessarily wrong, but that the mode of thought is single and linear. "On the contrary," he argues against the optimists, "there is almost always associated with the suggestion of advance in biological phenomena an opposite idea, which is its essential complement." Wells does not simply champion retrogression against the optimists' view of progression; he asks for a contrapuntal view of biological history that will accept both directions even in their contradiction: "The toneless glare of optimistic evolution would then be softened by a shadow; . . . the too sweet harmony of the spheres would be enhanced by a discord."

The translation of biological argument into aesthetic terms is revealing; it points to the basis of Wells's philosophical position: he is not simply the informed evolutionist enforcing accuracy, he is also the artist who cares for unity, complexity, depth, and above all, contrast and balance. "There is, therefore, no guarantee in scientific knowledge of man's permanence or permanent ascendency. . . . The presumption is that before him lies a long future of profound modification, but whether that will be, according to present ideals, upward or downward, no one can forecast" (p. 168). And then, on top of this up-down antithesis, Wells superimposes yet another antithesis:

> Still, so far as any scientist can tell us, it may be that, instead of this, Nature is, in unsuspected obscurity, equipping some now humble creature with wider possibilities of appetite, endurance, or destruction, to rise in the fulness of time and sweep *homo* away into the darkness from which his universe arose. The Coming Beast must certainly be reckoned in any anticipatory calculations regarding the Coming Man.

Wells's point in this suggestive passage is not a moral one, nor is it a warning about the future; rather it is an argument for a way of thought which proceeds by considering and balancing opposites.

Throughout his early essays we can see Wells delighting in opposition, often for its own sake. In "The Rediscovery of the Unique," he sees antithetical reversal as a truth in itself. "Order," he concludes, "seems now the least law in the universe; in the days of our great-grandfathers it was heaven's first law. So spins the squirrel's cage of human philosophy."[13] Earlier in the same essay, after accusing science of imitating religion by claiming that its ability to predict substantiates its claims, Wells scornfully declares, "Thus the whirligig of time brings round its revenges."[14] Though Wells is making a specific point about the pretensions of modern science, at a deep level he is enjoying, not the single truth he postulates, but the irony of contradiction itself. When, a decade later, in "The Discovery of the Future," he challenges his own earlier skeptical nominalism, he is also performing a further twist in this dialectical play.

Such opposition is the essential mechanism of Wells's imaginative strategy in all his early work. We can best understand how it works by seeing the way it treats central dilemmas of the human situation. For our purposes, the primary opposition, which in its turn generates a series of important secondary oppositions, is that between the freedom of human thought and the fatality of natural fact. The conflict can be formulated in many ways. We see it in classical debates about determinism and freedom, in Lévi-Strauss' antithesis between nature and culture, or even in Yeats's perception of the irreconcilability of reality and justice. Wells's version of it is best treated as a conflict between evolutionary and ethical imperatives. Stated thus, the conflict has a distinctly Victorian flavor; the Darwinian revolution gives the issue currency, and the terms themselves are from T. H. Huxley's Romanes Lecture of 1893, "Evolution and Ethics."[15] One can see how the issue in this form might serve to distract thought from other conflicts: for instance, neither imperative seems to address the problem of the way class interests function in modern capitalist civilization. But as the example of *The Time Machine* proves, as long as the opposition between evolution and ethics is seen as a genuine conflict and not simply as a pessimistic irony that by implying the futility of all thought justifies any course of action, such an opposition includes these issues and serves well to bring into focus irreducible problems of social existence that repeatedly arise as humans try to understand their place in the world and their relationships to each other.

The evolution-ethics conflict is inescapable. Mind, whatever its source or actual powers, exists as a determining force unlike anything else in nature and makes human society, despite its numerous parallels to various animal groupings, distinct and open to possibilities that do not exist elsewhere in nature. The baboon and the ant, though they participate in intricate social organizations, do not have the power to choose or to change their governing structures, economies, or modes of production. Humanity, without changing biologically, has lived under various governments and economies, has developed new modes of production, and, more remarkably, has undertaken the transformation of one form into the other. Yet, while choice and freedom are a part of human social experience, humans and their social organizations are also subject to natural laws. As the social sciences testify, individuals and groups act in consistent and predictable ways. Yet, even if mind exerts only a miniscule determining force against nature, if mind is, in T. H. Huxley's term, an "epiphenomenon," nevertheless from the perspective of acting and thinking humankind, mind is still balanced against nature, a source of growth and choice, of friction and frustration. Our future depends on the way we deal with this conflict, and our ability to think about the future of society is directly related to our sensitivity to the importance of the conflict.

In his early work, both nonfiction and fiction, Wells adapts issues at the heart of the debate about evolution and puts them to his own purposes. The aesthetic mode set forth in "Zoological Retrogression" is both a way of following his mentors, Darwin and Huxley, and a way of performing an essential and important break from them. In order to understand what Wells has done we need to understand the dilemmas Darwin posed and the way Huxley formulated them.

The first reviewers of *The Origin of Species* were aware of two major changes Darwin was asking them to entertain about their place in the world.[16] The first charge made against Darwin, one with which we are generally familiar, was that he was obliterating the traditional separations between humanity and the rest of nature. Darwin showed that species that now are separate and incapable of fertilizing each other do not represent permanent, stable categories but are separate groups that have grown out of previous unions. In the case of the human animal, this means that we cannot claim the entire independence from all other creatures that the earlier theories of special creation would have sanctioned.

The second, less commonly recognized charge against Darwin was that he was putting into doubt the relation between the orders the human mind posits for nature and the orders nature itself generates. At times Darwin suggests that the orders biological science establishes are mere "conveniences" and are not essential to the phenomena themselves. The metaphysical problem has a moral dimension: to what degree is humanity capable of establishing a system based on reason and to what degree is humanity bound to "follow nature"? The final issue is, thus, how much is civilization itself merely natural, and how much is it an intellectual and perhaps ethical construct of human will and thought superimposed on nature?

The problem of the relation of humanity to the rest of nature has, beyond the obvious moral and ontological consequences, a logical implication. Bishop "Soapy Sam" Wilberforce's attempt to humiliate T. H. Huxley by asking him whether he traced his descent from the ape on his grandfather's or grandmother's side,[17] though petty and ignorant, reveals in its way the horror he felt at the loss of contrast and distinction Darwinism seemed to imply. Even among professional scientists the issue led to a frantic quibbling as a way of undermining Darwin's massive and serene hypothesis. When in the opening lines of his introduction to *The Origin of Species* Darwin describes himself as having been "much struck with certain facts in the distribution of the inhabitants of South America," Sir Richard Owen finds the word *inhabitants* bothersome: "Mr. Darwin must be aware of what is commonly understood by an 'uninhabited island;' he may however, mean by the inhabitants of South America not the human kind only, whether aboriginal or otherwise, but all the lower animals. Yet again, why are the fresh-water polypes or sponges to be called 'inhabitants' more than the plants?"[18] We see here Owen's sound intuition that once you break down the border between humanity and the rest of nature you cannot simply redraw a line a little "lower."

Without question Darwin consciously uses the word *inhabitants* broadly and with edges that extend indefinitely. In the seclusion of his notebooks he could become quite belligerent in his assertions that humanity is but one species within nature,[19] and throughout *The Origin of Species* he uses the word *inhabitants* with broad sweep:

No one ought to feel surprise at much remaining as yet unexplained in
regard to the origin of species and varieties, if he make due allowance for
our profound ignorance in regard to the mutual relations of the many
beings which live around us. Who can explain why one species ranges
widely and is very numerous and why another allied species has a narrow
range and is rare? Yet these relations are of the highest importance, for
they determine the present welfare and, as I believe, the future success
and modification *of every inhabitant* of this world. Still less do we know
of the mutual relations of the innumerable *inhabitants* of the world during
the many past geological epochs in its history.[20]

What Darwin is doing here and what his early critics were aware of
and perhaps afraid of is restructuring the conventional logical categories by which we think about humanity in the world. And since
much behavior, even the definition of civilization, then and now, is
based on the assurance of the absolute and eternal borders between
such categories, to bring them into question is to jeopardize long-
standing moral assumptions. To put it another way, it is most easy
to justify domination if you can prove separation and inferiority.[21]

In the last paragraph of his review of *The Origin of Species* Owen
addresses the second issue, the deep problems Darwin's analysis of
species raises about the nature and meaning of classification itself:

The essential element in the complex idea of species, as it has been
variously framed and defined by naturalists, viz., the blood-relationship
between all the individuals of such species, is annihilated on the hypothesis of "natural selection." According to this view a genus, a family,
an order, a class, a sub-kingdom,—the individuals severally representing
these grades of difference or relationship,—now differ from individuals of
the same species only in degree: the species, like every other group, is
a mere creature of the brain; it is no longer from nature. With the present
evidence from form, structure, and procreative phenomena, of the truth
of the opposite proposition, that "classification is the task of science, but
species the work of nature," we believe that this aphorism will endure;
we are certain that it has not yet been refuted; and we repeat in the words
of Linnaeus. "*Classis et Ordo* est sapientiae, *Species* naturae opus."[22]

Owen believes that Darwin is not just saying that humans are animals
that have evolved, but is out to deprive the idea of species of the neat
borders that the creationist theory with its ahistorical mode of classification gives it. Owen wants the fact that different species are incapable of fertilizing each other to be "natural" and definitive, but

Darwin takes pains to show that such borders are blurred and shifting, that the separations we now recognize are modern and did not necessarily exist in the past. Louis Agassiz tried to refute Darwin on just this issue and to reinstitute clear separation in nature by pointing to the class of birds as completely unrelated to any other class of animal. but as Ernst Mayr observes, "by a curious coincidence this statement was published exactly one year before the description of *Archaeopteryx*, a virtually perfect intermediate between birds and reptiles."[23] Once we accept the historical dimension of evolution, the classifications that we make show up as true only for now. They are not universal; nor are they simply "nature."

Owen's alarm may arise from Darwin's assertion near the end of *The Origin of Species* that "we shall have to treat species in the same manner as those naturalists treat genera, who admit that genera are merely artificial combinations made for convenience."[24] To a certain extent Owen has just clouded the issue: Darwin would not have denied Linnaeus' axiom; species are, after all, defined by what modern biology calls "reproductive isolation," a quality that no one would deny is "from nature."[25] But Owen is correct in seeing that in denying species the sanction of permanent *type*, in arguing that species are changeable and the product of evolutionary process, Darwin has moved in the direction of nominalism.[26] In the first edition of *The Origin of Species* he could go so far to undermine the natural integrity of species as to argue that "the only distinction between species and well-marked varieties is, that the latter are known, or believed, to be connected at the present day by intermediate gradations, whereas species were formerly thus connected."[27]

For the anti-Darwinist, and even for some Darwinists, the problem such thinking raises is that it suggests that the order established by human thought is not necessarily identical with the "order of nature." Surely one of the comforting strengths of creationist theory was its claim to find the discriminations humans make confirmed by nature. It is precisely the threat to this identity that upset Professor Sedgwick when he wrote Darwin and insisted that,

> There is a moral or metaphysical part of nature as well as a physical. A man who denies this is deep in the mire of folly. 'Tis the crown and glory of organic science that it *does* through *final cause*, link material and moral. . . . You have ignored this link; and, if I do not mistake your meaning, you have done your best in one or two pregnant cases to break it.[28]

Darwin, a shy metaphysician, is finally ambiguous about how he thinks the orders of nature and of reason are related, but we can understand how *The Origin of Species* might be seen to open the way for the liberation of reason.

In Darwin we do not see the possibilities of this separation of reason and nature worked out, but in the thought of T. H. Huxley the separation becomes central. In his first book, *Man's Place in Nature* (1863), Huxley faces the issue directly. After establishing humanity's physiological links with the rest of creation and thus making explicit Darwin's implied breakdown of any separation between humanity and the rest of nature, Huxley argues that the human being's intelligence sets it apart from the rest of nature:

> I have endeavoured to show that no absolute structural line of demarcation, wider than that between the animals which immediately succeed us in the scale, can be drawn between the animal world and ourselves; and I may add the expression of my belief that the attempt to draw a physical distinction is equally futile, and that even the highest faculties of feeling and of intellect begin to germinate in lower forms of life. At the same time no one is more strongly convinced than I am of the vastness of the gulf between civilized man and the brutes; or is more certain that whether *from* them or not, he is assuredly not *of* them. No one is less disposed to think lightly of the present dignity, or despairingly of the future hopes, of the only consciously intelligent denizen of this world.[29]

An important word in this passage is *civilized*. Civilization is the expression of human intelligence devising an order, based on ethical ideals, different from nature.

Nature, Huxley argues, is devoid of ethical significance. It is the human intellect that creates the categories of desert and blame on which any ethical system is based, and the absence of intellect in lower life makes any ethical considerations irrelevant in nature. There are no morals to be drawn from nature; nature, Huxley would eloquently argue in *Evolution and Ethics*, is an ethical horror:

> If there is one thing plainer than another, it is that neither the pleasures nor the pains of life in the merely animal world, are distributed according to desert; for it is admittedly impossible for the lower orders of sentient beings to deserve either the one or the other. If there is a generalization from the facts of human life which has the assent of thoughtful men in every age and country, it is that the violator of ethical rules constantly escapes the punishment which he deserves; that the wicked flourishes

like a green bay tree, while the righteous begs his bread; that the sins of the fathers are visited upon the children; that, in the realm of nature, ignorance is punished just as severely as wilful wrong; and that thousands upon thousands of innocent beings suffer from the crime, or the unintentional trespass of one.[30]

In place of "the unfathomable injustice of the nature of things" the human intellect creates civilization, which struggles to establish an order founded on an ethical ideal. That does not mean that civilization has no connection with nature; Huxley readily agrees that our ethical ideals may have evolved just as other natural phenomena have, but since the "immoral sentiments" are products of the same evolutionary process, the connection is not a defining one. "The thief and the murderer follow nature just as much as the philanthropist. Cosmic evolution may teach us how the good and evil tendencies of man may have come about; but, in itself, it is incompetent to furnish any better reason why what we call good is preferable to what we call evil than we had before" (p. 80). The ethical life, whatever its origins, grows into an independent, self-conscious, self-creating order that justifies itself by reference to its own intellectual ideals, not by any reference to nature. "The history of civilization details the steps by which men have succeeded in building up an artificial world within the cosmos" (p. 83).

But separation is not enough; ultimately the ethical system of civilization must invert the values of nature. The "artificial world" is based on a systematic antithesis: civilization calls criminal the natural instincts that link the human being to the rest of nature, the very instincts that originally enabled it to survive competition in nature:

> In proportion as men have passed from anarchy to social organization, and in proportion as civilization has grown in worth, these deeply ingrained serviceable qualities have become defects. After the manner of successful persons, civilized man would gladly kick down the ladder by which he has climbed. He would be only too pleased to see "the ape and tiger die." But they decline to suit his convenience; and the unwelcome intrusion of these boon companions of his hot youth into the ranged existence of civil life adds pains and griefs, innumerable and immeasurably great, to those which the cosmic process necessarily brings on the mere animal. In fact, civilized man brands all these ape and tiger promptings with the name of sins; he punishes many of the acts which flow from them as crimes; and, in extreme cases, he does his best to put an end to the survival of the fittest of former days by axe and rope. (p. 52)

Though Huxley's irony here bespeaks his awareness of certain difficulties and drawbacks of civilization, the basic opposition is clear enough. Civilization is seen as entailing a profound transformation of the mere animal and enforcing a reversal of polarities.

> The practice of that which is ethically best—what we call goodness or virtue—involves a course of conduct which in all respects, is opposed to that which leads to success in the cosmic struggle for existence. In place of ruthless self-assertion it demands self-restraint; in place of thrusting aside, or treading down, all competitors, it requires that the individual shall not merely respect, but shall help his fellows; its influence is directed, not so much to the survival of the fittest, as to the fitting of as many as possible to survive. It repudiates the gladiatorial theory of existence (p. 82).

Civilization represents, not merely an alternative to nature, but an anti-nature ordered by the human will and intellect. "Let us understand, once for all, that the ethical progress of society depends, not on imitating the cosmic process, still less in running away from it, but in combating it" (p. 83).

Since the ethical life can exist only in the context of civilization, the latter is for Huxley to be chosen over nature, in spite of the awareness that civilization is not an unmixed blessing. Huxley acknowledges that "The garden was apt to turn into a hothouse," and that civilization, while curbing some forms of pain also leads to an "enlargement of the capacity of suffering" (p. 55). He is also aware of the unheroic aspect of modern civilization, the loss of that "frolic welcome" with which the Homeric hero faced the "thunder and the sunshine" (p. 77). But whatever ambiguity or sense of loss are entailed in choosing civilization and rejecting nature, they are suppressed or at best given expression by irony. For Huxley the ethical ideal, however, artificial and leading to whatever drawbacks, must be maintained; he repudiates the order of nature in favor of that of rational, ethical civilization.

Though the Darwinian view of nature has certainly helped shape Huxley's argument, it would be misleading to claim that the argument could not have been made without Darwin. Many of Huxley's arguments are anticipated by J. S. Mill in "Nature," written in the decade before the publication of *The Origin of Species*,[31] To some extent Huxley is speaking in *Evolution and Ethics* less as a scientist than as a philologist: it is usually not apparent in the selections printed of the lecture that one of Huxley's main theses is that the modern view of nature can be found in the writings of the ancient Stoics. Yet the

Darwinian view of nature gives a tension to the opposition Huxley develops that is generally missing from earlier versions of the idea. Nature, though it may be rejected in favor of an ethical ideal, exerts an insistent and undeniable pressure that at times lends an air of tragic futility to the vision of high civilization. What Sedgwick feared, the breakdown of the correspondence between nature and the morality that human reason affirms, leads not to despair or confusion, but to a stoic, one might say typically late Victorian, commitment to an ethical code in the midst of nature's overwhelming darkness.

Wells's genius is to grasp the logical base of Huxley's antithesis and to treat it, not as part of a single argument leading to a single answer, but as the generative source for a whole series of arguments and a wide range of answers. In "Human Evolution, an Artificial Process" (1896) Wells sets out to suggest that the important changes in humanity over the last ten thousand years, perhaps over the last hundred thousand years, have not been the result of natural selection but have been the work of the human mind. Wells follows Huxley in distinguishing between nature and civilization, but he goes on to argue that the natural process of evolution is essentially static in civilized humanity due to the large time spans evolution would require and the tempering mechanisms of civilization itself. Wells argues that the "artificial process," which depends on the shaping power of such purely cultural phenomena as tradition, art, and government, accounts almost entirely for the difference between modern and stone age humanity.[32] The separations Wells establishes here are very close to those Huxley develops, but in place of Huxley's forthright ethical heroism we have an opposition that verges on comic incompatibility rather than tragic disjunction:

> In civilized man we have (1) an inherited factor, the natural man, who is the product of natural selection, the culminating ape, and a type of animal more obstinately unchangeable than any other living creature; and (2) an acquired factor, the artificial man, the highly plastic creature of tradition, suggestion, and reasoned thought. In the artificial man we have all that makes the comforts and securities of civilization a possibility. That factor and civilization have developed and will develop together. And in this view, what we call Morality becomes the padding of suggested emotional habits necessary to keep the round Palaeolithic savage in the square hole of the civilized state.[33]

The difference between Wells and Huxley is a matter of tone, but that tonal difference denotes an essential logical difference. The end of this passage is particularly telling: Huxley's high ethical ideal has been reduced to "the padding of suggested emotional habits" whose purpose is to prevent wobble and rattle. Nature and civilization here have become an antithesis that is essentially value-free: that is, one is not to be preferred to the other, and it takes the two together to define humanity.

By allowing nature a value which Huxley's ethical argument rejects, Wells restores a balance to the opposition that Huxley's commitment to civilization will not tolerate. And once the ideas of nature and civilization have attained balance, they can express a series of secondary and more precise oppositions. Nature can represent immoral regression from the high ethical attainments of civilization, but it can also represent energetic wholeness against civilization's decadent hypocrisy and formality. Or, while civilization may express an ideal of efficiently ordered distribution against nature's chaos and waste, nature can represent a welcome animal joy against civilization's stultification and ennui. It is the denotative richness of the two terms, the complexity of values that attaches to each, and the stark clarity of their opposition that makes them so imaginatively and logically useful for Wells.

To understand how such contradictory but balanced thinking works we shall study closely the forms of opposition and identity in Wells's fiction. I have used the term opposition loosely in this essay, and I don't see much to be gained by enforcing a philosophically rigorous definition. But some sense of how opposition works is necessary. For purposes of practical analysis it will be useful to follow C. K. Ogden, who sees three essential kinds of opposition: opposition by "cut," opposition by "scale," and opposition by a combination of the two. In the cut there is a simple either-or distinction, such as left-right, and "opposition begins, as it were, immediately the line is crossed."[34] In the case of the scale matters get immensely more complex. There are degrees of opposition on either side of the cut. Thus, black-white can be treated as extreme terms on a continuous scale of gray (p. 66), and one can envision infinite subtleties of discrimination in opposition depending on the placing of the cut and the refinement of the perceiver's sense of values of gray. The third type of opposition puts two scales in series with the cut between them as a neutral point. Hot-cold is an example of such an opposition: one scale is hot——non-hot (i.e., tepid); the other is non-cold (i.e., tepid)——cold.

CUT
Hot————Tepid // Tepid————Cold

Opposition is achieved in this case, not by simple negation, since the mere negative marks the cut, but by an antithetical positive on a different scale. Such a system can function both as a simple cut, in which once one crosses the cut one has established opposition, or as a simple scale, in which distance from the cut is necessary to the perceived opposition.

In thinking about fiction we will find this third form the most useful model, and usually in its first sense, as opposition by cut rather than by scale. Any point on the cold scale will establish a symmetrical opposition with any point on the hot scale. The cut, therefore, becomes a crucial logical device. It sets up a system in which a simple difference can be treated as opposition and, importantly, in which a very loose likeness—a likeness that in other circumstances or according to a differently placed cut could itself be perceived as an opposition—can be treated as identity. The cut, as it announces a separation and an opposition, at the same time identifies a point of similarity, for it locates the point at which the opposites are not opposites at all. Therefore, in order to establish an opposition, one must also establish an identity, which in the universe of opposition is defined by the cut. Wells tends to mark such cuts with what I shall call "mediating symbols."

It is worth emphasizing that this is a logical system. We are not observing an allegory in which an image is tagged with an idea which can be translated out of the image language into a more abstract, discursive statement. We are interested in how images relate with other images in their own fictive universe. In order to elucidate this kind of thought we need to watch closely what the prose itself is doing and to direct our attention, not to themes or conclusions, but to the shape and texture of the story, to the way it moves, to the connections it achieves and the divisions it discovers. It is not enough to say that Wells is optimistic or pessimistic or to try to define a single, consistent attitude towards, say, technology or capitalism. Directed thought strives to achieve such unambiguous positions, but the undirected thought that we shall explore holds together oppositions and lives with them. The virtue of undirected thought lies in its openness to the genuine conflicts in the world it examines.

Though undirected, such openness is not unmethodical. What to the casual observer may appear simply as a flight of untrammeled fancy is in fact the product of a consistent, rigorous, and unflinching imagination. Though a degree of negative capability is essential to the mode, it is neither factless nor reasonless. Wells, as we shall see in detail, thinks by means of symmetrical, ironic opposites. He uses fiction to meditate deeply, almost unconsciously, on a problem. In a loose way his early fiction resembles a system of totemic classification in Lévi-Strauss' interpretation: the work constitutes a categorization of the field of interest, a charting of connections and divisions; it aims, not to predict natural or social phenomena, nor to argue moral positions, but to fill out a logical system that is primarily satisfying, not for its explanatory value, but for its own completeness.[35]

CHAPTER 2

Thinking by Opposition

Stories of Two Worlds

The coexistence of opposites is a fundamental structural element in all of Wells's early fiction. When at the beginning of *The Time Machine* he develops a theory of four dimensions that will allow for time travel, he is doing more than merely justifying the "science" of the story,[1] he is invoking a structure that allows our world and the world of 802,701 to share the same space. That this "two world structure" is important to Wells's imagination is shown by the comparatively large number of stories in which he develops no plot or moral, but in which he takes considerable pains simply to establish a juxtaposition of two incongruous worlds.

In a story like "The Remarkable Case of Davidson's Eyes," Wells seems to have no other aim than to work out the ways the two worlds fit and don't fit. Davidson, an acquaintance of the narrator, is working in a laboratory with electromagnets when lightning strikes close by and suddenly he sees, instead of a laboratory in London late on a stormy afternoon, a semiarid south-sea island early in the morning. Since his body resides in London, Davidson has a difficult time getting around, for what he sees has no relation to the physical world he actually inhabits. The story spends some time working out oppositions—it's day there when it's night here; at times he thinks he is going underground and gets claustrophobia; at other times he thinks he's suspended in midair and gets vertigo. At the end of the story evidence is produced which strongly suggests that Davidson was not hallucinating but was seeing an actual antipodal island. Neither of the opposite worlds is of any particular interest: that is, nothing of narrative consequence is happening in London, and the island is drab—its filthy penguins could hardly interest even an ornithologist. There is no mystery to be solved, no plot to be worked out in either world. Davidson does not want to escape London, and the island is no paradise. Clearly the fascination of the story, for author and for reader, lies in the juxtaposition itself, the superimposition of one world on the other. Well's imaginative energy has gone to bringing together two discrepant worlds.

A number of early tales work out variations on the two-world system that "Davidson's Eyes" gives us in a pure form. "The Crystal Egg," though it hints at plots tangential to the central structure—Mr. Cave's home life is very unhappy and the customers who want to buy the crystal egg have an air of intriguing mystery—is at its core exactly like "Davidson's Eyes." The crystal egg is the device, like the twist to Davidson's sight, that links drab London and a strange (in this case Martian) landscape. Nothing derives from the opposition; the juxtaposition is an end in itself and sufficient. "The Plattner Story" ornaments the two-world structure further by raising the issue of fraud (is Plattner merely perpetrating a hoax?), by making the other world a world of the dead, and, towards the end, by giving us a vignette of a dying husband and his greedy wife. But nothing develops from these suggestions of plot, and ultimately they are secondary to the central dichotomy of the two worlds and the odd links between them. "Under the Knife" similarly juxtaposes a living and a dead world, and again there is no consequence. The opposition is itself the pleasure.

What we have in these stories, then, is an imaginative structure that is central to Wells's art. We can see it in increasingly disguised form in many of his other stories and novels, and we can see how by a series of fairly simple transformations a number of other oppositions in Wells's early fiction derive from this basic two world structure. Before we do that, however, we should consider what it is that makes this elemental structure important and distinctive. First, the structure itself is free from moral suggestions; the oppositions it sets up are purely physical and we cannot apply to them the moral terminology of good and bad. Thus, it is not a matter of showing that one world is to be preferred to the other. Second, the principle behind the opposition is narrative. The point of such stories is not to describe a change, but to set up a static antithesis and then to fill in the relation between the two elements. Third, in such a structure neither world in itself holds our interest; what is important is the two of them together and the linked opposition they establish. Wells himself draws

our attention to these aspects of the two-world structure near the end
of "The Plattner Story" when he has the narrator point to the absence
of plot. In part this is a conventional device for asserting the "truth"
of the story, but then the narrator adds that the real value of the story
lies not in its truth so much as in a particular sensation that the bare
opposition of the two worlds generates:

> But quite apart from the objectionableness of falsifying a most extraor-
> dinary true story, any such trite devices [of conventional plot] would
> spoil, to my mind, the peculiar effect of this dark world, with its livid
> green illumination and its drifting Watchers of the Living, which, unseen
> and unapproachable to us, is yet lying all about us.[2]

We should note that the "peculiar effect" derives in part from the
"greenness" of the other world, but that greenness is essentially interesting for being so near the ordinary light of our own world and
yet unperceived. While the two-world structure lends itself to a number of possible developments, its main function is the pleasure it itself
provides.

In one of Wells's earliest novels, *The Wonderful Visit*, we can see
him move from the elementary pleasure of the two-world structure
toward a satiric perspective, but what is important for our purposes
is the way *The Wonderful Visit* stops short of realizing its satiric potential. The reasons are instructive: the instinct towards balance and
the rule of opposition counter any consistent satiric viewpoint, and
the two-world structure itself shows up repeatedly as a pleasurable
and energizing incongruity.

In *The Wonderful Visit* an Angel, who lives in a world to which we
are blind but of which we occasionally dream, by some accident never
satisfactorily explained "falls" into our world, which angels never actually see but of which they occasionally dream. Each world is the
other's dream, though the Angel's world is heavenly to our eyes and
our world is nightmarish to the angel's. Vicar Hilyer, who should be
an authority on the relation of the two worlds but who really knows
no more about them than does anyone else, wounds the Angel with
birdshot, befriends him, and takes him home. The incongruity of the
customs of the two worlds leads to many comic misunderstandings,
but most people account for the Angel by fitting him into their con-

ventional ways of seeing and understanding. The Angel's state of un-
dress simply scandalizes the curate's wife; his wings interest the doctor, but only as an anatomical curiosity; his violin playing charms the
neighbors, though some of them think they saw him playing in Vienna;
and his entire innocence of the ways of our world is repeatedly taken
for rudeness by the townsfolk. Only the Vicar understands that the
Angel is from a different world; all the others think he is either an
eccentric or an impostor. Frequently he is seen as the anarchist figure
Wells develops in other early stories: he is called a foreigner, a freak,
a "sans culotte," uncivilized, an eccentric genius. Of course all these
labels miss the point: he is a profounder anarchist than any social
revolutionary. As a pure moral force he threatens civilization totally,
but as pure innocence he is completely victimized by civilization.

The two-world system of *The Wonderful Visit* generates an insistent
irony to which the Angel is almost as vulnerable as the townspeople.
Though he has the potential for becoming the expression of a terrible
innocence that will punish the world, the Angel is unable to realize
that unambiguous righteousness and instead becomes a somewhat
pathetic sufferer who by his own blunders undercuts the possibilities
for huge moral statement. When little boys throw stones at him, we
sympathize with him, but any anger must be tempered by the understanding of our anger's futility, by the awareness that the little boys
represent not moral atrocity, but simply the daily meanness of common human nature. Similarly, when the innocent Angel asks why the
plowman works when others don't, the potential attack on the economic system is tempered by the fact that the example of leisure
juxtaposed to the laborer is the Vicar, the most—perhaps the only—humane figure in the story.[3] And the mild and innocent Angel sins most
when he is most just and in blind rage beats Sir John Gotch, a cruel
landowner, senseless. The Angel thinks he has killed the man, though
later, like a more famous Sir John, Gotch gets up and after rubbing his
wounds contemplates setting "spring guns and man traps" in the
future (p. 269). The Angel has committed a human crime, but his act
has reformed nothing.

It is this ironic rather than satiric view that the two-world structure
generates that seems to account for Wells's fondness for it. Early in
The Wonderful Visit, when the Angel and the Vicar are discovering the
mechanics of the two-world situation, they seem to speak for Wells:

> "You call men real [said the Angel], and angels a myth. It almost makes
> one think that in some odd way there must be two worlds as it were. . ."

"At least Two," said the Vicar.

"Lying somewhere close together, and yet scarcely suspecting. . ."

"As near as page to page in a book."

"Penetrating each other, living each its own life. This is really a delicious dream!"

"And never dreaming of each other."

"Except when people go a-dreaming!" (p. 135)

The Vicar, who "loved geometrical speculations" (p. 136), finds this "delicious dream" a pleasure in itself. Toward the end the novel points out that the important dilemmas derive not from the dominance of one world over the other but from their equality. When Sir John Gotch takes out a summons against the Angel for damaging his barbed wire, the Vicar meditates:

> I really do not know what to say. We must face our circumstances, I suppose. I am so undecided—so torn. Its the two worlds. If your Angelic world were only a dream, of if *this* world were only a dream—or if I could believe either or both dreams, it would be all right with me. But here is a real Angel and a real summons—how to reconcile them I do not know. (p. 239)

It is the total system with its inherent opposition and paradox that makes for the novel's interest.

But, if the whole system itself is more central than the satiric possibilities of using one world to criticize the other, that does not mean that the novel is not interested in ways of seeing. There is an ideal of humaneness represented by the Vicar and the Angel, and that humaneness is linked to their ability to see both worlds. All the other characters in the novel are limited to the vision of a single world. The only other character who comes close to seeing two is the Tramp who gives the Angel a useful criticism of English civilization and education. He compares education to "pithing":

> "Ever hear of a pithed frog?"
>
> "Pithed frog?" said the Angel. "No!"
>
> "It's a thing these here vivisectionists do. They takes a frog and they cuts out his brains and they shoves a bit of pith in the place of 'em. That's a pithed frog. Well—that there village is full of pithed human beings."
>
> The Angel took it quite seriously. "Is that so?" he said.
>
> "That's so—you take my word for it. Everyone of them 'as 'ad their brains cut out and chunks of rotten touchwood put in the place of it. And you see that little red place there?"

> "That's called the national school," said the Angel.
> "Yes—that's where they piths 'em," said the Tramp, quite in love with his
> conceit. (p. 209)

The plowman is the Tramp's example of the pithed human being; if
he hadn't been pithed, the Tramp claims, the plowman would "be
paddin' the hoof this pleasant weather—like me and the blessed Apos-
tles." Pithing is a fine metaphor for the limited civilized imagination
that resigns its free scope and accepts things as they are. Yet, if the
pithed man is complacent, he is also content, and though he is the
victim of economic oppression, he is blind to it. And out of this insight
the Tramp goes on to offer the most serious criticism of civilization
to be found in the novel, but it is a criticism hampered by being too
much involved in the values of the world it attempts to criticize:

> But speaking serious, ain't it ridiculous?—centuries and centuries of civil-
> isation, and look at that poor swine there, sweatin' 'isself empty and
> trudging up that 'ill-side. 'E's English, 'e is. 'E belongs to the top race in
> creation, 'e does. 'E's one of the rulers of Indjer. It's enough to make a
> nigger laugh. The flag that's braved a thousand years the battle an' the
> breeze—that's 'is flag. There never was a country was as great and glorious
> as this. Never. And that's wot it makes of us. (p. 210)

If such a passage reveals the Tramp's insight into the failure of civilization, it also reveals the limits of his criticism: he is still closely
bound to the imagination of the world he attacks, and though he sees
through some injustices, he still echoes its prejudices, patriotisms,
and chauvinisms. He too gives evidence of being pithed, and the only
alternative his imagination can offer to civilization is vagrancy. The
Vicar and the Angel are capable of more radical imaginings due to
their vision of two worlds. As the Vicar admits, he had taken life as it
is in nineteenth-century England "as a matter of course" until the
Angel arrived. The "pleasure of the incongruity" between the two
worlds has "enlarged" his "imagination" so that he is able to look at
his own world anew (pp. 147, 168). Pithed characters are incapable of
such imaginings; they can see only one world.

We can see in *The Wonderful Visit* how the two-world system becomes a source of imaginative energy which allows for, not satire on
civilization, but a reconsideration of it. But, partly because the world
that the Angel comes from is a never-never land, not a concretely
realized antithesis, in this novel such reconsideration remains an

ideal. In this it is like those other two-world structures we have looked at: the two worlds exist as aesthetic antitheses, as a systematic balance, but though the idea of reconsideration is more present in *The Wonderful Visit* than in the short stories, the novel still shies from the detailed imaginative work.

Stories of Fraud

It is not by accident that the Time Traveller has the reputation of being too ingenious to be believed.[4] At the edge of the two-world structure inevitably lurks the question of fraud. The extraordinary truth is impossible to prove, and the narrator takes pains to point out supporting evidence, to analyze his sources' motives, and in general to persuade us that unlikely as it may seem the two-world opposition has occurred. In "The Plattner Story" the narrator concedes that the whole thing may be Plattner's hoax, and many characters in *The Wonderful Visit* see the Angel, not as a refugee from another world, but as a con man. Thus, the primary physical juxtaposition generates a secondary one between the true and the false, and even when the two-world construct is missing the structure of the tale of fraud presents us with a very similar kind of opposition. Both oppositions generate a static structure which is content to express the elementary contradiction; ordinary concerns for plot, character, and meaning are secondary to this initial delight in opposition. And both types seem to enjoy most an opposition that remains balanced to the end, that is, the contradiction is not to be resolved simply by disqualifying one half of it. The reader has to hold both sides of the contradiction together at once. So, just as in the case of two-world stories the purest are content simply to establish a situation, so too in the stories of fraud we have simply the mechanics of deception, the fact that the same set of events can be read two different ways.

This static quality of the tale of fraud can be seen clearly in "A Deal in Ostriches." An Eastern Padishah on shipboard loses a valuable diamond and complains that one of five ostriches, he cannot tell which, ate it. A European named Potter buys the whole lot of ostriches and sells them one at a time by auction to a group of Europeans who gleefully and ruthlessly take advantage of the Padishah's bad luck. At the end of the simple story the diamond has not been found and we learn that Potter and the Padishah may be friends. This piece of evidence forces a thorough reinterpretation of all the events of the story: the Padishah's hysteria may have been skillful acting; the Europeans' racist smugness and lack of pity become blindness. Like the stories of two worlds, "A Deal in Ostriches" enforces an overlap of contradictory structures which is satisfying in itself. Any consequences are irrelevant: whatever pity the Europeans' callous treatment may have earned the Padishah is largely dispersed at the end when we see that it may have been necessary to the success of the trick. The story may let us feel some sense of poetic justice at the end, but that is severely qualified by the fact that the Europeans do not seem to know that they have been taken, if they have. If the story celebrates anything, it is the ingenuity that creates such intellectual optical illusions.

"A Deal in Ostriches" asks the reader to reinterpret events; in "The Diamond Maker" Wells leaves two different readings entirely open at the end. In this story an obviously poor man claims to have manufactured a diamond which he is unable to sell; in fact he claims that his scientific triumph has not only impoverished him, but it has led to such distrust that he has been called an anarchist. The narrator, a cautious and worldly man, suspects too good a bargain, declines the man's offer of the diamond at a very low price, but then at the end wonders whether he has not been too wary and missed his chance. The story offers us two structures: according to one the diamond maker is simply a confidence man. But the same series of narrative facts allows for the possibility that he is an unrecognized genius who has devoted himself to a vision of scientific truth—he has even gone without food in order to buy coal to keep the fires of his furnace going. This second reading is compromised, however; the man's driving vision is not of truth but of the money such an invention will earn, and when he fires his diamonds he knowingly risks the lives of his unsuspecting and innocent neighbors. Yet, perhaps this very mercenary ruthlessness lends plausibility to the man's claim to be telling the truth. The point of the story seems to be to create a puzzle; the ambiguity at the end forces the reader to contemplate the double structure and prevents him from simplifying the juxtaposition into an easy but narrow "meaning."

Thought about the tale of fraud leads directly to important questions about fiction itself, which is, after all, the quintessential confidence trick. This self-reflective dimension of his art is developed with exceptional acuteness by Wells in one of his shortest and least plotted stories, "The Triumphs of a Taxidermist." The story is simple: an old, drunken taxidermist tells the reporter, Bellows (the name hides that of the author), about the "secrets" of his profession. The greatest triumph of taxidermy has been, not merely to stuff well a damaged pelt, not merely to make a whole specimen out of the few shreds of the original, but to create species:

> "I have *created* birds," he said in a low voice. "*New* birds. Improvements. Like no birds that was ever seen before."
>
> He resumed his attitude during an impressive silence.
>
> "Enrich the universe; *rath*-er. Some of the birds I made were new kinds of humming birds, and very beautiful little things, but some of them were simply rum. The rummest, I think, was the *Anomalopteryx Jejuna. Jejunus-a-um*—empty—so called because there was really nothing in it; a thoroughly empty bird—except for stuffing. Old Javvers has the thing now, and I suppose he is almost as proud of it as I am. It is a masterpiece, Bellows. It has all the silly clumsiness of your pelican, all the solemn want of dignity of your parrot, all the gaunt ungainliness of a flamingo, with all the extravagant chromatic conflict of a mandarin duck. *Such* a bird. I made it out of the skeletons of a stork and a toucan and a job lot of feathers. Taxidermy of that kind is just pure joy, Bellows, to a real artist in the art."

This odd-lot creation—much like the art of bricolage that Lévi-Strauss sees as analogous to that of the mythmaker—is exactly what the novelist, especially the novelist of "scientific romances," performs. Both the novelist and the taxidermist create worlds that don't exist but which might exist and which people like Old Javvers may even think do exist. Javvers may get pleasure from a benign deception, but the real pleasure, the "pure joy . . . to a real artist" belongs to him who can see both worlds. We are back with the Vicar in *The Wonderful Visit*, though here the second world arises through fraudulent art rather than miracle.

Such happy indulgence in deception raises problems which the story blithely leaves open. The storyteller's fraud seems harmless, but science claims to be true and in that realm false creation becomes criminally deceptive. The taxidermist exists in a borderline area: his fraudulent activity is both a triumph of "art" and a betrayal of "truth." But in this "The Triumphs of a Taxidermist" falls into line with other stories of fraud: all find a symmetry between the luxuries and arts of civilization and criminal activity; it is always under the guise of high civilization that the fraud is perpetrated. Thus, the tale of fraud works a further twist of paradox: it is neither for nor against civilization, but uses civilization against civilization.

The possibilities of an infinitely regressing paradox are neatly pictured in "The Triumphs of a Taxidermist"; the question of fraud infiltrates all levels of trust. When the taxidermist claims to have created a mermaid we are moving into the realm of the sailor's tall tale, and the fraud may not be in the stuffing but in the telling. The story's closing lines point us directly to the problem of words:

> The reader unacquainted with the dark ways of the collector may be perhaps inclined to doubt my taxidermist, for so far as great auks' eggs, and the bogus stuffed birds are concerned, I find that he has the confirmation of distinguished ornithological writers. And the note about the New Zealand bird certainly appeared in a morning paper of unblemished reputation, for the Taxidermist keeps a copy and has shown it to me.

The questions this passage raises form a lengthy regression: can one trust a newspaper to tell the truth? Is the newspaper itself genuine? May not the taxidermist have forged it also? Finally, are we to trust Bellows when he says he has seen it? Wells does not settle such questions; he finds the friction of contradictory possibilities more attractive than a smooth resolution in favor of one or another.

Civilization and Nature

Though the structure of opposition seems pleasurable in itself, it is also an essential device by which Wells can meditate on specific deep contradictions that he finds in human experience. As he argued in "Human Evolution, an Artificial Process," the natural Paleolithic savage in us exists in uneasy tension with the moral creature of civilization;[5] throughout his early tales Wells is busy charting these tensions and conflicts, and the structure of opposition, because it does not seek easy union or resolution but delights in the symmetry of balanced antithesis, allows him to do this with a certain wry, even exuberant honesty.

In "The Flowering of the Strange Orchid" we can see the abstract and static oppositions translated into meaningful plot. Wells is here working on the problem, which Huxley also perceived, of civilization's developing into a decadent oversensitivity.[6] The opposition set up at the beginning of the story is between the hothouse civilization of Mr. Winter-Wedderburn, a collector of orchids to whom "nothing ever happens," and the primitive, violent, natural world of the Andaman

Islands where the orchid collector, Batten, died. Wedderburn's world is comically tame. When he has a premonition "that something is going to happen to me to-day" he means he may buy a new type of orchid. His housekeeper, even more cautious than Wedderburn, finds all ideas of "something happening" threatening, "for, 'something happening' was a euphemism that meant only one thing to her." The orchid is the link that allows Wedderburn to meditate on the opposite sort of life, that of Batten: "That orchid-collector was only thirty-six— twenty years younger than myself—when he died. And he had been married twice and divorced once; he had had malarial fever four times, and once broke his thigh. He killed a Malay once, and once he was wounded by a poisoned dart. And in the end he was killed by jungle leeches. It must have all been very troublesome, but then it must have been very interesting, you know—except, perhaps, the leeches." The housekeeper can only respond as she has before that she is "sure it was not good for him." This opposition between a passionate, active, but deadly life in the antipodal jungle and a quiet, secure, but dull life in London is a form of the two-world structure with which we are familiar.

But in this story there is a plot: an orchid Wedderburn buys turns out to be a beautiful but murderous blood-sucker that almost kills Wedderburn as it has previously killed Batten. Wedderburn is saved by his housekeeper who smashes the greenhouse and destroys the plant. The plot of the story performs a set of inversions on the original opposition. Wedderburn becomes, in effect, Batten. The housekeeper's worst fears about the meaning of "something happening" prove true. The calm of the London suburb is broken by the smashing of the greenhouse. The world is so transformed that even the odd-job man, hearing the glass breaking and seeing the housekeeper with bloody hands hauling out the body, "thought impossible things." Adventure, violence, and passion have momentarily become possibilities again. Though in terms of degree the passion and energy of the end is trivial compared to Batten's, because the "cut" has been crossed that separates Wedderburn's world of complacent nonaction from Batten's world of risk and adventure, we can see Wedderburn's passion and the housekeeper's violence as *like* Batten's and as a balanced opposition to Wedderburn's earlier domestic quiet. And it seems to be the story's purpose to perform this reversal and restoration, to link the two worlds which in a story like "Davidson's Eyes" remain in static opposition.

"The Flowering of the Strange Orchid" in its light way asks questions about protective moral civilization and its separation from predatory nature. It would be a mistake, however, to read the story as simply an exultation of the primitive over the civilized. The balance we see elsewhere in Wells is skillfully achieved here. The antithesis between the two worlds is mediated by the orchid, which is both an image of a decadent and listless civilization and a creature of predatory and dangerous nature. When Wedderburn is overpowered by the orchid's scent the contradictory elements come together; the language of pure nature is the same as that of an almost rococo decadence:

> And, behold! the trailing green spikes bore now three great splashes of blossom, from which this overpowering sweetness proceeded. He stopped before them in an ecstasy of admiration.
> The flowers were white, with streaks of golden orange upon the petals, the heavy labellum was coiled into an intricate projection, and a wonderful bluish purple mingled there with the gold. He could see at once that the genus was altogether a new one. And the insufferable scent! How hot the place was! The blossoms swam before his eyes.

At this moment aesthetic civilization ("ecstasy of admiration," "wonderful bluish purple,") and the jungle overlap. And once the orchid has transformed the civilized hothouse into a murderous tropical jungle, the housekeeper restores civilization by smashing the windows and letting in "the cold outer air." This is an exact inversion of her earlier role, for before she had insisted that Wedderburn carry an umbrella even though the weather was clear. She enforced caution and protection from nature; now she acts rashly and violently to let that nature in. What should be observed here is that the antithesis has gone full circle, that her act of passionate violence, so directly opposed to the world she enforces at the beginning, restores that world. The oppositions of the story maintain a constant and balanced reciprocity, and the one cannot exist without the other.

While "The Flowering of the Strange Orchid" plays symbolically with how a decadent civilization incorporates violent nature, that same violence which civilization controls is the explicit subject of the first story of Wells's first collection of stories. The central conflict of "The Stolen Bacillus" is between an anarchist who steals a test tube of cholera bacteria with the intention of poisoning London's public water supply and a bacteriologist who at the beginning shows the anarchist the test tube and later pursues him to prevent his crime. This elegantly simple story is useful to us at this point for two reasons: it is an example of a story that has the potential for making a serious moral about order's conquest of disorder but declines to do so, and it is an example of the way Wells can introduce considerable complexity into a story by the simple device of setting up a dichotomy within one of the terms of the initial basic opposition. The two sources of our interest are related, for it is the complexity of the pattern Wells creates out of his simple elements that prevents a unified and reductive moral theme from asserting itself.

The central opposition between the anarchist and the bacteriologist develops ironies that undercut its potential moral simplicity. The end of the story inverts and trivializes the beginning: at the start we see the anarchist as a weak, incompetent, unscientific man, but his seeming harmlessness reveals itself to be deadly. At the end of the story the anarchist's deadly threat proves to be harmless, and his vision of planned destruction is foiled by an accident: the anarchist, the figure of disorder and imbalance, breaks the test tube while trying to maintain his balance in a lurching cab. Finally, by drinking what he thinks is cholera but which is really only a bacterium that will stain him blue, the anarchist fulfills the bacteriologist's wish at the beginning of the story: "I wish, for my own part, we could kill and stain every one of them [i.e., living cholera bacilli] in the universe." The anarchist, a kind of moral cholera, has been stained and has been rendered trivial.

If Wells has treated the moral opposition represented by the scientist and the anarchist ironically and comically, in a subplot he creates an even more telling reversal. At the moment when the bacteriologist discovers the test tube is missing and anarchy most threatens, instead of focusing on the moral issue, the story turns to comedy: the bacteriologist's wife, Minnie, offended at the sight of her husband "running about London—in the height of the season too—in his socks," grabs his street clothes and joins the chase. Just as the scientist does his duty by chasing the anarchist, she does hers by chasing "her vagrant husband." As the scientist tries to save civilization from physical catastrophe, his wife tries to save it from a more trivial disaster by enforcing a set of clothing conventions. Minnie sees her husband as an agent of disorder: "'He has gone *mad*!' said Minnie; 'it's that horrid science of his.'" At the end of the story the conquest is Minnie's; she restores a civilized order, but one devoid of moral or physical function. She insists her husband dress properly, and in the story's closing lines he replies, "Put on my coat on this hot day! Why? Because we might meet Mrs. Jabber. My dear, Mrs. Jabber is not a draught. But why should I wear a coat on a hot day because of Mrs. —? Oh! *very* well." The opposition between civilization and anarchy as represented by the scientist and the anarchist is undermined by the presence of Minnie. She becomes a pole in a second opposition within the term civilization which repeats the major opposition of the story but reverses its values, for here our sympathies are on the side of the "disorder" represented by the bacteriologist against the petty and conventional order represented by Minnie, and it is this deadening order's victory that more than anything else undercuts the sense of melodramatic triumph we might otherwise expect to feel at the story's end.

The scientist is the enigmatic center of the story's oppositions, a middle term linking comedy and melodrama, symbol and function. His cry, "Blue ruin!" at the moment he discovers the theft of the test tube coyly reveals that he already knows that civilization is not at stake, that what appears to be catastrophe is really trivial. His own moral status is also a problem, for if he is the agent who will rescue civilization, he is also the creator of the bacillus, and it is an irony not to be overlooked that it is not the anarchist but the scientist who fully imagines the reign of death the cholera might bring. In the final balance the anarchist is as trivial as Minnie: though he tries to be the agent of death, he is powerless without "horrid science's" techniques and imaginings, and his motive is not a vision of justice, but of fame. Like Minnie, he cares in his own way about what Mrs. Jabber says. The scientist's middle position between these two "threats" to meaningful civilization is given as a visual emblem in the cab chase—Minnie chasing her husband chasing the anarchist. The scientist is pursued and pursuer, the salvation of civilization and the participant in a series of comic misconstructions. And the cab men, as they cheer the chase on, reiterate this ambiguity by converting a serious, functional activity (catching an anarchist) into a symbolic game (a horse race). Thus, at every level, the story raises serious problems but insists that they be the subject of *play* rather than of resolution.

"The Flowering of the Strange Orchid" and "The Stolen Bacillus" reveal a common symmetrical opposition: anarchy is transformed into harmless order; harmless order is transformed into a kind of natural anarchy. The fact that both stories end up with a restoration of order, though it may seem to display commitment on Wells's part to civili-

zation itself, actually does nothing of the sort. In both cases the restoration of order is deeply ironic and a further operation of the principle of opposition. In "The Stolen Bacillus" the anarchist's vision of
success is upset by the accidental breaking of the test tube, and the
threat of chaos becomes a threat of nonsensical order. In "The Flowering of the Strange Orchid," after the placid, cautious life of Wedderburn and his housekeeper has been upset by the murderous orchid, order is restored by an act of violence. In both cases what we
might see merely as a restoration of order is really an inversion of the
activities of the first part of the story. This symmetry is important for
our understanding of Wells's method in these stories, for it disqualifies
a dependence on any kind of simple moral message. Neither the
disruption nor the order can be seen as good in itself, but each is
expressive only insofar as it is part of a system that contains its complementary opposite. Both stories, though simple, give us structures
that force us to acknowledge a civilized and an uncivilized element
and to stay alert to the tension between them.

Just as each story sets up a symmetrical opposition within itself,
the two stories together form a complementary pair. In both stories
one aspect of civilization is represented by women who take care to
see that their men are well-clothed, and in both stories there is a
discontinuity between the weather and the apparel: "Mrs. Jabber is
not a draught"; the sky is clear but Wedderburn's housekeeper insists
he take his umbrella. But clothes represent different things in the two
women's minds. In "The Stolen Bacillus" clothes are important as
symbols of social convention and have no physical function. The housekeeper in "The Flowering of the Strange Orchid" is not at all concerned with social convention; for her clothing is a protection against
any physical contingency. If Minnie is the defender of an overly symbolic civilization, the housekeeper stands for an overly protective one.
The common imagery expresses contradictory excesses; civilization
can be studied from many angles, and we understand an essential
quality of Wells's method if we see that his images have a real logical
function. They are not symbols whose meanings come from outside
and persist from work to work. Each work develops its own inner
logic.

The simple structure of opposition that shapes these two stories
can be further complicated by very simple means. We have seen how

by setting up a "subordinate opposition" in "The Stolen Bacillus" Wells severely modifies the already ironic primary opposition in the story. On the model of the sentence, we can think of such a structure as a "complex opposition." The other elementary structural complication available is, on the same model, the "compound opposition" in which two oppositions are set up without subordination, in tandem, and connected by the narrative equivalent of *and.* "The Lord of the Dynamos" illustrates this structure of opposition in its purest form.

The opening opposition of "The Lord of the Dynamos" is between chauvinistic, technological civilization and superstitious primitivism. The former is embodied in Holroyd, the chief attendant of the dynamo, a complacent bigot, a thorough materialist, and an ardent imperialist. "He doubted the existence of the Deity but accepted Carnot's cycle, and he had read Shakespeare and found him weak in chemistry." The latter is embodied in Azuma-zi, Holroyd's native assistant whom he persecutes cruelly and whom he instructs in the worship of the "Gord" of the Dynamo. Though the difference between the two figures is striking, they also have a large area of similarity. Holroyd's materialism is as much an irrational worship as Azuma-zi's spiritualization of technology. Like the orchid in "The Flowering of the Strange Orchid," the dynamo itself participates in civilized and primitive visions; as both a technological marvel and a source of pure, raw power it links Holroyd's sceptical materialism and Azuma-zi's religion. As in the other tales we have looked at, the stark basic opposition is founded on an identity.

In the first half of the story Azuma-zi resolves the opposition by electrocuting Holroyd as a sacrifice to the dynamo. We can see here a similarity to "The Stolen Bacillus": Azuma-zi is like the anarchist, and Holroyd represents loosely the civilization he threatens. There are important differences between the two stories, however. "The Lord of the Dynamos" has little of the comic trivialization that prevents us from treating "The Stolen Bacillus" as a moral parable. Also, in "The Lord of the Dynamos" the values of the main opposition have been inverted: whereas we could not sympathize with the anarchist, we side with Azuma-zi. And fittingly Azuma-zi succeeds in his "crime" whereas the anarchist failed. But "the Lord of the Dynamos" is not simply a tale of third-world vengeance; Wells balances the implicit attack on imperialist civilization with a second opposition: after the successful murder of Holroyd, the event is reenacted with a new figure, the "scientific manager," in Holroyd's place. This second murder attempt fails. Then Azuma-zi, like the anarchist in "The Stolen Bacillus," tries to commit suicide by turning the tool of the intended murder on himself, and he succeeds. In this second unit of the story a reversal of values has taken place: the scientific manager, though hardly a vivid figure, is noticably unlike Holroyd, and Azuma-zi's attempt to murder this innocuous man loses its justification. If in the first part of the story Azuma-zi is seen mainly as an innocent sufferer, a victim of white, technological imperialism, and his violence as a kind of heroic justice, in the second part his homicidal urge has lost the personal dimension and the aspect of justice and has become a generalized murderousness in the name of superstition. Azuma-zi in this second version is simply a native run amok.[7] Thus the revolutionary implications of the first half of the story are neatly balanced by a conservative version.

The coda of the story plays on this balance. Azuma-zi's suicide is, in its way, a primitive heroic act that recalls the just nihilism of the first half of the story, but then the scientific manager restores civilization by recircuiting the current and getting the trains running again.[8] Finally the narrator combines the two treatments of Azuma-zi's violence in the closing lines of the story: "So ended prematurely the worship of the Dynamo Deity, perhaps the most short-lived of all religions. Yet withal it could at least boast a Martyrdom and a Human Sacrifice." These lines are doubly ironic. Azuma-zi's superstition and Holroyd's materialism are both parodied in the comparison to religion, but they are also elevated, and the primitive natural forces that civilization in the form of the scientific manager generally ignores are acknowledged even as they are mocked. We might also note that the link between Holroyd and Azuma-zi is again made strong here, for either one can fulfill either role, martyr or sacrifice.

Toward Science Fiction

The opposition between civilization and nature in these tales is not there to be settled; it is a perpetual tension inherent in the human condition. We can understand how the imperative of the dilemma could drive Wells to seek and discover new forms of mediation and thereby to begin to write, not just parables of civilization, but stories alert to new possibilities. "The Flying Man" is, in its way, an evolutionary link between the conventional short story and what would become Wellsian science fiction, for in it a mediation is discovered which works elegantly to bridge the story's opposition but which makes no claim, either explicitly or allegorically, to any solution outside the story itself. We have here the logical structure of Wells's great science fiction without the explicit meanings that make other longer works so important.

"The Flying Man" explores a two-world structure. Initially the opposition is expressed by the location of two settlements: the English camp is downstream and the Chin village is upstream in the wilderness. The English expedition's task is to go from one to the other and back. Since there is no road, to get to the Chin village the expedition must use the river:

> When we went up we had to wade in the river for a mile where the valley narrows, with a smart stream frothing round our knees and the stones as slippery as ice. There it was I dropped my rifle. Afterwards the Sappers blasted the cliff with dynamite and made the convenient way you came by. Then below, where those very high cliffs come, we had to keep on dodging across the river—I should say we crossed it a dozen times in a couple of miles.

The allegory here is clear; the Lieutenant narrator relinquishes an important symbol of British power, enters a world "slippery as ice," and is forced to dodge his way forward. The loss of the rifle is just the first movement away from civilized forms toward some more elemental, savage, natural being. When the expedition reaches the village it is attacked by the Chin and loses the mule that carries provisions and utensils. And as the English are deprived of their civilized tools, the Chin seem to gain them: they have guns, albeit not rifles, and the Lieutenant describes them, not as figures of nature, but in terms of civilization: "We became aware of a number of gentlemen carrying matchlocks, and dressed in things like plaid dusters." Thus, what at first looked to be a somewhat unbalanced horizontal opposition between technological civilization and primitive nature gradually becomes a balanced vertical opposition. The expedition gets trapped on a high ledge, while down below runs the river patrolled by the Chin. The ledge is completely safe but lacks water and offers no way out. The river is dangerous, but is life-giving and a route back to camp. The Lieutenant resolves the dilemma by improvising a parachute and leaping from one world to the other and escaping.

The act of flying is the central unifying gesture in the story. In flying the Lieutenant finally moves from the English world to that of the Chin, both by bridging the physical gap, and, importantly, by unintentionally committing an act of elemental savagery:

> Then I looked down and saw in the darkness the river and the dead Sepoy rushing up towards me. But in the indistinct light I also saw three Chins, seemingly agast at the sight of me, and that the Sepoy was decapitated. At that I wanted to go back again.
>
> Then my boot was in the mouth of one, and in a moment he and I were in a heap with the canvas fluttering down on the top of us. I fancy I dashed out his brains with my foot. I expected nothing more than to be brained myself by the other two, but the poor heathen had never heard of Baldwin, and incontinently bolted.

Just as the Chin have decapitated the Sepoy, the Lieutenant dashes out the brains of a Chin. Under the fluttering canvas the union of Englishman and native is complete, and when the Lieutenant arrives at the English camp to summon help he is mistaken for a Chin by the sentinel who fires on him. If flying, becoming "the gay lieutenant bird," means in part becoming a savage again, it also means transcending the human altogether by an act whose suicidal potential is strongly underlined in the story. Before he thinks of parachuting the Lieutenant contemplates simply jumping off the cliff: "It seemed a pleasant and desirable thing to go rushing down through the air with something to drink—or no more thirst at any rate—at the bottom." After he parachutes, two of the Sepoy jump, and it is unclear whether they intended suicide or hoped to fly. As in Greek myth, the Daedalian triumph entails Icarian tragedy. In giving over civilization (suicide) and entering nature (becoming a bird) the Lieutenant becomes one with the natives below and also becomes a myth.

The act of radical mediation, it should be noted, is then rejected, but not before it has transformed the world. The Lieutenant does not accompany the rescue squad: "I had too good a thirst to provoke it by going with them." The story closes with him reaffirming his bond with British civilization by drinking whiskey and soda. But the ethnologist, to whom the Lieutenant narrates the tale, complains that the Lieutenant's act has permanently upset the purity of the opposition he has come to study: "Here am I, come four hundred miles out of my way to get what is left of the folk-lore of these people, before they are utterly demoralised by missionaries and the military, and all I find are a lot of impossible legends about a sandy-haired scrub of an infantry lieutenant."

"The Flying Man" uses a familiar structure of opposition. By the act of radical mediation, by focusing on the "cut," however, it goes beyond the other stories we have looked at and opens the way for thought about the connections and disjunctions within the universe of opposition. The imaginative exercise does not solve the puzzle of the relation of civilization to nature. It brings the opposites close together; it discovers an image in which the opposition is an identity. Such a story in its elegant and simple way is a model for Wells's more intricate meditations on the problems of civilization.

CHAPTER **3**

The Time Machine

W̶ELLS'S use of balanced opposition and symbolic mediation as a way of thinking finds its most perfect form in *The Time Machine*. If the novella imagines a future, it does so not as a forecast but as a way of contemplating the structures of our present civilization.[1] At one level *The Time Machine* presents a direct warning about the disastrous potential of class division. But at a deeper level it investigates large questions of difference and domination, and rather than settling the issues, it constructs unresolvable conflicts that return us to the central dilemmas that have characterized the evolutionary debate we looked at in the first chapter.

The Time Traveller's insights into the benefits of civilization are paradoxical. In his first interpretation of the meaning and structure of the world of 802,701 he finds a complex pleasure in the union of idyllic ease and evolutionary decline:

> To adorn themselves with flowers, to dance, to sing in the sunlight; so much was left of the artistic spirit, and no more. Even that would fade in the end into a contented inactivity. We are kept keen on the grindstone of pain and necessity, and, it seemed to me, that here was that hateful grindstone broken at last! (p. 43)

If there is regret at lost keenness here, there is also joy at escaped hardship. By the end of the novella, when he realizes that the decline has not conferred quite the benefits he anticipated and that the structure of civilization has degenerated into a primitive horror in which the Morlocks, the slothlike descendents of the laboring class, slaughter and eat the Eloi, the species descended from the upper classes, he entertains a different set of conflicting emotions. Now he balances a sense of the ironic justice of this situation with an irrational sympathy for the humanoid Eloi:

> Then I tried to preserve myself from the horror that was coming upon me, by regarding it as a rigorous punishment of human selfishness. Man had been content to live in ease and delight upon the labours of his fellow-man, had taken Necessity as his watchword and excuse, and in the fulness of time Necessity had come home to him. I even tried a Carlyle-like scorn of this wretched aristocracy-in-decay. But this attitude of mind was impossible. However great their intellectual degradation, the Eloi had kept too much of the human form not to claim my sympathy, and to make me perforce a sharer in their degradation and their Fear. (p. 81)

If the moral view, which would find satisfaction in the Eloi enslavement, is not adequate to the situation, it nevertheless works against the sense of pity, which is also, in itself, inadequate. Such nodes of conflicting insights and feelings are the expressions of tensions developed by the brutal oppositions on which the whole novella is built.

We can isolate two large, separate realms of opposition which operate in *The Time Machine*. One, essentially spatial, consists of the conflict between the Eloi and the Morlocks. Though the Time Traveller first views the 802,701 world as free from opposition, the novella traces his discovery of the radical oppositions that actually define that world; what begins as a vision of benign decay and carefree pastoral ends up as a vision of entrapment wherein the economic divisions of the present have become biological and territorial. The other opposition is temporal; it entails the opposition between the civilization of 1895 and a set of increasingly less civilized, more purely natural worlds of the future. Of these, the world of the Eloi-Morlock conflict is of course the most important. Towards the end of the novella the Time Traveller moves further into the future; he sees darkness and cold advance on the earth until life is diminished to huge, sluggish crabs and then finally to a football-sized organism that hops fitfully on the tideless shore.[2]

Because the Time Traveller arrives in 802,701, not by a process of incremental progressions, but by a single leap, the structure of the novella poses a puzzle: what is the relation of the future to the present? The Time Traveller and the reader are engaged in the same activity: they try to understand the nature of the temporal contrast presented and then to discover connections. Like evolutionary biologists, they must first understand what distinguishes two species and then they must reconstruct the evolutionary sequence that links them; the difference between Eohippus and the modern horse is like that between the modern human and the Eloi or the Morlocks. Unlike the biologist, however, the Time Traveller and the reader are engaged in negotiating a pattern more complex than a simple genealogical sequence. We must figure out what bonds exist amidst the differences between the Time Traveller and his and our distant grandchildren. The mental act of reconstructing the evolutionary connection involves more than just taxonomic description; it is not simply a perceiving of a pure two-world system; it entails examining a whole series of ambiguous moral conflicts.

During the course of the novella, as the truth reveals itself and the meanings of the discovered oppositions change, one relation between the present and the future persists: the future is a *reduction* of the present.[3] The future offers a simplification of issues that is much like that which occurs in conventional pastoral: economic and social complexities have disappeared, and the issues of the world are those determined by elementary human nature. But to compare *The Time Machine* to a pastoral is somewhat misleading; though both diminish the importance of civilized forms and conventions, in *The Time Machine* the main agent of change is a biological regression not found in the conventional pastoral. The inhabitants of the future have lost much of the erotic, intellectual, and moral energy that we generally associate with human beings and which it is the purpose of the usual pastoral to liberate. The society of the future is reduced to what in 1895 might be considered childish needs and pleasures, and it is under the terms of this radical diminution that the systems of spatial opposition work.

Such a reduction certainly simplifies social issues, but the first question it raises is how human or how bestial are these distant cousins of present-day humanity. The split between the Eloi and the Morlocks raises this question from opposite directions: the Eloi seem subhumans, the Morlocks superanimals. The Time Traveller certainly considers Weena the most human creature he finds in the future, but as he acknowledges, he tends to think of her as more human than she is.[4] Her humanoid appearance tends to obscure how much she is a pet rather than a human companion. At the other extreme, the Morlocks, though they too are supposedly descended from present-day humanity, because they look like sloths, always seem bestial to the Time Traveller. For much of his time in 802,701 he does not realize

44

their importance; he treats them first as "ghosts," then as lower animals, then as servants to the Eloi. Even at the end when he comprehends their domination of the Eloi he never really conceives of them as human. Thus the novella sets up a symmetrical illusion: the Eloi, because of their appearance, seem more human than they are; the Morlocks, again because of appearance, seem less.

The Time Traveller's relation to the Eloi engages special problems because it involves, not simply identification, but affection across the abyss of species difference. Critics have found the Time Traveller's attention to his "little woman" disturbing and have treated the hints of repressed sexuality, of pedophilia, as a novelistic blunder.[5] I would suggest, however, that the unease generated by this relationship is apt, for at issue is the whole puzzle of human relations to nonhumans. The Time Traveller himself is confused by Weena. He can treat her as an equal and contemplate massacring Morlocks when he loses her, but he also forgets her easily. The tension and the ambiguities of their relationship derive from the impossibility of defining either an identity or a clear difference. To render such a state Wells plays on the inherently ambiguous relationship between adults and children.

The puzzle of Weena's sexuality is reflected and reversed by the Time Traveller's relation to the Morlocks. When he first meets the Eloi he allows them to touch him: "I felt other soft little tentacles upon my back and shoulders. They wanted to make sure I was real. There was nothing in this at all alarming" (p. 30). Similar behavior by the Morlocks, however, leads the Time Traveller to an hysterical smashing of skulls. At first, the touch of the Morlocks is hardly distinguishable from that of the Eloi: it is as if "sea anemones were feeling over my face with their soft palps" (p. 57). But this same intimate approach becomes sinister as the Time Traveller becomes aware of the Morlocks' real intent, and he feels horror later, at night in the forest, when he becomes aware that "Soft little hands, too, were creeping over my coat and back, touching even my neck" (p. 93). The reasons for the different reactions to this intimate approach are obvious; what we need to observe, however, is the area of identity here. If the repressed sexuality of the relation with Weena leads to a passive and childish activity (weaving flowers, dancing to burning matches), the Morlocks' almost seductive aggression leads to an antipathy which generates violence and ingenious invention.[6]

The central mystery of Eloi and Morlock humanity and of the Time Traveller's relation to it is emblematized by the statue of the sphinx that the Time Traveller sees when he first arrives in 802,701. The symbol works at a number of levels. It stands for the paradox of a progress that is a regression: the future is represented by a monument that we associate with early civilization. Thus, the future is a return to the past, to the childhood, so to speak, of human society. The sphinx herself is also a poser of riddles: when Oedipus met her she asked him the riddle of man who appears in different forms. This connection is clearly in Wells's mind, for no sooner has the Time Traveller seen the statue than he begins speculating about the possibilities of the human form in this distant future. But it is in her own appearance that the sphinx raises the most perplexing puzzle, for she represents a literal combination of human and animal: woman and lion. We ask whether Weena is a woman or not, whether a Morlock is a beast or not; here in the sphinx we have a creature which is both. The sphinx marks the cut; it is a union of a crucial opposition and, like the flying man, points to the possibility of transcending the contradiction. This important mediating symbolism is repeated in a striking but diminished form by the statue of a Faun which the Time Traveller later discovers (p. 77), another literal mixture of human and animal.[7]

Just as the sphinx and the faun render visually the puzzle of the relation of human and beast and offer a union of the supposed dichotomy, they also denote the areas of human and animal activity that have been diminished by the decline into the future. The sphinx, the poser of riddles, is a figure of the very intellectual prowess that the childish creatures of the future lack. Similarly, the faun embodies the sexual energy that is noticeably absent. Thus, while the statues link the human and the animal, they do so ironically; they suggest a potential for accomplishment and for civilization of which the Eloi and the Morlocks are biologically incapable.

While such issues of the relation of present-day humanity to these future creatures pervade the novella, the opposition between the Eloi and the Morlocks themselves, of which the Time Traveller becomes increasingly aware as he learns more about the future's underworld, has an important social meaning. In the split between the two species we see a split intrinsic to technological civilization itself. This is no dark secret of the tale, of course:[8] the Time Traveller's final interpretation of how the split developed refers directly back to the division of labor in contemporary England. But the values that initially caused the split persist in the far future, and, in ways that are not generally recognized, the two species represent and at the same time parody values that belong, not merely to British capitalist civilization, but to all technological cultures. Though the Morlocks are hairy, have an apelike posture, cannot bear light, and live in burrows of a sort, any simple equation of them with the lower animals won't do. They live amidst thudding machines, and their habitat is artificially ventilated. The passage down which the Time Traveller climbs to visit them has a ladder with iron rungs. Unlike the Eloi, the Morlocks function as a group; they are individually weak, but they cooperate. Thus, though their specific intellectual and emotional capacities remain largely unknown, symbolically they subsume one aspect of what we admire in civilization: organized technological mastery. And the Eloi with their trivial, careless aestheticism embody the alternative leisure aspect of civilization, the pure delight in beauty, gaity, play. They live for these and as much as possible avoid even thinking about necessity and pain. The Morlock-Eloi split may be the result of today's class divisions, but in its final form it expresses two high and apparently contradictory values of human civilization: mastery and aesthetic leisure.[9]

The landscape of the future becomes an extension of the contradictions represented in Eloi and Morlock. The surface of the countryside, while much hedged and walled, is devoid of meaningful divisions; the ruined castles of the Eloi hardly differentiate inside and outside; at one time the Time Traveller even gets lost because the field in which he has landed is indistinguishable from any other; only the presence of the statue of the sphinx defines it. But a radically different world exists beneath the Eloi pastoral, and so it is *down* that the Time Traveller must go to find an alternative. Up and down, therefore, become an important expression of the basic Eloi-Morlock opposition. The same opposition is expressed in the opposition between light and dark. The imbalance of the opposition is symbolized by the fact that the Morlocks can intrude on the Eloi above-ground preserve at night.

The cut between the two opposed realms is marked most concretely by the strange palace of green porcelain that the Time Traveller visits when seeking to recover his lost time machine. The building is made of material that reminds the Time Traveller of Chinese porcelain and has an oriental look to it; it seems a special version of the palaces the Eloi inhabit. But within this aestheticized exterior is a museum of technology, a "latter-day South Kensington." It thus partakes of both the worlds of Eloi aesthetics and Morlock technology. But most importantly it blurs the line between up and down. As he walks along one of the galleries, the Time Traveller finds himself unexpectedly underground. He confesses he wasn't even aware of the slope. And then, as if to underline the importance of this transition, but also to offer a new way of treating it, the editor, a person who appears no-where else in the novella, supplies a curious footnote: "It may be, of course, that the floor did not slope—but that the museum was built into the side of a hill" (p. 85). By translating the up-down division into a lateral one, the museum ingeniously mediates the division's absolute separation. That is not to say that it resolves the split: Weena is still afraid of the dark, and the Time Traveller retreats back to the light. But it is an important symbolic possibility in an otherwise destructive and rigid opposition.

Though a treasury of the present in the future, the museum of green porcelain also stands for the important mediating possibilities of modern technology in the face of the future's natural antithesis. The diminished intelligence of the creatures of the future prevents them from understanding or using the museum; only the Time Traveller is capable of realizing the museum's potential. The Time Traveller thus becomes the main mediator in the future system of static oppositions because by means of his human intelligence, passion, and morality he is able to bridge its dichotomies. He reconciles in himself the masterful and aesthetic aspects of culture that are at war in the future: at the end of the story he displays to his audience a flower, the token of Eloi aestheticism and affection, but he also vigorously demands a piece of meat, a token of Morlock carnivorousness. The future is a horror in part because the divisions that are for us in the present still capable of modification and correction have become a purely natural competition, a predatory antithesis that does not allow for exchange or change. The Time Traveller offers some hope because by using tools and by acting ethically he is able to break down the bounds of the otherwise rigid, hostile evolutionary categories.

It is his mastery of fire that gives the Time Traveller his most distinctive mediating power. That power is complex, however, and as in the cases of the other mediating images, involves contradiction and operates on a number of planes of meaning simultaneously. In *The Time Machine* fire defines civilized humanity. It is an image of both domestic security and war. It has an aesthetic function and a technological one. Finally, it is an emblem of the paradox of degenerative progress that dominates the whole novella.

The Time Traveller himself makes the link between fire and present-day humanity when he observes how rare fire is in nature:

I don't know if you have ever thought what a rare thing flame must be in the absence of man and in a temperate climate. The sun's heat is rarely strong enough to burn, even when it is focussed by dewdrops, as is sometimes the case in more tropical districts. Lightning may blast and blacken, but it rarely gives rise to wide-spread fire. Decaying vegetation may occasionally smoulder with the heat of its fermentation, but this rarely results in flame. In this decadence, too, the art of fire-making had been forgotten on the earth. The red tongues that went licking up my heap of wood were an altogether new and strange thing to Weena. (p. 92).

Implicit in the absence of fire is the question we have looked at earlier of the actual "humanity" of either the Eloi or the Morlocks. In this formulation of the issue, fire is a symbol of human control over nature, a control that the future has lost. Such innocence has ambiguous value; earlier in the story, before the Time Traveller has realized that the Eloi are victims, he approves of such ignorance. It is night; he has lost his time machine; searching for it he blunders into the dilapidated hall of the Eloi and, after striking a match, demands his machine from them. Their confusion conveys two things to him: that "they had forgotten about matches" and that they had forgotten about fear (p. 46). The link between the two forgettings is casual but significant. To forget about matches is to lose as aspect of today's technology, to revert to a primitive state in which tools are unknown. But to forget fear, one would expect, is to live in a world of complete security, to have escaped the primitive natural situation in which fear is necessary for survival. Thus, while the forgetting of matches suggests regression, the forgetting of fear suggests progress. At this early stage in his acquaintance with the future the Time Traveller interprets both forgettings as the privileges of progress, as the evidence of a carefree pastoral idyll. Under these circumstances the paradox that progress has led to regression is not dismaying.

So long as he does not understand the real situation of the future the Time Traveller has no conception of the importance his mastery of fire has, and he uses his matches merely to entertain the Eloi, to make them dance and laugh. The irony of such trivialization is that it actually prevents knowledge, as is clear in the following passage:

I proceeded, as I have said, to question Weena about this Underworld, but here again I was disappointed. At first she would not understand my questions, and presently she refused to answer them. She shivered as though the topic was unendurable. And when I pressed her, perhaps a little harshly, she burst into tears. They were the only tears, except my own, I ever saw in that Golden Age. When I saw them I ceased abruptly to trouble about the Morlocks, and was only concerned in banishing these signs of her human inheritance from Weena's eyes. And very soon she was smiling and clapping her hands, while I solemnly burned a match. (p. 66)

By using fire as a toy the Time Traveller diverts Weena from exhibiting "signs of her human inheritance." His instinct to avert tears is understandable, but the completeness with which the concern for Weena's innocence overrides the concern with the facts about the Morlocks has signs of panic. The other time that the Time Traveller uses matches to entertain the Eloi is also after they have been "distressed" by his inquiries about the Morlocks (p. 61). In both cases the match is used for entertainment at the expense of further knowledge, to sustain a complacent happiness which is, in fact, an illusion.

Though he is capable of using matches to preserve an innocent decorum, the Time Traveller is not simply a Victorian gentleman intent on preventing children from learning or expressing the grim truth. The match may be a toy, but it is also an instrument for seeing. When he first looks for the time machine the Time Traveller uses a match. When he looks down one of the Morlock wells he uses a match. And when he enters the underworld he uses a match: "The view I had [of the Morlocks' cavern] was as much as one could see in the burning of a match" (p. 70). When two paragraphs later he chides himself for coming to the future ill-equipped, the Time Traveller emphasizes the importance of matches for his investigation: though he might prefer a "kodak," the match, feeble as it is, is the single "tool" that he has brought. For the Time Traveller to be master of fire is for him to have an intellectual dominance, and the safety match becomes a symbol of that aspect of present-day technology.

Intellectual dominance leads to other kinds of dominance. The ambiguous potential of fire is most forcefully realized when the Time Traveller uses it, not for entertaining or seeing, but as a weapon. The match becomes an important defensive tool which allows the Time Traveller to move across the boundaries of this world. And after he visits the green porcelain palace and comes away with matches and camphor, the Time Traveller begins to use fire as a tool of aggression. With the intention of "amaz[ing] our friends," he sets a pile of wood on fire. Now when Weena wants to dance and play with the light, the Time Traveller prevents her. A little later he is forced to start a second fire.

What is important for our understanding of the symbol is that the fires fail him in diametrically opposite ways. The second, beside which he goes to sleep, goes out and the Morlocks, unhindered by the fire, almost overcome him. But the first, forgotten and left behind, starts a forest fire which threatens to destroy even the Time Traveller himself. We have here an expression of the danger of dependence on the very technology that allows for mastery: it can either fail to perform even its elementary expectations, or it can go wild and overperform. In both cases the human is betrayed by his own technological sophistication. Fire, which up to this point has been a symbol of technology's ability to mediate, here develops its own destructive opposition between too much and too little. The puzzle that a dependence on technology presents is again rendered a little later in the novella when the Time Traveller, mounted on the time machine's saddle, confidently tries to light a match to drive off the assaulting Morlocks and discovers that he has safety matches that won't strike without the box.

Yet it is just at the moments when fire gets out of control that the Time Traveller performs his most radical mediations. When the fire goes out he is forced to lay about with his other tool, a makeshift club, and when he is overtaken by the forest fire he comes to feel pity for the Morlocks. In both cases, though in different ways, he bridges the distance between himself and these alien beings.

In the first instance what starts as an act of self-defence becomes more aggressive until the Time Traveller is enjoying destroying others:

> It was indescribably horrible in the darkness to feel all these soft creatures heaped upon me. I felt as if I was in a monstrous spider's web. I was overpowered, and went down. I felt little teeth nipping at my neck. I rolled over, and as I did so my hand came against my iron lever. It gave me strength. I struggled up, shaking the human rats from me, and holding the bar short, I thrust where I judged their faces might be. I could feel the succulent giving of flesh and bone under my blows, and for a moment I was free. (p. 95)

The striking word, "succulent," in the last sentence conveys both the pleasure the Time Traveller gets from such battery and the strange similarity between such violent activity and Morlock cannibalism. The Time Traveller here reveals himself as like the Morlocks and quite unlike the passionless and passive Eloi.

A more direct acknowledgment of his union with the Morlocks occurs after the first fire overtakes them all and the Time Traveller stops clubbing the "human rats" and becomes a victim with them. "I followed in the Morlocks' path" (p. 96). In the face of the larger catastrophe of the forest fire, the discriminations and hostilities that have kept the Time Traveller and the Morlocks apart are abandoned, and the Time Traveller, "assured of their absolute helplessness and misery in the glare," refrains from his aggressions. Even when the thought of the "awful fate" of Weena whom he has lost in the confusion moves him "to begin a massacre of the helpless abominations" about him, the Time Traveller "contains" himself.

The logical distinctions to be made at this point are complex. The Time Traveller is both identical with the Morlocks and separate from them. In the morning, exhausted, shoeless, with grass tied to his feet to protect them from the hot soil, he is only remotely the master scientist. He has been reduced to a bare forked thing and forced to acknowledge his bond in suffering with the other creatures of this world. But with the difference between himself and the Morlocks overwhelmed by their common fate as victims of the fire, the Time Traveller reasserts a distinction, not by exhibiting mastery of some sort over the others, but by restraining himself, by mastering his own brutal nature.

The Time Traveller's self-control has a complex symbolic function. It marks his difference from both Morlock and Eloi, since neither species seems capable of such conscious mastery of the self. It is his ability—a distinctly human ability—to bridge distinctions, to recognize an area of identity within a difference, that sets him apart from the other forms of life which will presumably remain locked in opposition. The Time Traveller is able to assert an ethical view in the face of the evolutionary competition that rules the future. He offers the promise of, if not resolving, at least comprehending the problems inherent in the conflict between evolution and ethics. In place of absolute antagonism between classes and between species, he acknowledges momentarily the bonds that extend across those divisions. Such an act of sympathizing with a different creature is an important gesture in Wells; we will explore it more fully in the next chapter. What interests us right now, however, is not the particular thematic issue, but its structural fitness: the act both acknowledges difference and momentarily bridges that difference. In this way it reflects the central pattern of *The Time Machine* itself: its art is to create emblems of difference and separation and then to meditate on the balances, the antitheses and the identities that are possible.

In saying that reconciling both sides of a conflict is the central act of *The Time Machine*, I do not mean to suggest that the novella is without explicit moral point. The Time Traveller's latest interpretation of the division between Eloi and Morlock foresees and fears the transformation of an economic social division into a biological one, of an ethical issue into an evolutionary one. Clearly, Wells's moral point here is to impress on an audience which tends to accept the economic divisions of civilization as "natural" the horror of what it would mean if that division were truly natural. More narrowly, one may perhaps legitimately examine the novella as a treatise on possible evolutionary directions and study it as a prediction of sorts. But in isolating such moral ideas in the novella, one needs to be aware of the danger of distorting the deepest mechanisms of Wells's imagination: he is not the sort of writer who hides an esoteric meaning which is available only to the painstaking exegete. The difficulty one has deriving a clear reading of the future from *The Time Machine* comes from the large, unresolved oppositions of the tale. Instead of trying to "settle" ambiguities, to find out the one true reading, we should focus on the specific and powerful contradictions the story sets up. To see contradiction clearly in all its appalling and irresolvable conflict, and then to try by whatever imaginative means possible to mediate that disjunction: that is the true and deep moral of *The Time Machine*.

In the last paragraphs of the novella Wells offers us an explicit instance of how to read this way, to accept both sides of a contradiction. The Time Traveller has disappeared on his second journey three years ago, and the narrator speculates about his fate.[10] Wells here enforces ambiguity. And one understands why: any plot resolution would resolve the earlier tensions in such a way as to diminish the complexity of the whole vision. In this final stasis of opposition, not only does the frame distance us, as Robert Philmus has argued,[11] but the narrator proposes an attitude diametrically contrary to that of the Time Traveller. "I, for my own part," the narrator confesses,

> cannot think that these latter days of weak experiment, fragmentary theory, and mutual discord are indeed man's culminating time! I say, for my own part. He, I know—for the question had been discussed among us long before the Time Machine was made—thought but cheerlessly of the Advancement of Mankind, and saw in the growing pile of civilization only a foolish heaping that must inevitably fall back upon and destroy its makers in the end. (p. 117)

Here again we see the two attitudes of promise and hubris implicit in the symbolism of the matches. And then the narrator tries to combine the two in a single stance: if the Time Traveller's vision of bleak decline is the true one, the narrator argues, "it remains for us to live as though it were not so." He finally settles on an image that echoes the more hellish imagery of the novella itself and also alludes to the image of the feeble light shed by the match of science at the end of "The Rediscovery of the Unique": "But to me the future is still black and blank—is a vast ignorance, lit at a few casual places by the memory of his story."[12]

We see Wells here balancing pessimism and optimism. But the novella achieves an even more essential balance between a vision of change and a vision of no change. If we recall the two realms of opposition with which we began this essay, we can see that they themselves create an opposition. The horror of the split between the Eloi and the Morlocks lies in the fact that the divisions of modern civilization have not changed but have, by a process of speciation, become intrinsic in nature. But the other opposition, that between the present and the future, is a vision of change, of entropic decline. The first opposition implies that the essential injustice, the conflict of classes, will not change. On the other hand, the second opposition argues that in spite of all humans might do, things will change. The processes of entropy and evolution will continue, and any vision of humanity's place in the universe must take into account these large movements that are outside our control. This conflict between a vision of change and a vision of stasis undermines any simple thematic reading at the deepest level. Viewed as a prediction, the novella contradicts itself: the economic pessimism foresees a grim permanence; the cosmic pessimism sees an equally grim movement. And if the cosmic has the last word, that does not disqualify the economic: in terms of mere hundreds of thousands of years the cosmic process, by dividing the classes into species, merely confirms the continuity of the economic. Only on the scale of millions of years does the division of classes cease to be a controlling factor. So we face a problem as we try to derive a message from *The Time Machine*. But the problem is not a flaw: such unresolved, antithetical conflict is central to the way Wells's imagination works and gives his fiction a profundity, based on the ambiguities of human desire and experience, that is rare in thought about the future.

It may help us see exactly what Wells has achieved in *The Time Machine* if we briefly observe how George Pal in his film of *The Time Machine* (1960) avoids facing the very conflicts that define Wells's work. First of all, Pal erases the issue of evolution and ethics by making the Morlocks monsters and the Eloi simply badly educated humans. Though for a while the film allows us to think there may be a genetic problem, by the end the Eloi, who have spoken English from the beginning, show that they are human in every way: they become social; Weena, a starlet, falls in love; a male Eloi learns to fight; they use records (the talking rings); and in the end the Time Traveller (here H. George Wells) returns with books to repair the educational gap that has prevented the Eloi from succeeding. These people are not involved in any evolutionary or cosmic process; they are simply humans living in a "dark age." And while the Eloi are beautiful humans who can be reindoctrinated, the Morlocks represent nothing but horror. More than simply a softening of Wells's pessimism has taken place here: the intellectual tensions of the conflicts, both between the present and the future and between the values represented by the Eloi and the Morlocks, have disappeared.

If Pal ignores the biological issue so central to Wells, he evades the economic issue as well. In place of Wells's vision of class difference developing into species difference, Pal gives us a vague history of the first part of our century as it is defined by its wars. We know that the wars went on and that the bombs got more destructive until finally the human race "split." The conflict is not in capitalism itself, but in the opposition of capitalism and communism. The clear hint is that the Morlocks are, loosely, the Russians; the story of the Time Traveller's final return to revive Eloi culture is, thus, an allegory of the liberation of peoples oppressed by totalitarian communism. The sense of catastrophe, individual, social, racial, cosmic, that so darkens Wells's end, is entirely missing from Pal's. Like Nunez in Wells's "The Country of the Blind" (see chapter 6, below), the film George seeks a society he can dominate, and this time there seems no chance of the kind of ironic development that keeps Nunez from ruling the country of the blind.

It is important that we understand how Pal has changed the very nature of the story's thought. Wells's myth develops systematically a set of logical oppositions as a way of making us confront contradictions latent in our society and begin to think anew about our civilization, but Pal's myth lacks a logical base; our values and our civilization, except that they have wars, are not questioned. The future need only be returned to the present for all to be well; it can be "cured" by discipline and books. Wells has created a static nightmare which has the virtue of forcing us to reconsider our own world; Pal, by envisioning a change, a restoration, has freed himself from that stasis but has also avoided thought about the need for change in the present or the future. He has robbed Wells's story of the essence of its conflict and replaced intellectual tension with melodramatic conventions that inspire unreflective affirmation.

CHAPTER 4

The Logical Web

THE *Time Machine* is extraordinary because in its simple and stark way it establishes Wells's subject and sets up the language in which he will think about it. The novella's long gestation may be accounted for in part by the difficulty of the project, but it in turn accounts for the importance of the work. In the major works that follow *The Time Machine* Wells uses very different styles, plots, and situations, but despite these surface variations, the deep methods and preoccupations of *The Time Machine* persist. We can see these other novels as studies of details of the large issues of *The Time Machine*. And just as an enlarged photograph of a detail of a painting leads us back to the painting itself with new insight and appreciation, so the study of these other novels repeatedly leads us back to *The Time Machine*.

The technique of thinking by means of oppositions and mediations informs the structure of all of Wells's work in this period. It is a process of energetic imaginative creation according to rules which do not limit the range but which enforce focus. And then, most importantly, it is a process of prolonged pressure and endurance, of sustained attention. Though no "answer" is finally produced, the act of such meditation makes the author and his audience alive to the complex dynamics of the problems.

I am calling the set of oppositions and mediations a system, but I do not mean that Wells has a machine that produces art or thought, much less answers. A small repertory of essential images of opposition permits Wells to pose in various ways central puzzles of evolution and ethics, civilization and nature. In this early work opposition tends to be expressed biologically, by having humans confront some type of alien being, and spatially, by creating a landscape in which indoors and outdoors, up and down, denote important divisions. Wells then mediates these oppositions by images of union, like the sphinx or the green museum in *The Time Machine,* and by technological images, in particular the "misused tool" and fire. In this chapter we will examine the body of Wells's early work as an expression of this structure of thought, and at the end we will focus on a single work, *The War of the Worlds,* as a recapitulation of the whole.

Humans and Nonhumans

To even a casual reader of Wells it must be obvious that the meeting with alien life is a frequent, even a dominant theme for him. There are, of course, important stories that do not explicitly imagine some strange, new, nonhuman being, but such stories mark the exception rather than the rule. Eloi, Morlocks, Beast People, Martians, Selenites in the novels and the multitude of strange creatures—curiously seldom humanoid—in the stories constitute a tribe that owns an important territory of Wells's imagination. Once we start to think of the subject we can find that bit by bit the domination of aliens expands until even the supposed exceptions fit into the scheme. We can move from Martians to Morlocks to Eloi, so why not on to primitive natives and to anarchists? And, taking the same sized steps, why not the blind people in "The Country of the Blind" or even the invisible man in the novel of that name? Or to move in another direction, one can step from the Octopuslike Martians to the organized octopi in "The Sea Raiders" to the military ants in "The Empire of the Ants" to the blood-sucking orchid in "The Flowering of the Strange Orchid" to the cholera bacillus in "The Stolen Bacillus." We can see that in a sense Wells's stories and novels aspire to a rendering of all the possibilities of human confrontation with other forms of (conscious) life.

The very completeness of the web suggests that Wells is interested in trying out the various bonds and antipathies that can exist between beings. In general in the short stories he deals with creatures with whom no communication is possible (ants, octopi, orchids, Aepyornis). In the novels, however, he sets up a system of relationships between humans and creatures who one way or another express an aspect of what we value in humanity while at the same time remaining alien. We have discussed how the Eloi and the Morlocks in their diminished way blanket civilization's virtues. In the Martians of *The War of the*

Worlds, the Selenites of *The First Men in the Moon,* and the beast men of *The Island of Doctor Moreau,* Wells focuses on precise attractions and antipathies: the Martians, while physically repulsive, are superior to humans in intellect; the Selenites, also repulsive, are skilled in social organization; the beast men occupy a middle ground, uneasily human in appearance, dully human in intellect.

In general Wells's heroes feel a bond with creatures like the Eloi, who share the human appearance, but antipathy with creatures who, whatever their intellect, look nonhuman. As we shall see, one of the processes of the novels is to transcend that instinct.[1] Also, the higher the intellect of the alien, the more threatening it is. This is important because a paradox develops: the more intellectually superior creatures are, that is, the more capable they are of establishing an ethical relationship with other forms of being, the more likely they are to engage in evolutionary competition, while creatures of inferior intellectual accomplishment are occasionally able to achieve a more ethical relationship.

Every confrontation between the human and the nonhuman involves the evolutionary-ethical puzzle. The nonhuman, as a different species, exists in an unstable relationship with the human, and insofar as the human's and nonhuman's needs overlap the two are going to compete and a struggle for survival is going to occur. As Huxley argues, ethical questions are out of place in pure nature. The natural relation between wolf and deer entails predation and suffering without any kind of moral judgment (or, if we are going to condemn, we should condemn not the wolf, but the wolf's creator for developing a creature whose function it is to kill deer). If humanity were living simply in a state of nature no one could blame it for brutality or domination. But humanity's intelligence, Huxley argues, leads to a civilization in which the ethical imperative replaces the evolutionary.

Wells's early fiction probes two questions that arise out of such issues. The first is, when, if ever, do the demands of survival obviate the ethical criteria? When is nonethical behavior justified? In a curious way this question is not limited to conflicts between different species. The confrontation between human and nonhuman is simply a type for a whole series of confrontations which includes those between humans of different races, nationalities, and classes. It may not be extravagant to say that all difference leads to imbalance and the threat of domination and generates the puzzle of evolution and ethics.

If human intellect leads to ethics, it is reasonable to expect alien intelligence also to be ethical. The second question is, at what point, if any, does the nonethical behavior of the alien obviate the human's ethical imperative? The solutions to such questions must come from moralists; the role of Wells's fiction is not to answer such questions but to create structures that make us rethink them.

Wells's main probings of the ways evolutionary and ethical imperatives conflict and of the kinds of obligations that can extend across species difference occur in the novels, but the tale, "Æpyornis Island" gives neat, concise expression of the problem and its ramifications and demonstrates how the work will establish opposite expressions as a way of setting up and balancing the situation. The main narrator in "Æpyornis Island," a man appropriately named Butcher, recounts how he was stranded on an atoll for four years, the first two of which he spent in the company of a growing giant bird, the Æpyornis, now, alas, extinct. The core story tells how much Butcher enjoyed the bird's company ("You'd be surprised what an interesting bird that Æpyornis chick was"), the difficulties that occurred as the bird reached full growth (he was "about fourteen feet high to the bill of him, with a big broad head like the end of a pickaxe"), and the final battle between the two when the bird got ornery. Butcher takes the bird's unpleasant disposition to heart:

> I don't suppose I ever felt so hurt by anything before or since. It was the
> brutal ingratitude of the creature. I'd been more than a brother to him.
> I'd hatched him, educated him. A great gawky, out-of-date bird! and me
> a human being—heir of the ages and all that.

This little passage is interesting for the way it combines a genuine affection with a more questionable pride. Butcher tries to link himself and the bird ("I'd hatched him") and set himself apart from him ("And me a human being"). By naming the chick Friday, Butcher has worked a similar double transformation: he has raised a pet to human status and lowered a companion to servant status. When Friday becomes truly murderous and prevents him from coming on shore, Butcher devises a bolo, snags the bird's gawky legs, upends him, and saws through his throat with his pen knife. But no sooner has he won the battle for survival than he regrets his victory:

> I don't like to think of that even now. I felt like a murderer while I did
> it, though my anger was hot against him. When I stood over him and saw

him bleeding on the white sand, and his beautiful great legs and neck writhing in his last agony . . . Pah!

With that tragedy loneliness came upon me like a curse. Good Lord! you can't imagine how I missed that bird. I sat by his corpse and sorrowed over him, and shivered as I looked round the desolate, silent reef. I thought of what a jolly little bird he had been when he was hatched, and of a thousand pleasant tricks he had played before he went wrong. I thought if I'd only wounded him I might have nursed him round into a better understanding. If I'd had any means of digging into the coral rock I'd have buried him. I felt exactly as if he was human. As it was, I couldn't think of eating him, so I put him in the lagoon, and the little fishes picked him clean.

Here the identification across the species difference is clear and powerful. In place of competition he envisions companionship, and in place of justified self-defense he sees murder.

The puzzle this simple event expresses is brought into clear prominence by the contrast afforded by the subplot of the story. Butcher and two "native chaps" originally set off looking for fossil eggs. When one of the natives, bitten by a centipede, drops and breaks an egg, Butcher "hit[s] him about rather." In revenge the two natives try to abandon Butcher on the island. Butcher shoots one and later finds the other dead from the centipede bite. Butcher never thinks of calling the killing of the native murder, nor does he ever regret beating the native. By disregarding the ethical view of his atrocities, Butcher is, in effect, enforcing a separation between himself and the natives and treating them as nonhuman. Thus, the subplot mirrors, in the sense of echoing and reversing, the main plot in which Butcher feels impelled to stress the link between himself and the large bird. The story probes the issue of ethical obligation by presenting us with two opposite extremes: a savage and callous murder treated without ethical considerations, and a justifiable act of evolutionary self-defense treated ethically.

That Butcher cannot eat Friday is one of the signs of a closeness that overrides species difference. Throughout Wells's early work cannibalism is a test of difference: if cannibalism or the fear of cannibalism is involved (as with the Morlocks and the Eloi), then the two species are really one, but if it is not involved, then they are separate. Cannibalism is a transformation of the sense of murder Butcher felt: if the other species is different from ours, murder is not involved, but if it is the same, then murder is involved. The problem is raised acutely

near the beginning of *The War of the Worlds.* The narrator has met
a group of soldiers and told them about the Martians. They get into
a discussion:

> "Crawl up under cover and rush 'em, say I," said one.
>
> "Get aht!" said another. "What's cover against this 'ere 'eat? Sticks to
> cook yer! What we got to do is to go as near as the ground'll let us, and
> then drive a trench."
>
> "Blow yer trenches! You always want trenches; you ought to ha' been
> born a rabbit, Snippy."
>
> "Ain't they got any necks, then?" said a third, abruptly—a little, contem-
> plative, dark man, smoking a pipe.
>
> I repeated my description.
>
> "Octopuses," said, he, "that's what I calls 'em. Talk about fishers of men—
> fighters of fish it is this time!"
>
> "It ain't no murder killing beasts like that," said the first speaker. (At-
> lantic Edition, vol. 3, p. 259)

The separation between Martians and men is made from two directions here. Since the Martians use their weapons to "cook" men, they
are themselves drawing a line, otherwise they would be cannibals. But
also the fishiness of the Martians allows the first speaker to avoid the
accusation of murder. It is significant that the reference to cooking
puts men below the Martians (as does the next accusation of a man
being like a rabbit) while the later discussion treats the Martians as
just fancy fish and therefore below humanity. The point to be made
is that it doesn't matter which way the hierarchy goes so long as there
is a clear division. Even if the Martians are superior to humans, the
evolutionary "doctrine" of survival of the fittest justifies killing them.
According to these soldiers, ethics enters only if the two are of the
same species.

In other parts of *The War of the Worlds* this ethically sterile situation
is challenged. As the narrator points out, it is disgusting to watch the
Martians kill and use human beings for food: "I think," he modestly
cautions, "that we should remember how repulsive our carnivorous
habits would seem to an intelligent rabbit." The role of victim leads
us to give an ethically weighted significance to even the most purely
evolutionary situation. The special perspective enjoined by *The War
of the Worlds* places humanity, not at the top of the natural hierarchy,
but in a middle position, the predator of lower nature (ants, wasps,
rabbits, dodoes, even Tasmanians) and the victim of the superior Martians. This structure makes us acutely aware of the ethical horror of

natural evolutionary behavior and makes us reconsider the relations that can exist across species lines.

Near the end of *The War of the Worlds* the narrator has a moment in which he experiences the possibility of a different way of dividing life, a way which cuts across species and acknowledges the bonds of intelligence that transcend biology. As the last Martian dies, the narrator, wandering through a London deserted of all intelligent life except for the marginal figures of wild dogs and black, carnivorous birds, becomes aware of how much the Martians themselves can be seen as partners to humanity rather than as enemies: "Night, the mother of fear and mystery, was coming upon me. But while that voice sounded the solitude, the desolation had been endurable; by virtue of it London had still seemed alive, and the sense of life about me had upheld me" (p. 434). If there is division in species, there is a union in intellect, and, for a moment anyway, the narrator perceives the quality of this latter union as more important than the competitive division. As the novel ends all the machinery of decline and fall that has been set up and which we have been led to anticipate to be designed for humanity, comes down on the Martians; the tragedy of the novel is theirs.

In *The Island of Doctor Moreau* the sympathy with nonhumans is rendered more difficult by the absence of anything like real human intellect in the Beast Men. But that lack does not mean that no bonds exist. If in *The War of the Worlds* the reader moves from the easy antipathy of the soldiers, based on appearance, to the moment of union on the basis of intellect, in *The Island of Doctor Moreau* the reader studies the middle ground in which the relation of human and alien is always problematic. The novel develops a symmetrical system in which for every symbolic link between human and beast there is a symbolic separation, and often the very terms of union contain within them the seeds of division.

The basic symmetry of the situation is clear; for one half of the novel Prendick feels uneasy about the beast men because he thinks that they are humans who have been surgically modified by Doctor Moreau, and then for the second half of the novel he has anxieties because he is aware that they are not human at all, but humanized animals. While the nature of the biological link occupies much of Prendick's and our attention, and while from a Wilberforcean point of view it should make a major difference whether the beast men are degenerate humans or superior animals, the issue is ultimately irrelevant in determining the obligations that exist between humans and beast men.

Though the humans on the island hold themselves aloof from the beast men, the distinction they maintain is always in danger of being blurred. When Prendick first sees M'ling he perceives him as a "mis-shapen," "deformed man with a black face" and a "singular voice." Even when one knows exactly which is which the distinction keeps slipping away:

> I say I became habituated to the Beast People, that a thousand things that had seemed unnatural and repulsive speedily become natural and ordinary to me. I suppose everything in existence takes its colour from the average hue to our surroundings: Montgomery and Moreau were too peculiar and individual to keep my general impressions of humanity well defined. I would see one of the bovine creatures who worked the launch treading heavily through the undergrowth, and find myself trying hard to recall how he differed from some really human yokel trudging home from his mechanical labours; or I would meet the Fox-Bear Woman's vulpine shifty face, strangely human in its speculative cunning, and even imagine I had met it before in some city byway. (Atlantic Edition, vol. 2, pp. 106–7)

One has to learn to see the differences. Similarly, the beast men are confused about Prendick's status: they check his hands to see if they are malformed (p. 67), and in the huts they debate, not whether Prendick is human, but to what level of beast man be belongs (p. 74). For all the biological differences between humans and beast men, the final enforcer of their separation is the revolver, the "fire that kills."

The law that the beast men recite seems to set up a neat, systematic distinction between human and beast, but in fact it creates an illusion of separation:

> Not to go on all-Fours; *that* is the Law. Are we not Men?
> Not to suck up Drink; *that* is the Law. Are we not Men?
> Not to eat Flesh or Fish; *that* is the Law. Are we not Men?
> Not to claw Bark of Trees; *that* is the Law. Are we not Men?
> Not to chase other Men; *that* is the Law. Are we not Men? (pp. 72–73)

The ironies of this attempt to cross a biological boundary by means of ethical self-definition are multiple. First, there is an inherent paradox in the law itself: only a nonhuman would need such a rule to be human. And the law describes a line that is disproven in the very act of invocation, for we are aware that those here asserting "are we not men?" are definitely not men. Clearly, what defines the human is something other than what these monstrosities assert; they draw a line, but it is a trivial one. And finally, despite its precision, the line marks nothing, for in the course of the novel we see real humans repeatedly trespass across the boundary the law establishes. We see Prendick himself on all fours; Montgomery teaches M'ling how to cook a rabbit; at the beginning of the novel we see men in a lifeboat planning cannibalism, and it is only because they are clumsy that cannibalism does not occur. When he is rescued at the beginning of the novel Prendick drinks something that "tasted like blood," and at the end of the novel Montgomery drinks brandy the way beasts drink blood. Throughout the novel the activity of distinguishing between human and beast is mirrored by the activity of bridging that carefully defined boundary.

Such trespass does not, however, disqualify the distinction; human and beast constitute a difference even if the line between them cannot be clearly established biologically or the criteria of distinction settled. Humans can act bestial, and perhaps, though it is a rarer event, beasts can act humanely. M'ling is a possible instance of the latter: as the situation on the island gets more chaotic, he becomes more faithful to Montgomery, protecting him with his presence and perhaps even dying in his defense (p. 143). The possibility of bestial humanity is exquisitely rendered by the Captain of the *Ipecacuanha* who as captain should be a figure of civilized authority but turns out to be a drunken brute. Like the beast men, he invokes a "law": "I'm captain of the ship—Captain and Owner. I'm the law here, I tell you—the law and the prophets" (p. 16). Later, just as the beast men fall away from their law and attack humans, the Captain abandons the law he has invoked: "Law be damned! I'm king here" (p. 25). In place of civilized order the Captain asserts aggressive, impulsive force. His language gets childish and repetitive: he calls Prendick "Mr. Shut Up," a phrase that the beast men will proudly use (p. 71), and finally out of pure malice he casts Prendick adrift. Though his biology and his social role qualify him for humanity, the Captain is morally and intellectually bestial.

Montgomery and Prendick more consciously bridge the line between human and beast. Montgomery is able to regard the beast men "as almost normal human beings" (p. 105) and, never a very pleasant man himself, he becomes so generally misanthropic that towards the end he casts his lot with the beast men even going so far as to burn the boats to prevent a return to humankind. He and Prendick debate

how they should behave, and though Montgomery confuses the terminology, the standards remain clear:

> "You don't give drink to that beast!" I said, rising and facing him.
> "Beast!" said he. "You're the beast. He takes his liquor like a Christian.
> Come out of the way, Prendick."
> "For God's sake," said I.
> "Get . . . out of the way," he roared and suddenly whipped out his
> revolver.
> "Very well," said I, and stood aside, half-minded to fall upon him as
> he put his hand upon the latch, but deterred by the thought of my useless
> arm. "You've made a beast of yourself. To the beasts you may go."
> He flung the doorway open and stood, half facing me, between the
> yellow lamp-light and the pallid glare of the moon; his eye-sockets were
> blotches of black under his stubby eyebrows. "You're a solemn prig, Pren-
> dick, a silly ass!" (pp. 138–39)

His most radical jumbling of the distinction occurs a few moments
later when, leaving the teetotalling Prendick, he turns to the beast
men and invites them: "drink, ye brutes! Drink, and be men" (p. 139).
We prove our humanity by degenerating beneath it.

At the end of the novel Prendick the prig performs a similar but
opposite re-vision; like Montgomery he becomes a misanthrope, but
whereas Montgomery joins the beasts to escape the human, Prendick,
like Gulliver, sees beasts when he looks at humans: "I go in fear. I see
faces keen and bright, others dull or dangerous, others unsteady,
insincere; none that have the calm authority of a reasonable soul. I
feel as though the animal was surging up through them; that presently
the degradation of the Islanders will be played over again on a larger
scale." He has left London for the country because,

> in London the horror was well-nigh insupportable. I could not get away
> from men; their voices came through windows; locked doors were flimsy
> safeguards. I would go out into the streets to fight with my delusion and
> prowling women would mew after me, furtive craving men glance jeal-
> ously at me, weary pale workers go coughing by me, with tired eyes and
> eager paces like wounded deer dripping blood, old people, bent and dull,
> pass murmuring to themselves, and all unheeding a ragged tail of gibing
> children. Then I would turn aside into some chapel, and even there, such
> was my disturbance, it seemed that the preacher gibbered Big Thinks
> even as the Ape Man had done; or into some library, and there the intent
> faces over the books seemed but patient creatures waiting for prey. Par-

ticularly nauseous were the blank expressionless faces of people in trains and omnibuses; they seemed no more my fellow-creatures than dead bodies would be, so that I did not dare to travel unless I was assured of being alone. And even it seemed that I, too, was not a reasonable creature, but only an animal tormented with some strange disorder in its brain, that sent it to wander alone, like a sheep stricken with the gid. (pp. 171–72)

Wells here adapts a favorite device of satire, but how has civilized humanity earned the accusation of bestiality in the novel? or what justifies Prendick's skewed vision? The deep point of the passage is not simply satiric, but ontological: it is the confusion of animal and human, the collapse of all claim that a biological difference earns a moral position.

The dichotomy of human and animal is a kind of conceptual pun that crops up, almost inevitably, perhaps even unconsciously in the novel's language. Like some of Milton's puns, the second, discovered meaning is narrower and more precise than the first, more obvious meaning.[2] For instance, when Prendick, after he has learned of the animal origin of the beast men, calls them "inhuman monsters" (p. 101), he is at once making an emotional statement of moral and aesthetic revulsion and stating the cool facts: they are biologically "inhuman" and they are literally monsters. At another time, when he thinks the beast men are degenerate humans, he can in his revulsion accidently express the paradoxical truth when he remarks on "the inhuman face of the man" (p. 49). Toward the end of the novel Montgomery gives an important and telling ironic twist to the word "human" when he observes that he and Prendick have ethical responsibilities toward the beast men even though they are physically threatened by them: "We can't massacre the lot,—can we?" Montgomery asks bitterly. "I suppose that's what *your* humanity would suggest?" (p. 138). The pun here works on the evolution-ethics contradiction. In an evolutionary context Prendick's "humanity" pits him against the beast men and survival at all costs is his final imperative. Later when Montgomery is dead and he is alone, Prendick "had half a mind to make a massacre of them" (pp. 165–66). The other meaning of humanity sarcastically alludes to the usual hypocrisy of supposedly ethical humanity in slaughtering other creatures.

Just as the narrator of *The War of the Worlds* has a moment when by an act of sympathy he bridges the separation that has dominated the novel, so Prendick achieves a moment of true connection in spite of separation. Both moments occur when the other dies, but Prendick's is rendered especially difficult by the fact that he is not simply the witness of the other's death, but its killer. After he understands the genetic nature of the beast men, Prendick, assisting in the hunt for the leopard man who has reverted to carnivore, by chance comes upon him hiding:

> I saw the creature we were hunting. I halted. He was crouched together into the smallest possible compass, his luminous green eyes turned over his shoulder regarding me.
>
> It may seem a strange contradiction in me—I cannot explain the fact—but now, seeing the creature there in a perfectly animal attitude, with the light gleaming in its eyes, and its imperfectly human face distorted with terror, I realized again the fact of its humanity. In another moment other of its pursuers would see it, and it would be overpowered and captured, to experience once more the horrible tortures of the enclosure. Abruptly I slipped out my revolver, aimed between his terror-struck eyes and fired. (p. 120)

The moral dynamics are complex here, but it is clear that Prendick is performing an act of mercy. In the face of evolutionary chaos in which the animal and the human overlap and in which the conflicting obligations of evolution and ethics have become hopelessly tangled, Prendick responds with simple sympathy for a fellow creature, "perfectly animal" but endowed with the "fact of its humanity." Here the word "humanity" has broken free from any question of biological descent: instead of a pun that poses a puzzle, the word here challenges the whole evolutionary criterion. And yet Prendick's ethically motivated act is cold-hearted slaughter. The ethical impulse is contaminated by an almost spontaneous violence; when Moreau complains that Prendick should not have killed the beast, Prendick evades both Moreau's point and the ethical one: "'I'm sorry,' said I, though I was not. 'It was the impulse of the moment.'"

The Island of Doctor Moreau, while it may be Wells's most systematic study of the evolutionary dilemma, arrives at no conclusions. The prevailing mood is of a confused flux: the beast men are frightening and pitiful; Moreau is heroic and tyrannical; all Prendick can do is get sullen. The darkness of the book comes not from a real pessimism, but from a kind of muddiness that the inconclusive yet systematic separations and crossings create. Prendick himself is aware of the problem: just after killing the leopard man he again separates himself from both humans and beast men and meditates on the meaning of the situation:

> It was easy now for me to be alone. The Beast People manifested a quite human curiosity about the dead body, and followed it in a thick knot, sniffing and growling at it, as the Bull Men dragged it down the beach. I went to the headland, and watched the Bull Men, black against the evening sky, as they carried the weighted dead body out to sea, and, like a wave across my mind, came the realisation of the unspeakable aimlessness of things upon the island. (pp. 121–22)

All imperatives are pointless here where the most humane gesture is to kill. And if evolutionary and moral aimlessness occupies the center of the novel, the imagery of the beginning and the end expresses the problem exactly. Prendick begins and ends adrift: the oarless, open boat in the midst of a vast expanse of empty sea is a fitting image for the universe Moreau's genius has created.

If biology poses a clear distinction between human and nonhuman which is then overcome, intellect may offer a no less problematic criterion for discrimination. In *The Island of Doctor Moreau* the separation of human and beast is parallelled by the deep problem posed by Moreau himself, and to a slighter degree Montgomery. Moreau's genius is thwarted by society, and so he preys on society. As an intellect with no ethical sensibilities, Moreau is like the Martians, but without the physiological difference that enforces separation in *The War of the Worlds*. It is his action, not his appearance, that has driven Moreau apart. Whereas in the case of the Martians and the beast men the imaginative achievement of the novel is to bridge the antipathy physiology establishes, in the case of Moreau that gulf has been neutralized. To a certain extent the problem has been reversed: now the imaginative achievement is to get past an urge to admire Moreau as an exceptional human and to see how inhumane he is. In this respect, *The Island of Doctor Moreau* is structurally like *The Time Machine* in that the antithetical urges to see separation and to see union balance. But the important question of how a man like Moreau "fits" civilization is largely ignored in the novel. Wells isolates him on his island where he can play God without the inconvenience of considering his relation to civilization. Though he attains a certain grandeur, he looms as an

outcast in the tradition of Victor Frankenstein, tormented and alien-
ated by his genius and his egoism, but Wells does not follow Shelley
into the psychology of such a figure.

Yet, if Moreau alludes to issues left largely undeveloped in the novel,
he still represents an important figure in Wells's logic: he is the most
complex alien, the isolated scientist, the exceptional human. We see
him in the Time Traveller; we see him in Cavor in *The First Men in
the Moon*; and he is studied most concentratedly in Griffin in *The
Invisible Man.* The figure will always attract and bother Wells. While
the value placed on the isolated genius shifts radically in different
works, logically he remains constant: he is always solitary against a
crowd. The ambiguities inherent in the figure are those generated by
the individual in society: he saves society and he plagues it; society
nurtures him and it frustrates and persecutes him.

But if the scientist figure has a variety of permutations in different
works, in each work he is inflexible and undergoes remarkably little
revaluation. Griffin becomes more homicidal as the novel progresses
until Kemp realizes that the conflict is evolutionary: "Griffin contra
mundum." But such change is simply the following out of the beginning potential, and it is apt that this is the one novel in which we
never experience the kind of reversal of sympathies that is so important
to the others. In his early work the question that interests Wells is not
how to think about the exceptional person, but how to think about
civilization, and the genius is mainly interesting for the pressure he
puts on the mechanisms of civilization.

The Spatial System

We have seen how in *The Time Machine* Wells translates the central
Eloi-Morlock opposition into a spatial system of up-down. The elab-
oration is important because many of the mediational gestures are
transacted in terms of this secondary system rather than in terms of
the primary racial one. The green porcelain museum unites up and
down by a lateral movement. Like the museum, the sphinx that the
Time Traveller discovers when he first arrives in the future, in addition
to its allegorical significances, becomes a mediating structure in space,
for it is a hollow residence of the Morlocks and yet above ground. The
Morlocks can use it to capture the time machine without having to
move it downwards, and by entering the sphinx the Time Traveller

can penetrate the Morlock kingdom without abandoning the security of above-ground. The importance of horizontal rather than vertical movement is repeatedly emphasized in the novella: in the opening pages the Time Traveller defines the time dimension by comparing lateral movement, which is common and easy, with vertical movement, which is restricted and difficult. When he sets off in the time machine he describes the danger of stopping inside something in the future. Finally, when the Time Traveller escapes the Morlocks by moving away in time, because they had shifted the machine sideways into the sphinx, he arrives back in the present on the opposite side of the room from which he started. Horizontal movement causes only slight dislocation; had there been vertical movement disaster might have followed.

In *The Time Machine* up and down are particularly important, but in most of Wells's early fiction the crucial distinction is between inside and outside. Though frequently indoors corresponds to civilization and outdoors to noncivilization or nature, the meaning of the spaces is not absolute: indoors can, as in the hothouse in "The Flowering of the Strange Orchid," correspond to nature, and in that case the housekeeper's shattering the glass and letting in the air is, paradoxically, an ethical and civilizing gesture. The terms of indoors and outdoors, for all their appeal to a rigid and absolute symbolic import, are only significant as a pair; each is meaningful in relation to the other, and together they form a logical system by which Wells is able to negotiate his central oppositions. Given such a dichotomous structure, the imaginative interest centers on two issues: how does one move from one space to the other, from inside to out or from outside to in; and how does or can one space invade the other, that is, how can one make an outside inside or vice versa. Mediating structures, by introducing confusion into the rigidities of the inside-outside system, allow for movement between opposites.

In *The Time Machine* the indoors-outdoors dichotomy marks the overwhelming antithesis between the present, which is situated in the cozy indoors of the Time Traveller's study, and the future, which is by comparison outdoors. That pleasant outdoors with flowers and no wild animals expresses a complicated attitude, however. At first the Time Traveller envies the Eloi ease and security. He reasons that such an open life means that a static world of easy pleasure without predation has come about. Soon he learns that the same landscape signifies vulnerability and mental degeneration. Within this garden are the Eloi castles which suggest an indoors, but they are decrepit and lack the security of a true indoors; because the Eloi gather in them to sleep they may even make the Morlock roundup of their cattle easier, though that is not entirely clear. The green museum, which contains the reliques of high technological civilization, offers a more satisfactory indoors, but by penetrating underground it also deprives indoors of its security. And if the Eloi pasture is outdoors, the whole Morlock realm might be seen as indoors, but it is a sinister indoors, not at all like that of the Time Traveller's study. The novella moves from a civilized indoors to a pastoral outdoors to a sinister indoors.[3] The horrible irony of the Morlocks is exactly rendered here, for their indoors and the Time Traveller's study are antithetical products of the same economic system; the many differences between them should not blind us to the link. The Time Traveller, we are informed, has servants, but he prefers to keep them out of sight.

As we have already remarked, Wedderburn's greenhouse represents an instance of a building which creates an indoors which perverts the purpose of indoors. This motif of indoors becoming a trap is repeated in the next story of the volume, "In the Avu Observatory." Here the observatory itself, both a protective enclosure and a place from which to view the cosmic outside, is situated on the spur of a mountain in Borneo, between the "unfathomable blue of the sky" and the "black mysteries of the tropical forest beneath." It is a locus of civilization between two natural mysteries. It is the very construction of the observatory with its slit for the telescope which makes it vulnerable to the batlike monster that attacks the assistant astronomer, Woodhouse. And the ingenious structure which allows the beast to enter prevents Woodhouse from escaping. Like Wedderburn's greenhouse, Woodhouse's observatory, the building of high civilization that claims to mark neatly the distinctions between indoors and outdoors, renders the distinction ambiguous and may even cause us to question its value, for it is the protective quality that attracts the outside. This vulnerability of the indoors is again developed in "Through a Window," in which a native run amok attacks a sedentary man watching him through a window.

At this level the irony carried by the imagery is easy and clear: civilization by its very triumphs breeds weakness to the predatory outdoors. In Wells's system the heroic figures, like the housekeeper in "The Flowering of the Strange Orchid," actively link the two spaces rather than allow one or the other to exist alone. A minor detail at the

primitive creatures, but such weapons entail ambiguous consequences, for as often as not the dependence on fire as a weapon leads
to failure in one of two directions: either a fire goes out, or it spreads
out of control until it threatens, not only the enemy, but the lighter
of the fire himself. The two fires that the Time Traveller sets capture
this undependable quality of fire as a tool. Matches serve as an elab-
oration of this duality. Woodhouse tries to ward off the monster with
matches, but twice he fails to light them. When the invisible man
wants to set a fire that will complete his plan he cannot find the
matches. The Time Traveller discovers to his dismay that the matches
he has conserved to frighten off the Morlocks are safety matches and
won't light without the box. Simple as matches seem as a tool, they
express the paradox of technological sophistication that is at once the
mark of civilized achievement and control and at the same time an
alienation from the natural instincts and powers of animal humanity.
The point of the symbol, let me emphasize, is not to argue for or
against technology, but to set up ironic balances and oppositions that
will allow us to contemplate the full range of technology's possibilities
and dangers.

One further function of fire in Wells's logic is to perform a traumatic
obliteration of the careful distinctions and discriminations humanity
sets up. We see this happen near the end of both *The Time Machine*
and *The Island of Doctor Moreau*. In the latter novel fire is conspic-
uously absent through the first three quarters. We are told that the
beast men have no fire (p. 71); Montgomery honors M'ling by teaching
him how to cook a rabbit (p. 112); and the beast men mythologize the
revolver as "the fire that kills," but otherwise there are no signs of fire
and no references to it. In the last pages of the novel, however, fire
devastates the island. At the climax two fires occur. One is the bonfire
Montgomery makes of the boats to "prevent our return to mankind,"
and the other, accidentally set by Prendick when he tips over the
lamp, burns down Moreau's enclosure. Together they trap Prendick
and make it impossible for him to separate himself from the beast
men: he can neither flee to the sea nor lock himself up in the for-
tresslike enclosure. After such devastation he "became one among the
Beast People" (p. 154). In *The Time Machine*, when he and about forty
Morlocks are marooned on a hillock surrounded by fire, the Time
Traveller comes closest to being a mere brute and also comes closest
to sympathizing with the creatures which elsewhere he finds simply
and utterly repulsive. In both *The Island of Doctor Moreau* and *The*

Time Machine the catastrophic fire breaks down the distinctions between human and nonhuman to the point that the human acknowledges his similarity with that form of being from which he has carefully
separated himself.

Evolution and Ethics in *The War of the Worlds*

The dominant image of *The War of the Worlds* is sunset. It is an
image built on paradox: it is hot and cool, red and black, violent and
calm. And it marks a mediation between day and night. The sunsets
early in the novel are benign and calming and express the peace of
the narrator as he works on his paper on "the probable developments
of moral ideas as civilization progresses" (p. 220). The Martian cylinder
opens against a sunset that reveals itself as more and more violent,
becoming the "hot western sky" and finally the "burning sky." This
potential for violence in the midst of deep peace is apt, for the Martian
invasion is exactly such an intrusion of an evolutionary nature that
humanity has always been aware of but in its complacent ethical
civilization has not bothered to worry about. As the Martians rise out
of the pit their cylinder has dug they replace the fading light of sunset
with the light of their heat ray, and the aftermath of the heat ray is
much like sunset itself:

> The undulating common seemed now dark almost to blackness, except
> where its roadways lay grey and pale under the deep-blue sky of the early
> night. It was dark, and suddenly void of men. Overhead the stars were
> mustering, and in the west the sky was still a pale, bright, almost greenish
> blue. The tops of the pinetrees and the roofs of Horsell came out sharp
> and black against the western afterglow. The Martians and their appli-
> ances were altogether invisible, save for that thin mast upon which their
> restless mirror wobbled. Patches of bush and isolated trees here and there
> smoked and glowed still, and the houses towards Woking station were
> sending up spires of flame into the stillness of the evening air. (p. 241)

Martian violence has exploded on earth, but still the quietness of dusk
prevails in the midst of the burning houses of English civilization. The
image holds together the conflicting realities of evolution and ethics.
    One of the great scenes of the novel develops this image of sunset
to an extraordinary complexity. At the end of Book One, the narrator's
brother, escaping England on a ship, watches the *Thunder Child*, a
ram, smash two Martian fighting machines. For a moment there is

hope; it looks as if humanity had, in the ram, discovered a machine that might compete with Martian technology, but as the chapter ends the Martians counter with a weapon more devastating than even the heat ray:

> After a time, and before they reached the sinking cloud-bank, the warships turned northward, and then abruptly went about and passed into the thickening haze of evening southward. The coast grew faint, and at last indistinguishable amid the low bands of clouds that were gathering about the sinking sun.
>
> Then suddenly out of the golden haze of the sunset came the vibration of guns, and a form of black shadows moving. Every one struggled to the rail of the steamer and peered into the blinding furnace of the west, but nothing was to be distinguished clearly. A mass of smoke rose slanting and barred the face of the sun. The steamboat throbbed on its way through an interminable suspense.
>
> The sun sank into grey clouds, the sky flushed and darkened, the evening star trembled into sight. It was deep twilight when the captain cried out and pointed. My brother strained his eyes. Something rushed up into the sky out of the greyness—rushed slantingly upward and very swiftly into the luminous clearness above the clouds in the western sky; something flat and broad and very large, that swept round in a vast curve, grew smaller, sank slowly, and vanished again into the grey mystery of the night. And as it flew it rained down darkness upon the land. (pp. 359–60)

The ambiguity of the last sentence is important: in place of the expected natural darkness we get an artificial one, but one which is not distinguishable from the one we expected. The natural and the technological are confused, just as are the evolutionary and the ethical. Against such natural activities and against such weapons human activity and intelligence fail.

The image of total darkness as an eradication of the distinctions and discriminations that human intelligence sets up has occurred before in the vision of the end of life on earth in *The Time Machine*. In that work much is made of the difference between light and dark in the year 802,701. A million years later, when the earth has stopped rotating and a cool red sun hangs steadily in one part of the sky, the Time Traveller sees an eclipse:

> The darkness grew apace; a cold wind began to blow in freshening gusts from the east, and the showering white flakes in the air increased in

number. From the edge of the sea came a ripple and whisper. Beyond
these lifeless sounds the world was silent. Silent? It would be hard to
convey the stillness of it. All the sounds of man, the bleating of sheep,
the cries of birds, the hum of insects, the stir that makes the background
of our lives—all that was over. As the darkness thickened, the eddying flakes
grew more abundant, dancing before my eyes; and the cold of the air
more intense. At last, one by one, swiftly, one after the other, the white
peaks of the distant hills vanished into blackness. The breeze rose to a
moaning wind. I saw the black central shadow of the eclipse sweeping
towards me. In another moment the pale stars alone were visible. All else
was rayless obscurity. The sky was absolutely black. (p. 109)

Such blackness marks the complete dominance of a purely physical
nature in which human intelligence and choice have no place. Total
darkness marks the limit of human imagination, the point at which
pure, inevitable natural process rules. The Time Traveller climbs back
in the saddle of the time machine and returns to the present. Confronted with a similar darkness, the narrator of *The War of the Worlds*
gives up imagining the defeat of the Martians and resigns himself to
what the second book of the novel calls, "The Earth Under the Martians." But there is an important difference between the two dark-
nesses, for if in *The Time Machine* the agent of such defeat of human
imagination is entropy, the inexorable physical decline of the universe,
in *The War of the Worlds* the agent is the conscious, aggressive, purposeful, civilized Martian race. Each darkness has its horror, but the
Martian darkness combines the natural with the additional horror of
the denied potential for an ethical dimension.

The spreading of darkness is but one of the ways the Martians ravage
civilization. They repeatedly undercut the kind of systematic separations humans make and we have been studying. If the indoors-
outdoors distinction seems to function for humans, the Martians violate it by their fighting machines which create an indoors that is
outdoors. That topographic puzzle expresses exactly the moral one:
the Martians are evolutionary predators in a natural struggle of survival
of the fittest, and yet they are highly civilized and, we expect, capable
of ethical considerations and behavior. And if by the way they live the
Martians negate the indoors-outdoors distinctions, by their weapons
they deprive humanity of such distinctions for itself. The heat ray
smashes human houses, and to a large extent it is this ability to destroy
the conventional protections and boundaries that civilization has developed that accounts for the weapon's terror. The heat ray obviates
all discriminations; it levels the logical landscape.

It is this intelligent denial of civilization that constitutes the real problem of the Martians. Wells's imagery forces us to confront the disabling paradox of such aggression: though their intelligence makes them capable of ethical thought, the Martians' appearance and machines all invoke a language of purely natural process. They look like octopi; their heat ray and their black smoke pick up the imagery of uncontrolled fire and of total darkness, both of which suggest a pure natural destructiveness without an ethical dimension. And yet this "natural" presence is at the same time a highly intelligent, technologically sophisticated species capable of considering the rights and wrongs of their invasion. The paradox, of course, is not exceptional; the novel makes it very clear that the same inconsistency characterizes humanity's treatment, not only of other nature, but of other humans.

The image of sunset, which for much of the novel expresses violence in calm, toward the end of the novel expresses an opposite paradox. The extraordinary power of the passage describing the narrator's awareness of the death of the Martians derives in part from the way it picks up the important image and reverses its polarity. Again, as on Horsell Common, we see the Martian silhouetted against the sunset: "as I emerged from the top of Baker Street, I saw far away over the trees in the clearness of the sunset the hood of the Martian giant from which this howling proceeded" (p. 432). Twilight advances, and then suddenly the howling stops. We have already discussed this passage in a different context, but let us look at it again in terms of the imagery we are treating:

> The dusky houses about me stood faint and tall and dim; the trees towards the park were growing black. All about me the red weed clambered among the ruins, writhing to get above me in the dimness. Night, the mother of fear and mystery, was coming upon me. But while that voice sounded the solitude, the desolation, had been endurable; by virtue of it London had still seemed alive, and the sense of life about me had upheld me. Then suddenly a change, the passing of something—I knew not what—and then a stillness that could be felt. Nothing but this gaunt quiet. (p. 434)

If the descent of a darkness in which the Martians collaborated marked a triumph of a purely evolutionary vision at the end of Book One, now the complexities of an ethical view of the place of intelligence in nature is reasserted. The Martian voice is counter to that desolating night. Though the narrator's easy assurance of ethical progress is satirized at the beginning of the novel, here at the end an ethical idea reemerges, and it does so as an antithesis to the imagery of twilight and natural process that originally subverted it.

Wells treats the problem of ethical activity in the midst of evolutionary imperatives by giving us two characters who try to dismiss one or the other side of the contradiction. Both men are revealed to be inadequate models for humanity. The Curate whom the narrator meets early in the invasion has an absurdly ethical view, not simply of civilization, but of the universe, and he cannot see how he and England have deserved such a scourge. "All the work—all the Sunday-schools—What have we done—what has Weybridge done?" The narrator angrily asserts a version of Huxley's "unfathomable injustice of the nature of things":

> "Be a man!" said I. "You are scared out of your wits! What good is religion if it collapses under calamity? Think of what earthquakes and floods, wars and volcanoes, have done before to men! Did you think God had exempted Weybridge? He is not an insurance agent." (pp. 302–3)

The attack here on a smug ethical view that expects an easy and trivial security is clear. Later in the novel when the Curate discovers an ethical reading of disaster and sees the Martians as God's agents he appears just as foolish.

The opposite view, an evolutionary standpoint—which at first, given the facts of the invasion, might seem less absurd than the ethical view—is also satirized. The Artilleryman, whom the narrator meets early in the novel and again after the Martians are victorious, is the antithesis of the Curate: he faces the evolutionary situation boldly, and whereas the Curate had to be enjoined to "Be a man," the Artilleryman earns an enthusiastic compliment from the narrator, "'Great God!' cried I. 'But you are a man indeed!'" (p. 417). The Artilleryman dismisses any ethical argument: "This isn't a war. It never was a war, any more than there's war between man and ants." Humans are, in his view, simply "eatable ants" to the Martians. And yet, far from being upset by the prospect that lies ahead, the Artilleryman sees the reversion to a code of survival of the fittest as a needed purification:

> All these—the sort of people that lived in these houses, and all those damn little clerks that used to live down that way—they'd be no good. They haven't any spirit in them—no proud dreams and no proud lusts; and a man who hasn't one or the other—Lord! what is he but funk and precautions? They

just used to skedaddle off to work—I've seen hundreds of 'em, bit of breakfast in hand, running wild and shining to catch their little season-ticket train, for fear they'd get dismissed if they didn't; working at businesses they were afraid to take the trouble to understand; skedaddling back for fear they wouldn't be in time for dinner; keeping indoors after dinner for fear of the back streets, and sleeping with the wives they married, not because they wanted them, but because they had a bit of money that would make for safety in their one little miserable skedaddle through the world. Lives insured and a bit invested for fear of accidents. And on Sundays—fear of the hereafter. As if hell was built for rabbits! Well, the Martians will just be a godsend to these. Nice roomy cages, fattening food, careful breeding, no worry. After a week or so chasing about the fields and lands on empty stomachs, they'll come and be caught cheerful. (pp. 418–19)

The criticism of the Curate's vision and way of life is clear. Such people, the Artilleryman argues, are well off dead if the human race is to succeed. His argument is purely evolutionary: "We can't have any weak or silly. Life is real again, and the useless and cumbersome and mischievous have to die. They ought to die. They ought to be willing to die. It's a sort of disloyalty, after all, to live and taint the race" (p. 421). The Artilleryman plans a kind of underground action in which the worthy humans hide and plan and finally overthrow the enemy:

Just imagine this: Four or five of their fighting-machines suddenly starting off—Heat-Rays right and left, and not a Martian in 'em. Not a Martian in 'em, but men—men who have learned the way how. It may be in my time, even—those men. Fancy having one of them lovely things, with its Heat-Ray wide and free! Fancy having it in control! What would it matter if you smashed to smithereens at the end of the run, after a bust like that? I reckon the Martians'll open their beautiful eyes! Can't you see them, man? Can't you see them hurrying, hurrying—puffing and blowing and hooting to their other mechanical affairs? Something out of gear in every case. And swish, bang, rattle, swish! just as they are fumbling over it, *swish* comes the Heat-Ray, and, behold! man has come back to his own. (p. 422)

The tremendous irony here is that in coming "back to his own" man has simply become a Martian in a slightly different shape. The puzzle between ethical and evolutionary imperatives that might be said to define humanity is here simply ignored.

As we shall see, in just a few years Wells himself will attempt just such heroic simplifications as the Artilleryman here performs, but in *The War of the Worlds* the stance entails irony.[6] First of all, no sooner have we heard the Artilleryman's credo than it is undercut by the discovery that it is all bluster, that the man is a lazy hypocrite who has no intention of living up to his arduous declaration. But even without that deflation, one would have to see his idea as inadequate because the whole first half of the novel, in the repeated comparisons of the Martian destruction of humans to the European destruction of other animals and other humans, has made us strongly question a purely evolutionary criterion for intelligent behavior. While the Curate's petty insurance-agent God is clearly inadequate, there is a strong ethical element in the novel: humanity as a whole, despite the Sunday schools, has deserved the Martian invasion because as a whole humanity has lived by an evolutionary code itself. Though it had the chance to act ethically towards the rest of nature, it has not. Those who live by evolution will die by it.

That Wells himself felt some justice in the Martian invasion is evident from the pleasure he took in planning the book. In writing to Elizabeth Healy he identified himself with his Martians; "I completely wreck and sack Woking—killing my neighbours in painful and eccentric ways— then proceed via Kingston and Richmond to London, which I sack, selecting South Kensington for feats of peculiar atrocity."[7] Such ruthlessness, as V. S. Pritchett said, is central to Wells, but the novel is also, as Fredric Jameson notes, in part an imperialist "guilt fantasy."[8] At some point the destruction of other life ceases to be merely an evolutionary commonplace (wolf killing deer) and becomes a moral atrocity (the extermination of the Tasmanians). *The War of the Worlds* upholds an ethical ideal without relinquishing its admiration for evolutionary success. After *The Time Machine* it is Wells's clearest study of the moral dilemma of triumphant civilization.

CHAPTER **5**

Frustrating Balances

The Dialectic of Balance

THE system Wells has developed, while it forces an ironic vision which must become aware of contradiction, does not solve problems. In fact it delights in irresolvable problems. It enjoys the very conflicts that consume human beings. In this way it participates in, even sustains because they generate an entertaining stand-off, the processes it criticizes. This is not a position in which to rest content, and in Wells's next works the same intelligence and skill which went into creating the ironic system struggles to make it see beyond irony. The attempt is not entirely successful, but if Wells's next gestures are flawed, they should not be faulted too casually, for they are stabs at what in his letter to Bennett Wells called a new "system," ambitious and necessary. The failure we are now at the brink of, while it has its dose of egoism and pettiness, is in the main one of a mind which already has accomplished a major breakthrough and is attempting to go further. This section of our study, then, is the picture of the dilemma implicit in Wells's success, for it is the very completeness of the balance of such a work as "A Story of the Days to Come" that, while it marks a state of wisdom, prefigures a crisis. The ironic mode, if it is to be true to itself and not degenerate into conservative posturings, must acknowledge its own powerlessness, and, with full awareness, the writer must take sides if he is to do more than passively observe civilization's catastrophe.

The pressure Wells is feeling to get beyond balance leads him to a frustration with the purely imaginative in the face of the real. In the next chapter we will examine his nonfiction proposals and imaginings.

In the present chapter we begin to perceive the limits of the ironic mode he has mastered. Aesthetic balance, however pleasing it may be to the comfortable reader, however true it may be to conflicting urges in moral humanity, exists as a privilege. If we recall Prendick's killing of the leopard man, a moment of highly complex irony, we see that there is a cost in suffering that, even if only "imaginary," does not get wholly compensated for by the ironic awareness it generates. Irony, even the most aware, has its element of evasion. And the more Wells begins to think about the social possibilities of England, the more he becomes conscious of the inadequacy of his literary accomplishment.

I am beginning with *The First Men in the Moon* (1901) which, though it was published after "A Story of the Days to Come" (1897), poses a more fanciful world, more distant from the practical issues of our own, and therefore is closer imaginatively to the work we have been looking at. In *The First Men in the Moon* the conflicts are dealt with at the symbolic level. But an interesting twist occurs toward the end of this novel: since the Selenite civilization is Wells's most elaborate exercise in utopian fantasy, one might expect such an exercise to be liberating, but by a perverse paradox of imaginative economy, that flight of fancy leads to a kind of imagery which, however ironically intended, lays the foundation for a mode of thought which is intolerant of the tensions and conflicts that have made Wells's earlier work so vital.

The problem Wells faces shows up in a shift in the images he uses to structure his fantasy. In place of opposition, we see images that diminish contrast, that express coherence and unity rather than conflict. In *The First Men in the Moon* we see this aspect of the imagery explicitly in the vision of the Selenite world. In "A Story of the Days to Come" something a bit more disconcerting is at work: the imagery which at first seems to promise contrast and change turns out to deny it. Now, as Wells tries to think precisely about specific economic structures and what is to be done about them, the logical maneuvers that work so well in the more fanciful early works cause problems, and the mediating symbol that formerly allowed him to hold together opposites, as the focus changes, begins to obscure differences. In place of illumination we begin to see frustration. Wells seems as surprised as anyone at this development, as we shall see.

At this point in my argument a full perspective demands that we observe that a part of the problem we are about to begin to see in Wells is a product of the limitation of the mode of analysis I am employing. Just as irony reaches a point at which it ceases to be a mode of exploration and thought and becomes simply a habit of obliqueness, an evasion of commitment, so the analysis that seeks evidence of conflict and balance can become an interpretative machine that can see virtue only in those qualities that it is designed to discover. While I do not propose to renounce a method whose insights continue to explicate and expose strengths and weaknesses, I can nevertheless acknowledge here that there are other ways of valuing, other ways of seeing. A work such as *When the Sleeper Wakes*, for instance, which comes across in our reading as among Wells's weaker productions, has in spite of its shortcomings attracted readers and writers throughout the century. In chapter seven I will explore this phenomenon further; here it is sufficient to admit that Wells's imaginative world spreads in ways no single analytical method can encompass fully.

The Ambivalences of *The First Men in the Moon*

The First Men in the Moon is certainly one of Wells's finest scientific romances, and in many ways it partakes of the system we have been examining.[1] But the novel seeks something else, too. In *The First Men in the Moon*, more than in any other work we have looked at, Wells considers utopian solutions to the dilemmas of civilization. The whole novel is a kind of tentative testing ground for social ideas that are given a skeptical and distanced presentation. Irony is never absent, but here in place of the clarity of the earlier works we begin to see an escape into ambiguity and a blurring of precise opposition. Such ambiguity can generate fine satire, but as a cognitive tool it is weak; it allows one to think opposites without ever quite understanding or clarifying the conflict between them. It allows for a broadminded tolerance that ignores the real strife.

Before getting to the problem of such utopian imaginings, let us observe that in *The First Men in the Moon* the familiar techniques of balance and opposition are at work. The moon and the earth are opposed both as social ideas and as images: the earth is seen in terms of surface; the moon in terms of interior; the earth poses a disordered and competitive social system; the moon an ordered and cooperative one. The novel's two protagonists, Bedford and Cavor, represent two extremes of individualist ethic opposed to the Selenite hive: Bedford is a capitalist con man; Cavor is an eccentric scientist.

In Cavor, Wells brings together a number of figures of competence that have interested him before. Cavor joins the good-willed rationality of the Time Traveller with the absent-minded disregard for others of the Diamond Maker. Though his personality remains uncorrupted by the egomaniacal hatreds of Moreau and Griffin, he shares with them a blindness to the needs of society and to the consequences of his experiments: had the first piece of Cavorite been fastened down it would have pumped all of earth's air into space. As it is, when Cavor believes his three assistants to have died in the accident, he wastes no concern: "three martyrs—science" settles the matter for him.

But while there is a lethal narrowness to his intellectual pursuits, he is also admirably rational and curious, and on the moon he repeatedly challenges Bedford's xenophobia and argues for inquiry and discussion. Yet, enlightened as he is, he can still succumb to chauvinistic irrationality: under the intoxicating influence of lunar mushrooms he becomes as absurdly proud of his evolutionary good fortune as Bedford: "Insects!—and they think I'm going to crawl about on my stomach—on my vertebrated stomach!" (Atlantic Edition, vol. 6, p. 101). Nevertheless, at the end of the novel he has made an effort to overcome this pride, and the preoccupied mechanical genius of the novel's opening pages becomes a competent and resourceful figure in the last. Cavor is the focus of a cluster of ideas about the scientist: human, in the worst, proud sense, yet able to surmount his trivial pomps; preoccupied but capable of noble self-sacrifice and devotion to the truth; unworldly, but intensely interested in the world. In a broad way he is a charming figure and serves as a useful foil to Bedford, a more deeply problematic presence.

Bedford is a member of the fraternity of frauds that populates Wells's imagination. He is unscrupulous, but admirable for his ability to survive. A bankrupt, he has retired to a cottage to dash off a play by which he expects to recoup his losses; like the Artilleryman, however, his exhilarating ambitions amount to very little, and he is easily distracted from his project. But even in inactivity he has an eye to his fortune, and when his neighbor, Cavor, finding him a distraction, offers to buy his house, Bedford seriously considers the fraud of selling him the rented house. It is only the promise of greater gain to be obtained by latching onto Cavorite that keeps Bedford from cheating Cavor. Unlike other frauds, such as those who deal in taxidermy, diamonds, and art, Bedford is more interested in profit than in the fine art of deception, and this unimaginative drive comes under much criticism later in the novel.

Bedford's psychology leads him to treat all interchanges as competitive ones and all injuries as attacks; unable to see the Selenites as other than hostile aliens, he is quick to despair of negotiation and to resort to violence in dealing with them. We need to be careful here and not simply condemn Bedford as a fanatic racist: violent behavior has its value in Wells, and in confronting aliens such as the Martians it is merely suicidal to try to negotiate. But the Selenites are clearly not like the Martians in this respect. Cavor repeatedly argues for a more rational way of dealing with them. A particular crisis occurs when the Selenite guards try to get the two humans to cross a narrow bridge over an abyss. When the humans balk one of the guards prods Bedford with a spear, and he, wounded and angry, attacks the Selenites and leads Cavor on an "heroic escape." Cavor's response is not the praise for quick-wittedness that Bedford expects, but disgust: "You spoiled it all" (p. 136). It is a crucial scene for the way it plays with our own xenophobic, adventure-story instincts and then rebukes them.

The puzzle the passage raises and which Bedford confronts us with is not a simple one, and it is not confined to dealing with aliens; at this point Cavor and Bedford embody the ethical and evolutionary imperatives, and the novel does not settle easily for one or the other. Bedford may be a rash, greedy imperialist, and Cavor a humane, rational, and disinterested seeker of truth, but Bedord's energy is admirable in its paranoid ability to succeed, and Cavor's openness is both naive and in a strange way ruthless.

The last paragraphs of the novel force us to pit the two imperatives against each other. Cavor has told the Grand Lunar of earth's record of war and oppression[2] and has explained Cavorite to him. Then come the last fragments of a message:

"I was mad to let the Grand Lunar know———"
There was an interval of perhaps a minute. One imagines some interruption from without. A departure from the instrument—a dreadful hesitation among the looming masses of apparatus in that dim, blue-lit cavern—a sudden rush back to it, full of a resolve that came too late. Then, as if it were hastily transmitted, came:
"Cavorite made as follows: take———"
There followed one word, a quite unmeaning word as it stands—
"uless."
And that is all.
It may be he made a hasty attempt to spell "useless" when his fate was close upon him. Whatever it was that was happening about that appa-

ratus, we cannot tell. Whatever it was we shall never, I know, receive
another message from the moon. For my own part a vivid dream has
come to my help, and I see, almost as plainly as though I had seen it in
actual fact, a blue-lit dishevelled Cavor struggling in the grip of a great
multitude of those insect Selenites, struggling ever more desperately and
hopelessly as they swarm upon him, shouting, expostulating, perhaps
even at last fighting, and being forced backward step by step out of all
speech or sign of his fellows, for evermore into the Unknown—into the dark,
into that silence that has no end. (pp. 266–67)

Clearly the Selenites have for good reason silenced Cavor's radio, but
Wells forces us to remain sceptical about Bedford's account: he
"imagines" it; it is, after all, "a vivid dream," not an actual observation;
and the melodramatic battle is typical of Bedford's paranoid fantasies
but very unlike Cavor's rationalism. The cliches of xenophobic horror
are a projection that we have to doubt; the reality is probably more
tame and less violent than Bedford would lead us to believe.

Xenophobia is but one aspect of the imperialism criticized in Bedford. The profit motive itself, the inability to see things except in terms
of gain, leads to a vacancy of real personality that is the complementary
opposite of the egomania that leads Bedford to violence. Against
Cavor's pure scientific quest Bedford repeatedly enforces a crude doctrine of "use." When Cavor first proposes going to the moon, Bedford
keeps asking why. "It's just firing ourselves off the world for nothing"
(p. 37). It is clear that Bedford does not question the value of the trip
in the name of some higher ideal; he simply lacks imagination and
can value only what will profit him. On the moon itself he is baffled
by Cavor's curiosity: "It wasn't that he intended to make any use of
these things: he simply wanted to know them" (p. 129). When they
are drunk on lunar mushrooms and Cavor is expressing his vertebrate
pride, Bedford idealizes "projects of colonization":

> "We must annex this moon," I said. "There must be no shilly-shally.
> This is part of the White Man's Burden. Cavor—we are—*hic*—Satap—
> mean Satraps! Nempire Caesar never dreamt. B'in all the newspapers.
> Cavorecia. Bedfordecia. Bedfordecia. Hic—Limited. Mean—unlimited!
> Practically."
>
> Certainly I was intoxicated. I embarked upon an argument to show the
> infinite benefits our arrival would confer upon the moon. I involved myself
> in a rather difficult proof that the arrival of Columbus was, after all,
> beneficial to America. I found I had forgotten the line of argument I had
> intended to pursue and continued to repeat "sim'lar to C'lumbus" to fill
> up time. (pp. 100–1)

When he discovers that gold is a common metal on the Moon he has but one thought: how to get it back to earth.

This material single-mindedness, while it inspires him, also leaves him prone to fits of depression, the most overwhelming of which he experiences on the way back from the moon. Wells here uses the imagery of isolation, weightlessness, and timelessness to describe Bedford's "pervading doubt of [his] own identity." Cut off from the worldly drives that have structured him, he gains a radically new perspective on his whole life:

> I became, if I may so express it, dissociate from Bedford, I looked down on Bedford as a trivial incidental thing with which I chanced to be connected, I saw Bedford in many relations—as an ass or as a poor beast where I had hitherto been inclined to regard him with a quiet pride as a very spirited and rather forcible person. I saw him not only as an ass, but as the son of many generations of asses. I reviewed his schooldays and his early manhood and his first encounter with love very much as one might review the proceedings of an ant in the sand. . . . I regret that something of that period of lucidity still hangs about me, and I doubt if I shall ever recover the full-blooded self-satisfaction of my early days. (p. 190)

In a different kind of person such insights might lead to a change of life, but Bedford yanks himself back to the solidity of the economic battle by meditating on advertisements and financial announcements. As he says, the experience has deprived him a bit of "the full-blooded self-satisfaction" he had, but when he returns to earth he sets about turning his information to profit, and the old Bedford, the con man who knows no other way of being, resumes.

The opposition between what Bedford and what Cavor represent dominates much of the novel. By making Bedford the narrator, Wells encourages the reader to be skeptical about motives and reactions that Bedford takes for granted. If the reader has not taken such precautions from the start, Wells forces him to by having Cavor, at the beginning of his transmissions from the moon, criticize Bedford as being "impulsive, rash and quarrelsome" (p. 217). Bedford makes a defense of sorts and in doing so manages to imply that Cavor is not to be trusted entirely either, so that the final result of the point-of-view technique is to leave the reader free from both characters and intensely aware of the ways their attitudes conflict. Bedford is an advocate of evolutionary struggle who is only occasionally capable of appreciating more disinterested points of view. Cavor is the advocate of a rational, ethical attitude, but he too compromises the purity of the stance. In this respect the novel skillfully poses a conflict: instead of bridging it by symbols, the novel mediates it with the inconsistencies of human character itself. And, opposites though they are, Cavor in his drunken self-revelations moves toward Bedford, and Bedford in his resourcefulness resembles Cavor.

It is in the detailed imagining of the moon itself that we see Wells beginning to shift away from the engagement of conflict. The two much-discussed scenes of *The First Men in the Moon*—the coming to life of the moon with the rising of the sun, and the Selenite hive— together generate a structure that looks familiar: like the earth in the year 802,701, the moon consists of a garden above and a machine civilization beneath. For a moment the oppositions of up-down and indoors-outdoors appear. Bedford, like the Time Traveller, fears the underground-indoors; he smashes Selenites the way the Time Traveller smashes Morlocks; his escape up the blue-lit tunnels of the moon is parallel to the Time Traveller's trek back from the green museum to the sphinx.[3] But despite these parallels, a major change has taken place in the way Wells is imagining things, for in the moon there is no opposition. The Time Traveller is, as far as anyone can tell, in the midst of a genuine antithesis, but Bedford's imitation of the Time Traveller is more a response to his private fantasy of monstrous and insensitive aliens than to an actual situation. The moon, for all its contrast of surface and interior, turns out to be a unified, homogenous system.

Whatever contrast Bedford's adventures might imply, Cavor's final report makes it clear that as far as Selenite civilization is concerned, the surface is trivial, simply a mooncalf pasture. Cavor compares the body of the moon to a sponge (p. 219), and that image catches exactly the lack of contrast within the structure. There is gradation: as Cavor descends by balloon he observes the increasing blueness as one approaches the interior sea, but there are no lines marking boundaries. The contrasts of light and dark that define up and down, day and night in *The Time Machine* disappear in this world. The "everlasting blue" that upsets Cavor (p. 223) replaces color and darkness. The sun's effect is not to change the light, but only, by heating different parts of the moon, to generate air currents. The fact that these currents reverse suggests that even gravity can define only a weak up-down polarity to the system. Admittedly, at the fringes of the system are mazelike *terrae incognitae* in which lurk monsters, but these perhaps mythological threats are forgotten as soon as mentioned. Likewise, the inner sea contains fish and a particularly frightening tentacled animal that gives Cavor nightmares, but such curiosities of natural history do not much threaten or define the shape of the lunar social world. In fact they serve to reinforce the image of Selenite society as a homogenous whole, a core whose antitheses, such as they are, exist, not within or in parallel, but at the remote peripheries.

Lunar civilization is composed of a single species which occupies and masters the center of the satellite. As far as we know, the only other creatures on the moon are the monsters at the fringe and the mooncalves, which are hardly animals at all. The moon is, therefore, a "world state," a civilization in which evolutionary competition has been almost totally eradicated.[4] In this respect we can see how appropriate the end of the novel is: to allow commerce between the earth and the moon would be to reinaugurate evolutionary conflict. A staunch isolationism preserves the homogenous Selenite culture.

After ridding the lunar world of evolutionary conflict, however, Wells performs a significant logical trick; he reintroduces difference, not as species, but as individual gradation within the homogenous Selenite species. Again the contrast with *The Time Machine* is instructive. The Eloi and the Morlocks, though they share a common ancestor in present-day humanity, have evolved into separate species, each with its area of specialization, and they are locked in conflict. Among the Selenites there are individual creatures more different in competence and in appearance than any Eloi and Morlock, and yet, as versions of different possibilities of the single species, they avoid entirely the conflict that defines the world of 802,701 on earth.[5] At first Wells compares this multiplication of forms within a single species to earthly ants. Cavor, Bedford reports,

> does not mention the ant, but throughout his allusions the ant is continually brought before my mind, in its sleepless activity, its intelligence, its social organisation, and, more particularly, the fact that it displays, in addition to the two forms, the male and the female, produced by almost all other animals, a great variety of sexless creatures—workers, soldiers and the like, differing from one another in structure, character, power and use and yet all members of the same species. And these Selenites are of course if only by reason of this widely extended adaptation, incomparably greater than ants. And instead of the existing four or five different forms of ant that are found there are almost innumerably different forms of Selenites. I have endeavoured to indicate the very considerable difference observable in such Selenites of the outer crust as I happened to encounter;

the differences in size, hue, and shape were certainly as wide as the differences between the most widely separated races of men. But such differences as I saw fade absolutely to nothing in comparison with the huge distinctions of which Cavor tells. (p. 226)

The passage goes on, but the point is clear and insistently repeated: here is a model of radical difference without conflict. When Cavor is in a crowd he observes that "indeed, there seemed not two alike in all that jostling multitude." What Wells has done here is to replace class or species difference with individual differences. It is a mode of avoiding strong conflict that will attract him more and more over the next few years. For our purposes here it is enough to observe that by this new method of conceiving difference Wells never needs to see groups in conflict. These creatures do not prey on each other; they all work towards one end.

As we shall see later when we examine how Wells tries to think concretely about the future of civilization, this subtle shift away from conflict has profound and not entirely happy consequences. In the short run, however, it has virtues, the most significant of which is that it allows for satire of a sort that would be impossible in *The Time Machine*. Some of the satire is fairly conventional: the arrogance of Selenite intellectuals who are accompanied by "trumpet-faced news disseminators shriek[ing their] fame" (p. 239) is easy enough. At times, though, Wells can strike a note which probes to more difficult problems. For example, Selenite workers, when they have no work, are sedated until they are needed. Cavor's first reaction to seeing such a sleeping worker is that "the pose of his slumber suggested a submissive suffering," but then, fearing he may be projecting human prejudices, he withdraws the opinion. But in the next paragraph his ruminations force us to confront a terrible problem of what is the humane way for any civilization to treat its surplus:

To drug the worker ones does not want and toss him aside is surely far better than to expel him from his factory to wander starving in the streets. In every complicated social community there is necessarily a certain intermittency in the occupation of all specialised labour, and in this way the trouble of an unemployed problem is altogether anticipated. And yet, so unreasonable are even scientifically trained minds, I still do not like the memory of those prostrate forms amidst those quiet, luminous arcades of fleshy growth, and I avoid that short cut in spite of the inconveniences of its longer, more noisy, and more crowded alternative. (p. 243)

The ambiguities surrounding Selenite civilization spread and infect other areas. Is Cavor's unease "unreasonable?" Should a "scientifically trained mind" be blind to such ethical problems? The satire in such a passage arises from its ambiguities. Earlier, in a passage that is much quoted, discussing the techniques of introducing specialized difference into the Selenite world, Wells masterfully squeezes the reader between unacceptable options:

> The making of these various sorts of operative must be a very curious and interesting process. I am still much in the dark about it, but quite recently I came upon a number of young Selenites, confined in jars from which only the fore-limbs protruded, who were being compressed to become machine-minders of a special sort. The extended "hand" in this highly developed system of technical education is stimulated by irritants and nourished by injection while the rest of the body is starved. Phi-oo, unless I misunderstood him, explained that in the earlier stages these queer little creatures are apt to display signs of suffering in their various cramped situations, but they easily become indurated to their lot; and he took me on to where a number of flexible-limbed messengers were being drawn out and broken in. It is quite unreasonable, I know, but these glimpses of the educational methods of these beings have affected me disagreeably. I hope, however, that may pass off and I may be able to see more of this aspect of this wonderful social order. That wretched-looking hand sticking out of its jar seemed to appeal for lost possibilities; it haunts me still, although, of course, it is really in the end a far more humane proceeding than our earthly method of leaving children to grow into human beings, and then making machines of them. (pp. 240–41)

The satire works by playing off against each other two unsatisfactory alternatives.[6] Against frighteningly regulated society Wells sets a callously unconcerned one in which the citizen is also brutalized, but only after he has dreamt of better possibilities. Against total specialization from birth, he sets casual and inefficient education which requires Procrustean measures later. Against what is in effect a blatant class system, he sets a concealed class system.

It is worth inquiring into how Wells achieves here a balance by which the monstrous Selenite education system can be seen as better than that offered British youth. Wells works a piece of mental jiujitsu: he gets us leaning hard to be sure to overcome our human prejudices and chauvinisms, and when we are off balance, worrying about what we think of the "lost possibilities" of the young Selenite, he hits us with the atrocity of the human situation. In spite of what Cavor thinks he is saying, we must find the Selenite laboratory ethically intolerable. In accord with satiric tradition the "technical" language of the passage conceals horrors ("educational methods," "drawn out," "broken in"). Cavor's "unreasonable" affect is completely rational. And yet the nightmare of Selenite shaping can still be called "humane" in the face of ordinary human education.

In part, Wells is working on the confusion between ant and human: Selenite civilization is able to be seen as something other than a nightmare of regimentation and deformation because of the nonhuman aspect of the Selenites themselves. What would be intolerable as a way of bringing up humans is, at the least, hard to judge among insects.[7] The real opposition, therefore, is between a "natural" brutality on the one hand and a "social" horror on the other. We are back with the issue of evolution and ethics: we can no more blame the Selenites than we can the wolf. But in this game a line is in danger of being blurred: the Selenite hive is perhaps "natural," but it also has a social and ethical dimension, and that very union of the social and natural solves a logical problem for Wells. In Selenite society there is no evolutionary-ethical conflict. Its structure is both social and natural; it is without inner conflict. In later work Wells will seek to adapt this structure to human needs.

If *The First Men in the Moon* were the only thing Wells had written, we might be justified in treating the irony here as an expression of pure savage indignation. The possibilities of order and disorder confront each other and in their balance leave no position sound. But our acquaintance with other works by Wells, particularly his nonfiction of this period, leads us to see this passage in a different way: Selenite training would be morally offensive in human society; probably it is biologically impossible;[8] but nevertheless it represents an emblem of "admirable social order" that Wells cannot help but find attractive. It can be argued that all intense satire is in part attracted to that which it attacks, but in Wells's case we are talking about a mechanism that is not subconscious but conscious. Swift would not, whatever his deepest impulses, advocate eating paupers' children. Wells might with a kind of glee at his own daring and outrageous ingenuity move in the direction of control and elimination that is so ambivalently projected in Selenite society. In this passage we are witnessing a moment of perfect balance which then becomes a moment of transition from one form of thought (irony) to another (utopia).[9] The attraction of the utopian solution which lurks behind the horror here will never again leave Wells's thought, and the absolute imperative that he find such a solution will lead him to all kinds of contortions in his quest for the idea that will make order reign in place of muddle.

The Stasis of "A Story of the Days to Come"

The potential difficulty utopian fantasy poses for the balance of Wells's ironic system shows up as a real crisis in fictions about the comparatively near future which will evolve, without the intrusion of alien invasion, out of the world we already know. In "A Story of the Days to Come" and *When the Sleeper Wakes* Wells is imagining a world that he believes has a potential to be real; the pure play we have been looking at is now infiltrated by the serious attempt at prediction. A year or two later, in *Anticipations*, Wells will give full attention to this mode of thought. In these visions of the near future Wells tries to see and to imagine what life will be like. In some of the symmetries of "A Story of the Days to Come" we may detect evidence that Wells himself is a bit surprised at how awful the world of technological marvels will be, but in this novella he does not try to figure out a way to cure the world; he is content to watch his protagonists find their place in that world. In *When the Sleeper Wakes*, which we will look at in chapter seven, he undertakes to envision a righting of the nightmare his cool ironic intelligence has invented, and if the results are analytically disappointing, they are nevertheless revealing. That novel exposes the limits of the logical and symbolic mode of fantasy in the face of real political issues.

"A Story of the Days to Come" is often treated along with *When the Sleeper Wakes* as a dystopian story,[10] as an attack on a capitalist future. What may be true of the latter does not hold for the former: while capitalism clearly comes in for some intense criticism in "A Story of the Days to Come," to call the work dystopian distorts the method that is at work, for Wells's imagination here is still deeply intrigued with completing an aesthetic system, with rendering the whole symmetrical. The shape of the story is less an attack on the capitalist city than a meditation on forms of opposition and change. The story concludes with a reconciliation of various attitudes toward change and toward conservation, and though one can see how the ironic reconciliations of *We* and *Nineteen Eight-four* may be said to have their ancestors in "A Story of the Days to Come," Wells's conclusion is remarkable and important for the way it transcends irony and dystopian despair to imply a new aesthetic attitude which sees the old in a new way, and the new in an old.

Though the plot of "A Story of the Days to Come" is jagged on the surface, at a level just beneath that of plot stands a thorough and systematic coherence. The story begins with a strange—and in terms of plot, irrelevant—description of Mr. Morris, the nineteenth-century ancestor of the heroine's father, Mwres. After this introductory matter, the story proceeds through five linked but essentially independent chapters. One describes how the hero, Denton, wins Elizabeth after she has been hypnotized into not recognizing him and had been set to marry Binton, the villainous capitalist. Chapter two describes the poor lovers' attempt to leave the city and live in the country and the failure of that enterprise. Three depicts the couple's descent from middle-class comfort to lower-class serfdom as wards of the Labour Company. Four depicts Denton's education into the "high art of scrapping," his acceptance of the life of the laboring poor, and Elizabeth's rejection of it. And chapter five describes Binton's attempt to destroy the marriage of Denton and Elizabeth, Binton's liver disease, his final magnanimity, and his voluntary euthanasia. The story ends with a coda that shows Elizabeth and Denton restored to the middle class, living at the edge of the city, and contemplating the sunset.

Each chapter plays on a different genre of conventional story. Chapter one is a love story; chapter two a pastoral; three the tragedy of economic decline; four heroic fisticuffs; and five the insane rich man. And to compound the variety, the attention of the narrator keeps shifting: at times he is content merely to sketch the plot so as to set the conventions in motion, while at other times the story becomes detailed and realistic for short stretches. And ornamenting the whole fiction but seemingly never quite essential to the plot is the imagery of an advanced urban technology. On the surface "A Story of the Days to Come" is very unlike anything we have looked at so far; it appears a potpourri of plots, styles, and ideas, a kind of sketchbook filled with studies that Wells might use and develop more adequately in later work.

This surface variety conceals a symmetrical and balanced structure. The first and last chapters are about love, while the middle three deal with the couple's attempt to find a place in the future society, what we might call the "art of living." And each chapter has its own clear and distinctive conflict which is mediated by a figure or group which is able to link the two sides.

	SUBJECT	CONFLICT	MEDIATOR
Ch. 1	Love	Passion-Economics	Hypnotist
Ch. 2	Art of Living	City-Country	Shepherd
Ch. 3	Art of Living	Middle Class-Lower class	Labour Co.
Ch. 4	Art of Living	Gentility-Violence	Laborer
Ch. 5	Love	Possessiveness-Magnanimity	Doctor

What is immediately apparent is that the story is not progressive. It sets up minor structures which are mirrored and reversed at symmetrically opposite moments in the story. Thus, the first and last chapters about love use mediating figures from the future, the hypnotist and the doctor, one of whom is seen as evil, the other good. In the middle three chapters about economics the mediating figures of two and four come from the past, while at the center of the story is the Labour Company, which is both from the past and from the future.

A detailed examination of chapters two and four shows how pointed the opposition between the two is and yet how alike they are in the imaginative terms by which they approach life. Both chapters study the problem of living amid violence. The second sees a retreat to an earlier way of life as impossible because of the intrusion of violence, while the fourth sees the heritage of violence as inevitable and in its limited way admirable. Thus, if the second chapter arrives at a reluctant acceptance of the future, the fourth arrives at a stoic and equally reluctant acceptance of the inescapable past.

The two chapters constitute a detailed meditation on the possibilities of pastoral retreat. In chapter two Elizabeth and Denton, unable to afford a life in the city, perform an exodus to the now-abandoned countryside where for a week they live with a moderate happiness. Though not much is made of it, clearly they are already beginning to find this careless pastoral boring. They are forced to reconsider the mode of life by the attack of nature in the form of a violent storm and a pack of sheepdogs. They drive off the pack, Denton fighting with a sword he has brought with him, Elizabeth using an old spade as a club, but they realize that, though such a life of danger and heroism was once humanity's ideal, they are too much a product of civilization to be able to live it. Wells here treats the love of nature as a sentimental fantasy, and he forces his lovers to accept that absolute division between nature and civilization that in the nineteenth century is still blurred and able to be crossed. The distinguishing factor is violence. Civilization, both as social organization and as technological replacement of nature, has controlled the evolutionary pressures that the storm and the dogs represent, and the future human needs civilization's protection to survive.

In chapter four this point is balanced by one which, if not exactly a refutation of the attitude toward nature in chapter two, at least sets up different responses toward violence and toward the past. Denton on the first day of his new job with the Labour Company gets into a fight because he, a ruined gentleman, does not know how to accept a piece of bread that one of the workingmen, Blunt, offers him. Denton is snobbish and revolted. The offer, which seems to have begun as an act of charity, turns easily into an act of bullying, and a fight ensues in which Denton is quickly and soundly beaten. Then another man, an albino, tries to continue the fight, but Blunt stops it. Blunt befriends Denton, teaches him to "scrap," and finally sets up the situation in which Denton can trounce the albino. Denton returns home exultant. What is interesting here is that the romance of labor and the manliness of violence seem to be treated without irony or criticism.[11] The reversion to violence, which in chapter two was merely a source of despair, is given an heroic quality, and the pastoral ideals of labor, hardiness, and fellowship, despaired of in chapter two, are now sanctioned. Repeatedly in this chapter Wells tells us how progress, while eliminating violence and the sight of violence from the upper classes, has let it seep back in at the bottom. Thus, if chapter two says you cannot go back to the old ideals, chapter four says that you cannot escape them (or the old vices that require them).

Violence, we see, is both vanquished by civilization and allowed by it. We can follow this problem into new realms in the first and last chapters. In the first chapter the hypnotist is an important figure who causes change without physical violence. He hypnotizes Elizabeth and causes her to forget Denton, and then later he releases her from the hypnotic suggestion and thus restores the love. He performs the change, not for moral reasons, but for money. He is a nonviolent economic agent. Yet the way Denton convinces him to release Elizabeth from her mental bonds is, importantly, by violence: he grabs a lamp, fells the hypnotist, and then forces him to obey his will. If economics seems to have gained control, therefore, violence is an effective refutation. Later, in chapter four, when he is faced with fighting the albino, Denton remembers this event.

But if economics seems opposed to violence in chapter one, in chapter five economics itself is revealed to be an agent of violence. Bindon, hoping to regain Elizabeth, plots the couple's financial ruin, and his economic fantasy, by a natural progression, leads him to envision Denton "smashed and pulverised" (p. 253).[12] In this chapter the agent of change is the doctor who prescribes a medication that makes Bindon magnanimous. Unlike the hypnotist, the doctor is in the service of an idea of civilization. Bindon gets angry when a man he has "paid" to cure him lectures him on the improvement of the species at the expense of the individual. Bindon's economic violence is made symmetrically opposite to Denton's physical violence: first by being incapable of changing the mediating figure's actions, and second, by being the problem rather than the solution. That is, chapter five begins with the fact of economic violence and then foresees a nonviolent way around it, while chapter one begins with economic nonviolence and uses violence to counter it.

Behind the violence that recurs throughout the story as both problem and as solution is the problem of change: in a conflict how do you move from one side to the other? "A Story of the Days to Come" studies this problem systematically. We can treat the five chapters as covering a broad set of changes that are possible for the individual in his attempts to accommodate himself to civilization:

Ch. 1	Change mind (by hypnosis)
Ch. 2	Change place (by moving to country and back)
Ch. 3	Change class (by descending from middle to lower)
Ch. 4	Change behavior (by learning to scrap)
Ch. 5	Change nature (by giving Bindon medication)

It should be observed that these changes are not necessarily solutions or even improvements. They are tentative explorations, chartings of the links between opposites. In chapters two and four the change is momentarily successful, but it is quickly seen past. In chapter two the pastoral idyll is shown to be a sentimental dream, and the lovers return to the city. In chapter four a more complicated reassessment takes place: Denton's education in the "art of scrapping" seems, momentarily, a solution, and he comes home to Elizabeth proclaiming his exuberant sense of being a part of "life." But Elizabeth confronts him with a blank and stony contradiction: she more than ever dreads the degeneration to primitive mindlessness that lower-class life entails. She acknowledges that Denton "can be coarse and ugly, and still be a man," (p. 249) but finds the growing likeness between herself and the laboring women unendurable. Thus, the changes are not answers to the problems the various chapters raise; the mediators are agents of Wells's thought: they permit the mind to move back and forth between the contradictions the story sets up.

Though the oppositions within each chapter tend to balance and cancel each other out, the story offers two escapes: love and suicide. Love represents an alternative to the economic trap of civilization. Chapters two and three end with the lovers joining hands in spite of their failure to resolve the economic problem; the linked hands represent a transposition out of the economic dilemma into a purely personal world. Chapter four, significantly, ends without a joining of hands; instead Denton is left shaking his fist "at all that environed him about, at the millions about him, at his past and future and all the insensate vastness of the overwhelming city" (p. 250). The symbolism here is appropriate: earlier in the chapter Denton has given his hand to Blunt and by that act symbolically affirmed the world of men, labor, and economics and thereby been unfaithful to the alternative idyll that his marriage has up to this point represented. His unfaithfulness is not gratuitous, however. Wells is here working with a theme he will perfect to a high art, the erosion of young love in the face of time and economic lack, and he depicts with deft strokes the failure of Elizabeth and Denton's love to sustain them in spite of economic misery. Love is a source of hope and energy, but it cannot resolve the real problems the story raises.

Suicide represents an attitude symmetrically antithetical to love: if love offers the prospect of a meaningful spiritual world in place of the oppressive and enslaving economic world, suicide would challenge the economic world by denying all worlds. But just as love's alternative is ultimately contaminated by the economic world it tries to oppose, suicide in Wells's system, rather than posing an absolute alternative, ultimately constitutes a reaffirmation of the world it rejects.

In chapter four the complexity of suicide as a mode of change is made explicit by inconsistencies in Denton's attitude. In despair Denton wonders out loud whether he will go on, and then he immediately reverses himself and asserts that there is "not a grain of suicide in us"

(p. 245). But then soon he reverses himself again: after training with Blunt and finding himself exhausted and depressed he wonders "was it worth while that he should go on living?" At times, then, suicide appears as a logical alternative to oppressed life, but then at other times that alternative is denied.

This seeming contradiction makes sense, however, if we study the way self-annihilation functions elsewhere in the story. In chapter one when Denton does not see Elizabeth for a number of weeks and fears he may have lost her, he takes on a conventional lover's stance and decides that he must have her or die. In this future world die translates into forget: he will have the hypnotist make him forget her. The equation of forgetting with death is underlined by the hypnotist who points out that Denton is making himself less by such an act. Though Denton is prevented from suicide of this sort, the will was there, and it is imagined in terms of submission to the world as it is. The will for suicide appears also in the fifth chapter, but here it is Bindon who chooses suicide, and here it is successful. Bindon's doctor, after lecturing him on what a poor specimen of the human species he is, advises him to undergo euthanasia. Bindon at first rejects it, saying that he doesn't "approve of suicide," to which the doctor answers, "you've been doing it all your life" (p. 256). After his chemical conversion to charity Bindon rushes off to the euthanasia company and finally dies for love, just as Denton had contemplated. Bindon's suicidal life of debauch, his euthanasia, and Denton's going to the hypnotist all share one thing: they escape by using the tools of the civilization that is to be escaped.

We see this combination of rejection and acceptance in other stories too: the anarchist tastes what he thinks is cholera; Azuma-zi embraces the dynamo. Thus in Wells's logic the suicide reaffirms the world as it is, even while in the act of self-annihilation he tries to deny it. Denton's fluctuation between enthusiasm and despair in chapter four and his explicit rejection of suicide make sense; for him to commit suicide would be for him to sanction the world being rejected. Paradoxically, chapter three, in which there is no hint of suicide, entails a more severe criticism of civilization than do the chapters in which suicide of one sort or another is contemplated.

Though "A Story of the Days to Come" works through opposites, the circularity of the gesture of suicide exposes how those opposites exist within a larger closed system that does not allow opposition. It is at this level, rather than at the level of plot, that the imagery of the story becomes significant. The transportation systems of the world of 2100 stand as symbols both of the promise and of the frustration of the whole structure: they set up the expectation of some large alternative which is then never discovered. At the beginning of chapter two Wells argues that "improved means of travel and transport" revolutionized human life, that the railroad was the first step in changing England from a rural to an urban civilization, and that the "Eadhamite road," which allows for high-speed travel "ranks with the invention of printing and steam as one of the epoch-making discoveries of the world's history" (p. 207). Such roads seem to promise two kinds of freedom. They offer the possibility of movement between the city and some alternative world. But that promise is false, for there is no alternative. Also, the roads are graduated according to speed (more than one hundred miles per hour on the inner lane; less than twenty-five on the outer) and would seem to mediate between rest and high-speed motion, between stasis and movement. But again the promise is unfulfilled, for when Denton and Elizabeth leave the city they walk. The road represents not graduation but the epitome of the uncaring city that has no place for the lovers; it is "a rushing traffic, beside which they seemed two scarce-moving dots" (p. 212).

The more elaborate invention, the "moving ways" within the city, while they too offer the idea of gradation, become an explicit symbol, not of change, but of oppressive lack of change: technological marvels, they merely reproduce the conditions of the Victorian city street. The moving ways are the home of the poor, their only privacy. The ways blind and deafen with incessant, aggressive advertising. And while the Eadhamite roads at least offer the vague prospect of an alternative to the city, the moving ways lead nowhere else; they merely cycle passengers. They are the prime symbol of what Denton understands at one moment as "the monstrous fraud of civilization" (p. 247). They invoke the imagery of change and of mediation, but in fact they allow for no change.

Air travel offers the one kind of technological advance in transportation that might represent meaningful change. The landing stages are set at the edge of the city; from them you can see the stars; on a landing stage Elizabeth and Denton first fall in love, and it is to a landing stage they retreat when oppressed by the city and the moving ways. Here is a rest that is truly rest; here is a view that is something other than the unnatural stimulation of advertising. And in a vague way here is the promise of real escape to Paris or to one of the "pleasure cities." But again the system closes in: all cities are the same; only the rich can afford pleasure cities; there is no other place to go.

The sense of claustrophobia that "A Story of the Days to Come" exudes derives in large part from the homogeneity of the world as Wells imagines it. For Selenites such a unified, unconflicted environment may satisfy, but the unhappiness of Denton and Elizabeth's life demands an alternative of some sort. On the local level, each chapter has its moment of fulfillment when opposites are bridged, but at the level of the largest structure there is no opposition; therefore, there can be no mediation and no change. The future, as Wells here envisions it, has meant a gradual lessening of human possibilities. In a significant passage near the beginning of chapter two Wells says this:

> In the old agricultural days that had drawn to an end in the eighteenth century there had been a pretty proverb of love in a cottage; and indeed in those days the poor of the countryside had dwelt in flower-covered, diamond-windowed cottages of thatch and plaster, with the sweet air and earth about them, amidst tangled hedges and the song of birds, and with the ever-changing sky overhead. But all this had changed (the change was already beginning in the nineteenth century), and a new sort of life was opening for the poor—in the lower quarters of the city. (p. 209)

What that idealized eighteenth-century poverty offered was the possibility of change. The word *change* becomes insistent near the end of this passage; the change, however, is in the direction of the denial of natural change as represented by the "ever-changing sky."

At the beginning of chapter three Wells gives us a paragraph which captures the whole paradox. The paragraph starts by talking about the "World-changing inventions" that have wrought "an entire revolution in human life." But after this praise of technological change, the paragraph modulates into an attack on civilization for its failure to change:

> That any steps should be taken to anticipate the miseries such a revolution might entail does not appear even to have been suggested; and the idea that the moral prohibitions and sanctions, the privileges and concessions, the conception of property and responsibility, of comfort and beauty, that had rendered the mainly agricultural states of the past prosperous and happy, would fail in the rising torrent of novel opportunities and novel stimulations, never seems to have entered the nineteenth-century mind. That a citizen, kindly and fair in his ordinary life, could as a

shareholder become almost murderously greedy; that commercial methods that were reasonable and honourable on the old-fashioned countryside, should on an enlarged scale be deadly and overwhelming; that
ancient charity was modern pauperisation, and ancient employment
modern sweating; that, in fact, a revision and enlargement of the duties
and rights of man had become urgently necessary, were things it could
not entertain, nourished as it was on an archaic system of education and
profoundly retrospective and legal in all its habits of thought. (p. 221)

Wells's criticism of the future is a criticism of his own thought. Partial
change is merely corruption, the old forms debased. The dystopian
suggestions of "A Story of the Days to Come" derive from the failure
of the future city to generate and the failure of Wells to imagine an
opposite, an alternative.

We are now in a position to appreciate the true depth of the symmetry of "A Story of the Days to Come." Nothing in the story stands
unopposed, but instead of leading to change, all those potentials for
change have led only to greater stasis. Repeatedly Wells takes pains
to describe how things have changed, but every time the pessimistic
conclusion results that, whatever small changes have taken place, the
large structure is the same, only more oppressive. The opening pages
of the story criticize Victorian Mr. Morris for not realizing how much
the world that he thinks is permanent is changing, but then, in blatant
self-contradiction, the story shows us Mwres of 2100 who, with some
minor modernizations, is exactly the same as his Victorian ancestor.

And the almost obsessive balance of such a passage recurs in the
final pages of the novel, which again play on the issue of change that
leads to stasis. The lovers have at last been restored to an apartment
at the edge of the city, a place much like the landing stage where they
first fell in love, a point as far from the center of the city as the structure
permits. From this point they watch the sunset: "Very wide and spacious was the view, for their balcony hung five hundred feet above the
ancient level of the ground. The oblongs of the Food Company, broken
here and there by the ruins—grotesque little holes and sheds—of the
ancient suburbs, and intersected by shining streams of sewage, passed
at last into a remote diapering at the foot of the distant hills" (p. 261).
There is room for satire here, but to treat it merely as satire is to miss
the opportunity the scene offers for a new aesthetic and an appreciation of the benefits change has brought. Denton for a moment tries
to imagine the future, then recoils and contemplates the past and
concludes:

Men had been but the shapes of men, creatures of darkness and igno-rance, victims of beasts and floods, storms and pestilence and incessant hunger. They had held a precarious foothold amidst bears and lions and all the monstrous violence of the past. Already some at least of these enemies were overcome. . . .

For a time Denton pursued the thoughts of this spacious vision, trying in obedience to his instinct to find his place and proportion in the scheme. (p. 261)

Compared to the radical antitheses posed at the end of *The Time Machine* this is muted and merely ambivalent and, given the economic horrors the story has described, somewhat beside the point. So long as the object of such imagining is not to fix a political position, but by tentative and conflicting imaginings to begin to find a "place and proportion in the scheme," such moments are still of value. But for Wells now, like a more influential thinker before him, it is no longer enough to understand the world; he must change it.

CHAPTER 6

The Dreams of Reason

WHEN, in the letter to Bennett, Wells intuits a new system, he thinks he has found a way around the static potential we have just studied, and in a way he has, but it is a liberation that entails a great sacrifice. In this chapter we can track closely the logical shifts by which Wells evades the crucial issues of justice and translates the evolution and ethics conflict into the easy and undebatable issue of efficiency. It is a decline, and it is worth tracing, not because it demeans Wells, but because seen in its process it reveals the accomplishment that has preceded it. What is important for our understanding of the imaginative method is not the explicit solutions to the frustrating balances we explored in the last chapter, but the structure beneath them. We shall see Wells obliterating the evolution-ethics dilemma in opposite ways, at times negating the ethical side, at other times elevating the ethical to the whole. At the core both methods are alike in that they resolve tension into a unitary project.

Simplifying Choices

In *Love and Mr. Lewisham* (1900) Wells depicts the simplification of conflict inherent in choice. Though the novel has none of the scientific fantasy or prediction that have dominated the work we have been studying, the central issues of *Love and Mr. Lewisham* involve problems of the meaning of civilization and its relation to nature that are familiar to us. The two women in Lewisham's life, Ethel and Miss Heydinger, pose alternative possibilities, not only for love, but for ambition and fulfillment. When at the end of the novel Mr. Lewisham chooses Ethel over Miss Heydinger, he shows he has learned a lesson about the nature of civilization and the place of humanity in nature.[1]

Lewisham's choice is between being a middle-class reformer with a wife as intellectual partner, and being part of a deeper, biological reality, less romantic in conventional terms, but more in tune with the true imperatives of human nature and existence. Miss Heydinger offers intellectual companionship, career, and the fulfillment of Lewisham's youthful *schema* of sound, orthodox, liberal success. By finally declining Miss Heydinger's attentions and ambitions for himself, Lewisham frees himself for what the novel asserts is a more meaningful existence. Lewisham contemplates his coming fatherhood and discovers the meaningfulness of the purely biological.[2]

Near the end of the novel the ambiguities of Wells's prose catch the complexity of this final acceptance, but also suggest that it is a reduction. Sitting at his desk, Lewisham meditates on his approaching fatherhood and finds it not only sufficient, but transcendent and purposeful, for it gives him a place in the true scheme of things:

> "Natural Selection—it follows . . . this way is happiness . . . must be. There can be no other."
>
> He sighed. "To last a lifetime, that is.
>
> "And yet—it is almost as if Life had played me a trick—promised so much—given so little! . . .
>
> "No! One must not look at it in that way! That will not do! That will *not* do.
>
> "Career! In itself it is a career—the most important career in the world. Father! Why should I want more?
>
> "And . . . Ethel! No wonder she seemed shallow . . . She has been shallow. No wonder she was restless. Unfulfilled . . . What had she to do? She was drudge, she was toy . . .
>
> "Yes. This is life. This alone is life! For this we were made and born. All these other things—all other things—they are only a sort of play . . .
>
> "Play!" (Atlantic Edition, vol. 7, pp. 516–17)

The biological imperative transcends the ethical projects of his earlier days. In place of the tension between the natural and the civilized, Lewisham chooses an ideal of nature that reduces the ambitions of his *Schema* to a trivial game.

Such a choice of nature is not, however, simply a dismissal of all plans: Lewisham is, after all, at his desk, a figure much like Wells himself a few years earlier, ready to write, not for the "liberal interest," but for the true liberation of humanity. And Ethel, for all her dreariness, is the stepdaughter of the intellectual scoundrel, Chaffery, and there are hints that Lewisham may in some way intend to imitate his father-in-law. The seemingly more ordinary life of marriage and children that Ethel represents paradoxically frees Lewisham for a more honest career, both more instinctual and more intellectually daring. The word "play" in the above passage, while it diminishes the pretensions of the *Schema*, becomes deeply ambiguous as it is reiterated. It ceases to be simply a noun; it takes on shadings of an imperative. A few lines later Lewisham welcomes the "end of empty dreams," but that may open the way to *real* dreams, a vision of an unorthodox new career in which the very awareness of the inconsequence of individual intellectual activity liberates him. Lewisham has managed to see beyond the shams of civilization and career and is ready to undertake "real life," which is both more elementary and purely biological than his earlier fantasies, and, because of his rejection of the middle-class ethos, also more daringly playful and speculative than his earlier plans.

The transformation from the orthodox *Schema* of the beginning of the novel to the radical acceptance of the evolutionary world at the end describes the main change of the novel, but that change would lack meaning, would probably be impossible, without the mediating figure of Chaffery. He is an Autolycus figure who does more than simply influence Mr. Lewisham: his doctrine, if one can so dignify the rogue's rationalizations, is the key to an aesthetic and logic of survival that initially frees Mr. Lewisham from his romantic bourgeois dreams and finally permits the word *play* its provocative ambiguity. Chaffery represents Wells's most elaborate development of the fraud figure, and here, as in the other tales of fraud, Wells achieves unresolved balance rather than judgment.

The balance is intricate, however, for Chaffery stands for more than simply a lie in the face of truth. As he himself explains, he stands for honest lies in the face of civilization's hypocritical lies. Thus, he claims he is true to himself, whatever frauds he perpetrates on others. So, though in civilization's eyes (and in Mr. Lewisham's at first) he is an outlaw, he is also, paradoxically, a figure of integrity and self-knowledge. Chaffery's mystery remains even after the mechanics of his fraud are exposed. The question is not whether he is honest—he clearly is not—but how we are to value him.

Chaffery's lesson to Lewisham in chapter 23 is a tour de force of paradoxical reasoning, but it is worth going over the main lines of his self-justification because to some extent Chaffery's argument becomes Wells's own. Chaffery's main premise is that civilization is based on lies, that money, to use his example, is really a deception in which all members of civilization participate. The conventions of trust and exchange, in Chaffery's view, far from freeing humanity for "higher" occupations, are simply evasions of the real living situation. Chaffery's pride is that he continues to participate in the evolutionary struggle, to see life for what it is, while most civilized people fool themselves into thinking they have somehow transcended the elementary facts that money is not food and unless you get food you die:

> "Now I am prepared to maintain," said Chaffery, proceeding with his proposition, "that Honesty is essentially an anarchistic and disintegrating force in society, that communities are held together and the progress of civilization made possible only by vigorous and sometimes even violent Lying: that the Social Contract is nothing more or less than a vast conspiracy of human beings to lie to and humbug themselves and one another for the general Good. Lies are the mortar that bind the savage individual man into the social masonry." (p. 416)

Chaffery here performs a noteworthy transformation of the evolution-ethics opposition: ethics, in his rendition, is merely a way of concealing the evolutionary reality. "Money," he says a little later, "is just the lie that mitigates our fury" (p. 207)

Given the central evasion that constitutes civilization, the way to authentic self-knowledge is not through an attempt at intellectual honesty (impossible so long as one accepts civilization) but through fraud:

> Since all ways of life are tainted with fraud, since to live and speak the truth is beyond human strength and courage—as one finds it—is it not better for a man that he engage in some straightforward comparatively harmless cheating, than if he risk his mental integrity in some ambiguous position and fall at last into self-deception and self-righteousness? That is the essential danger. That is the thing I always guard against. Heed that! It is the master sin. Self-righteousness. (p. 420)[3]

Chaffery's self-justification has further ornaments (that people want to be cheated, that he comforts them with his lies, that those he defrauds can afford it) but this central axiom, that civilization itself is a lie, forms, as he puts it, the loom from which he weaves his defense (p. 418).[4]

If the confidence man is a hero, certain corollaries follow, the most important of which is a disregard for conventional ethical bounds. Chaffery's charm and his skill in arguing come from his liberation from moral rules. When at the beginning of their conversation Lewisham says to him of his fraudulent seance, "But it isn't right—it isn't straight," Chaffery dismisses the charge with a single word, "Dogma" (p. 407), and when pressed simply changes the subject. Whenever things get wildly speculative or when they threaten to get specific, Chaffery insists that "our present object is discussion" (p. 423). It is an evasion, to be sure, but one that has its virtues, for it prevents the argument from shying into defensive moral postures. When Chaffery defends his position by appealing to Matthew Arnold, "I've a nature essentially Hellenic" (p. 408), the marvellous irony is that he actually does share with Arnold an antipathy to dogmas. In his perverse way Chaffery is a bringer of sweetness and light in the face of Lewisham's plodding and unimaginative moralism. But whereas Arnold seeks an ethical insight in the great monuments of traditional culture, Chaffery is ready to junk them all in the name of evolutionary reality and the higher fraud. He is therefore a comic version of Arnold, a representative of an anarchy on the other side of the dogmatic attitudes that both men see demeaning life and civilization. Chaffery's triumph over civilized lies and moral dogmas gives him, finally, an almost total freedom. "But on your principles you might do almost anything," Mr. Lewisham complains. "Precisely!" Chaffery answers (p. 422). What Lewisham fears as a moral abomination, Chaffery celebrates as an imaginative liberation. The "everything is permitted" that appalls Ivan Karamazov, exhilarates Chaffery.

Chaffery's comic seriousness renders exactly the free play of speculative imagination that fires Wells's own scientific romances. Like the Time Traveller, Chaffery is too ingenious to be trusted. The brilliant lie is liberating; the dogmatic truth is death. Only through such explicit lies does one see through the obfuscating, often unrecognized fraud of civilization. Chaffery rightly puts himself in the tradition of G. B. Shaw: both cut through cant and find truth in outrageous paradox.

But such comedy and insight depends on our awareness of opposition: Chaffery works in the novel because he is part of a larger conflict, the other side of which is conventional moral civilization as represented by Miss Heydinger and the *Schema*. Neither side has the whole truth. Each illuminates the other, and truth lies in their tension. But if one extracts Chaffery from his context within the novel and makes him, not part of a comic balance, but a model for behavior and thought, his whole stance becomes absurd: his emancipation from civilization becomes trivial, self-serving hypocrisy. If his transcendence of moral dogma leads towards ironic insight, it also leads to a narrow pride in his ability to make tricks work, and Chaffery often, in a quite sinister way, evades the moral issue simply by taking refuge in the ingenuity of his gimmicks. Wells sees the dodge and treats the character ironically in the novel, but Chaffery himself is not aware of the irony. Therefore, though he works brilliantly in the novel, he nevertheless offers a weak, even dangerous, model for actual intellectual behavior and activity.

I make this obvious point because I think Wells himself in the letter to Bennett is confused about it. By putting together *Anticipations*, "The Discovery of the Future," and Chaffery's chapter he implies a view of Chaffery that deprives him of his ironic fictional status. The lumping together of such different genra suggests that Wells sees his own preachings in *Anticipations* and those of Chaffery in the novel as importantly similar and valuable. In *Anticipations* Wells too tries to avoid the difficulties of civilization by denying the ethical dimension; he too prides himself on his ingenuity and seems to believe that it is enough to make something succeed to justify it. And *Anticipations* is not alone. Much of the work that follows *Love and Mr. Lewisham* has its audacity and its attractive surprises, but it is too much like Chaffery. It is self-serving, and it abandons the real difficulties civilization and the future pose.

The Denial of Ethics

We can already see Wells moving away from ironic balance towards narrow and dogmatic solutions in *Love and Mr. Lewisham*, for the choice between Ethel and Miss Heydinger is finally resolved by a clear choice which ends up ignoring the values of that which is rejected. Such simplification, while one may understand the psychological usefulness of it, deprives the problem of its tension and significance. The end of *Love and Mr. Lewisham* is too easy and complacent about what is "right." The anxieties, doubts, and regrets that are so masterfully depicted in the middle of the novel are at the end trivialized or disregarded. In its unitary simplification the novel's resolution marks an evasion befitting Chaffery himself. It is a way of relieving the tensions of the problem that Wells attempts in almost all his writing of this period.

We can, for instance, see this same simplifying choice at work in "The Discovery of the Future," in which he argues that until recently past-oriented thought has dominated human action and that it is time for a future-oriented mode of thought and action to take over. What is important for us here is not the specific argument, which we have already examined, but its structure. Two ways of thought establish a dichotomy, and here Wells insists that we cannot entertain both sides, that we have to choose one side of the split:

> They are distinct methods, the method of reference to the past and the method of reference to the future, and their mingling in many of our minds no more abolishes their difference than the existence of piebald horses proves that white is black.
>
> I believe that it is not sufficiently recognized just how different in their consequences these two methods are, and just where their difference and where the failure to appreciate their difference takes one. This present time is a period of quite extraordinary uncertainty and indecision upon endless questions—moral questions, aesthetic questions, religious and political questions—upon which we should all of us be happier to feel assured and settled; and a very large amount of this floating uncertainty about these important matters is due to the fact that with most of us these two insufficiently distinguished ways of looking at things are not only present together, but in actual conflict in our minds, in unsuspected conflict; we pass from one to the other heedlessly without any clear recognition of the fundamental difference in conclusions that exists between the two, and we do this with disastrous results to our confidence and to our consistency in dealing with all sorts of things. (Atlantic Edition, vol. 4, p. 359)

Wells wants us to acknowledge the presence of a conflict here, not so that we can rise to a state of ironic understanding that accepts both sides, but so that we can make a clear separation that will dissolve the conflict altogether. The example in the first paragraph is telling: piebald horses constitute exactly the kind of image of union that in his earlier work would permit Wells to hold together both sides of an opposition. But here he rejects the mediating possibilities of the image and goes on to denounce the confusion that results from accepting both sides. He thus subverts the method we have seen at work earlier. His reason for doing so, we should note, is not that such simplification is somehow truer, but that it leaves us "happier," "assured and settled."

If the logical interest of Wells's early work lies in his willingness to tolerate and explore contradiction without restlessly seeking to simplify and resolve its tension, what marks this later mode and sets it importantly apart from the earlier imaginative style is a tendency to seek single answers and solutions, to see contradiction, not as the expression of the complexity of human desire and the contradictory seekings and interests that have so far prevented any easy settlement of social problems, but simply as muddle, a confusion that some clear, directed thinking will resolve. In this new mode, contradiction, which formerly was essential to the understanding, marks a crisis that must be resolved by attaining some kind of unity, usually by disproving or discarding one of the opposing elements of the contradiction.

The most agonizing contradiction for Wells and the one that he performs the most extraordinary contortions to get around remains that between evolution and ethics. At the very beginning of the last chapter of *Anticipations*, describing the men of the "New Republic" of the future, Wells makes what, given the contempt he shows for the Curate in *The War of the Worlds*, is a surprising prognostication: he foresees that the future will be religious in a special sense. These new men, "being themselves, as by the nature of the forces that have selected them they will certainly be, men of will and purpose, they will be disposed to find, and consequently they will find, an effect of purpose in the totality of things" (p. 243). Wells finds it necessary to go into the future humans' religious convictions so that a few pages later he can use this "axiom of purpose" as a way of solving the problem Huxley posed for him years before:

> If, like Huxley, we do not positively believe in God, then we may still cling to an ethical system which has become an organic part of our lives and habits; and finding it manifestly in conflict with the purpose of things, speak of the non-ethical order of the universe. But to any one whose mind is pervaded by faith in God, a non-ethical universe in conflict with the incomprehensibly ethical soul of the Agnostic, is as incredible as a black horned devil, an active material anti-god with hoofs, tail, pitchfork, and Dunstan-scorched nose complete. To believe completely in God is to believe in the final rightness of all being. The ethical system that condemns the ways of life as wrong, or points to the ways of death as right, that countenances what the scheme of things condemns, and condemns the general purpose in things as it is now revealed to us, must prepare to follow the theological edifice upon which it was originally based. If the universe is non-ethical by our present standards, we must reconsider these standards and reconstruct our ethics. (pp. 247–48)

This is an important passage. Whereas earlier Wells had translated
Huxley's distinction between ethics and evolution into a balanced and
systematic opposition, now in *Anticipations* Wells has eradicated the
opposition altogether: if we believe in the "final rightness of all being"
(i.e., if we are religious in the way Wells tells us future people will be)
then the evolutionary process is ethical, and any "ethics" which conflicts with evolution must be rejected. In other words, ethics as a
system chosen by humanity as a way of organizing civilization in
opposition to nature ceases to have meaning for Wells. The only meaningful imperative is the evolutionary one.[5]

We may ask why Wells felt it important to make this logical move.
Why exclude the ethical dimension? One simple answer is that only
by so excluding ethics can prophesy make any claim to "scientific"
objectivity and dependability. If you allow ethics, you allow choice,
the possibility that given various technological and social options a
people will choose some and reject some on the basis of their con-
ceptions of what is good and bad. We must negate such moral wan-
derings if we wish to predict with accuracy. In the purely evolutionary
context choice as such does not exist: the successful is the good. Thus,
the very idea of writing *Anticipations* requires a negation of ethics.
Even acknowledging (as Wells does not) that in such a diminished
and mechanical system prediction is extremely chancy, there are still
difficulties. *The Time Machine* is perhaps the best comment on the
whole enterprise, for it shows how difficult it is to evaluate "success."
Fitness in the short run may be disastrous in the long; the Eloi domination of the Morlocks has eventually led to their own overthrow. But
in *Anticipations* Wells ignores such dialectical ironies. The positing of
"universal purpose" and the incorporation of ethics within the evolutionary scheme are logical moves designed to simplify the world in
such a way as to make prediction feasible.

This tendency to deny conflict often leads to prose which obscures
issues with vague and ambiguous words. Consider the following passage in which Wells "solves" central problems of the use and distribution of wealth:

> And while the emergent New Republic is deciding to provide for the
> swarming inferiority of the Abyss, and developing the morality and ed-
> ucational system of the future in this fashion, it will be attacking that
> mass of irresponsible property that is so unavoidable and so threatening
> under present conditions. The attack will, of course, be made along lines
> that the developing science of economics will trace in the days imme-

diately before us. A scheme of death-duties and of heavy graduated taxes
upon irresponsible incomes with perhaps, in addition a system of ter-
minable liability for borrowers, will probably suffice to control the growth
of this creditor elephantiasis. The detailed contrivances are for the spe-
cialist to make. (pp. 279–71)

Wells's prose here is hiding complexity and conflict in order to give
the impression that solutions are simple, unitary, and obvious. The
word *irresponsible*, for instance, occurs twice, but with deep and
essential vagueness. Later in the passage he will condemn the "gambler" as a "mean creature who hangs about the social body in the
hope of getting something for nothing, who runs risks to filch the
possessions of other men exactly as a thief does." Whom does he
mean? Does he count the investor in the future such a gambler? The
ambiguities of the terms and the abstraction of the discussion, rather
than encouraging thought, hide the real problem: at what point does
optimistic hope become gambling speculation? What exactly is "irresponsible property?" Issues that any realistic person knows will be
a source of deep conflict and disagreement in any reorganization of
the world are treated as if they were clear and undebated. The economic revolution will simply be the work of "specialists" trained in
their respective "sciences."

  Though he invokes evolutionary mechanisms to justify his ethics,
in *Anticipations* Wells even deprives this reduced vision of the tensions
that have dominated his early work. In an extraordinary passage he
disclaims the dialectical aspect of evolutionary struggle itself:

> The insoluble problems of pain and death, gaunt, incomprehensible facts
> as they were, fall into place in the gigantic order that evolution unfolds.
> All things are integral in the mighty scheme, the slain builds up the slayer,
> the wolf grooms the horse into swiftness, and the tiger calls for wisdom
> and courage out of man. All things are integral, but it has been left for
> men to be consciously integral, to take, at last, a share in the process, to
> have wills that have caught a harmony with the universal will, as sand
> grains flash into splendour under the blaze of the sun. There will be many
> who will never be called to this religious conviction, who will lead their
> little lives like fools, playing foolishly with religion and all the great issues
> of life, or like the beasts that perish, having sense alone; but those who
> by character and intelligence are predestinate to participate in the reality
> of life, will fearlessly shape all their ethical determinations and public
> policy anew, from a fearless study of themselves and the apparent purpose
> that opens out before them. (pp. 252–53)

The movement into abstraction ("reality of life," "apparent purpose") and the bullying rhetoric ("little lives like fools," "those who by character and intelligence are predestinate to participate in the reality of life," "fearlessly," "fearless") take the place of real argument here. We may remember the complexity of the Time Traveller's awareness that "we are kept keen on the grindstone of pain and necessity" and the terrible ironies that awareness generates. A similar opportunity here leads only to vague praise of the heroic future.

The alien, a source of intensive questions earlier, is now irrelevant. Ultimately, this new mode of thought, evasive and intolerant of conflict, leads to demands for euthanasia and for a slow, "evolutionary" genocide. After saying that the selection process will not be racial, Wells says:

> And for the rest—those swarms of black and brown and yellow people who do not come into the new needs of efficiency?
>
> Well, the world is a world, not a charitable institution, and I take it they will have to go. The whole tenor and meaning of the world, as I see it, is that they have to go. So far as they fail to develop sane, vigorous, and distinctive personalities for the great world of the future, it is their portion to die out and disappear.
>
> The world has a purpose greater than happiness; our lives are to serve God's purpose, and that purpose aims not at man as an end, but works through him to greater issues. (p. 274)

To say "the world is a world, not a charitable institution" is a coarse way of denying Huxley's ethical dimension. To render the population "sane" is to rid it of conflict. As elsewhere in *Anticipations*, a profound vagueness lurks in the words which advocate the most radical measures. This late in the twentieth century we are educated to the sinister implications of Wells's program, but my point here is not historical—I do not see Wells as a prefiguration of Hitler—but goes to the structure of the imagination. As Wells's thought tries to be neat and free from conflict, it falls inevitably into a totalitarian scheme; it sidesteps concrete particulars and settles easily and disastrously into complacent abstraction.

The Denial of Evolution

It is a sign of the difficulty he now has maintaining the tensions that characterize his early work that a few years after *Anticipations*

Wells can, without apology or even an acknowledgement of inconsistency, upset the balance of evolution and ethics in the opposite direction and advance the ethical over the evolutionary. In *A Modern Utopia* (1905), explaining why the Samurai live by "the Rule," Wells asserts the importance of the ethical in a language that recalls his early essay on the artifice of civilization:[6] the Samurai "know quite clearly that civilization is an artificial arrangement, and that all the physical and emotional instincts of man are too strong, and his natural instinct of restraint too weak, for him to live easily in the civilised State" (p. 259).[7] As in Huxley, here the ethical ideal is in conflict with the natural, and in *A Modern Utopia* Wells comes closer to Huxley's strong ethical position than he has ever before: "there is no justice in Nature perhaps, but the idea of justice must be sacred in any good society" (p. 129). If in *Anticipations* he could argue for the ethical value of the natural, here in *A Modern Utopia* he rejects such a philosophical position with acerbity: "We of the twentieth century are not going to accept the sweetish, faintly nasty slops of Rousseauism that so gratified our great-great-grand parents in the eighteenth. We know that order and justice do not come by Nature—'if only the policeman would go away'" (pp. 153–54).

Along with this return to the nature-civilization opposition comes an emphasis on human will and choice that was largely absent in *Anticipations*. The connection is clear; immediately after the rejection of Rousseauism just quoted, Wells goes on, "These things [i.e. order and justice] mean intention, will, carried to a scale that our poor vacillating, hot and cold earth has never known. What I am really seeing more and more clearly is the will beneath the visible Utopia" (p. 154). Will, an ethical commitment, now drowns out the imperative of evolutionary necessity, and Wells can close Utopia with words that deny the inevitable altogether:

> The new things will be indeed of the substance of the thing that is, but differing just in the measure of the will and imagination that goes to make them. They will be strong and fair as the will is sturdy and organised and the imagination comprehensive and bold; they will be ugly and smeared with wretchedness as the will is fluctuating and the imagination timid and mean.
>
> Indeed Will is stronger than Fact, it can mold and overcome Fact. (p. 326)

If in *Anticipations* Wells could scoff at any ethics that did not conform to the brute "fact" of evolutionary sequence, here he exactly reverses his allegiance and denies the determinative power of the evolutionary altogether. Yet, opposite though the two positions are at the surface, underneath they are versions of the same intolerance of conflict; they both express simplifying resolutions.

Wells's new emphasis on will is not that of the resolved revolutionary who sees a long battle ahead, but that of an optimist who sees the process of history as a continuing movement away from conflict. He rejects Marx and classical economics: such sciences, he argues, posit a human nature that lacks an ethical dimension. "The fundamental weakness of worldly economics," the Voice of *A Modern Utopia* declares, "lies in that curious disregard of the fund of enthusiasm and self-sacrifice in men." All Utopian history, he declares,

> is pervaded with the recognition of the fact that self-seeking is no more the whole of human life than the satisfaction of hunger; that it is an essential of a man's existence no doubt, and that under stress of evil circumstances it may as entirely obsess him as would the good hunt during famine, but that life may pass beyond to an illimitable world of emotions and effort. Every sane person consists of possibilities beyond the unavoidable needs, is capable of disinterested feeling, even if it amounts only to enthusiasm for a sport, or an industrial employment well done, for an art, or for a locality or class. (p. 232)

Again, Wells evades conflict: what defines the human is exactly and only its ethical imperative. Our world, Wells argues, has not learned to harness this enthusiasm, but it is there nevertheless, and with proper foresight it can be made to shape the world to come.

This aspect of good will which has shaped human history and is responsible for civilization's progress becomes the key to Wells's whole socialist program. In place of models of conflict, he emphasizes the ethical element, "the Good Will in Man," the steady pressure in human history that has gently but inexorably forced an amelioration of the social condition. History, Wells asserts in *New Worlds for Old* (1908), is not chaotic; a little distance allows us to see,

> something that goes on, that is constantly working to make order out of casualty, beauty out of confusion, justice, kindliness, mercy, out of cruelty and inconsiderate pressure. For our present purpose it will be sufficient to speak of this force that struggles and tends to make and do, as Good Will. More and more evident is it, as one reviews the ages that there is this much more than lust, hunger, avarice, vanity, and more or less intelligent fear, among the motives of mankind. This Good Will of our race,

however arising, however trivial, however subordinated to individual ends, however comically inadequate a thing it may be in this individual case or that, is in the aggregate an operating will. In spite of all the confusions and thwartings of life, the halts and resiliencies and the counter-strokes of fate, it is manifest that in the long run, human life becomes broader than it was, gentler than it was, finer and deeper. On the whole—and nowadays almost steadily—things *get better*. There is a secular amelioration of life, and it is brought about by Good Will working through the efforts of men. (p. 5)[8]

For Wells the virtue of socialism is that it would "coordinate all the Good Will that is active or latent in our world in one constructive plan" (p. 204). Under present conditions this Good Will is frustrated by fragmentation and dispersion. Good Will is the key which permits Wells to replace the images of conflict, which have so dominated his early imagination, with images of harmony and unity.

If Good Will rather than "enlightened self-interest" shapes progress, then the vision of society that sees it as a version of the natural struggle is irrelevant, and conflict, whether between the individual and the mass or between classes, is not the deep truth of political science. Wells sees the problem of capitalism to be, not so much its injustice resulting from conflicts of interest, but simply the inefficiency of rampant individualism. In Wells's view socialism is preferable not because it rights injustice and suffering, but because it is efficient, because it is the best fulfillment of the rule that acknowledges "the superiority of order to muddle" (*New Worlds*, p. 22). Oppressors in this vision are generally not villains, but simply misguided owners who, if properly enlightened, would see their way to sharing their wealth with the rest of society. Under such circumstances, the socialist's main aim is to reeducate the capitalists, to emancipate the "Good Will" from the mistaken traditions and prejudices that prevent a more efficient distribution of society's and nature's benefits. The whole thrust of this argument is to see the social problem, not as one of conflicting interests, but as one of poor organization and miseducation. Whatever one thinks of such a view, one can see that a trust in essential Good Will is a logical necessity for it.

Society in this view, therefore, is an ethically oriented and controlled structure, and the paradigms of conflict that all Wells's early work explores are irrelevant to the social issues as now perceived. The history of the competition between Morlock and Eloi, far from illustrating a deep dilemma in technological civilization, becomes a case of mere ignorance leading to disaster. For Wells now, national and class interests are false idols, fetishes left over from a less enlightened and awkwardly civilized past of absurd and irrational distrust and aggression. In part this easy view of society may be a rhetorical ploy, a way of assuring his readers that socialism is in their interest since capitalism is really in no one's. But the picture of society satisfies Wells at a more essential level because by getting rid of the ethics-evolution problem he manages to make all problems simply matters of efficient engineering. If that is true, then he can turn the revolution over to the specialists, the social engineers. The struggle with nature may go on, but that is now confined to issues of technological efficiency; for Wells there is no ethical *problem* left because civilization has become purely ethical.

This position sounds like Huxley's; in Wells's thought here the Good Will in Man seems to have a natural origin but to sustain an ethical behavior that is opposed to the evolutionary struggle. But whereas for Huxley this leads to a universal division in which humanity must continually choose between the ethical and the natural and must live with the tension of the opposition, Wells undercuts any ethical heroics by arguing that there is no choice on these grounds since *all* social behavior is against human nature, that is, that any society, whatever its form, is completely artificial, not an expression of evolutionary nature. In answering the objection that socialism in particular is against human nature, Wells replies:

> That is true, and it is equally true of everything else; capitalism is against human nature, competition is against human nature, cruelty, kindness, religion and doubt, monogamy, polygamy, celibacy, decency, indecency, piety, and sin are all against human nature. The present system in particular is against human nature, or what is the policeman for, the soldier, the debt-collector, the judge, the hangman? What means the glass along my neighbour's wall? Human nature is against human nature. For human nature is in a perpetual conflict; it is the Ishmael of the Universe, against everything, and with everything against it; and within, no more and no less than a perpetual battleground of passion, desire, cowardice, indolence, and good will. So that our initial proposition, as it stands at the head of this section, is as an argument against Socialism, just worth nothing at all. (*New Worlds*, pp. 202–3)

While Wells may seem to be finding conflict here, he is in fact nullifying conflict by laying waste the field of discourse. By placing everything social "against human nature," he makes it impossible to argue that human nature is at all related to social form. It is like dividing by zero: it is an illegitimate operation that renders everything equal.[9] In Wells's hands any ethical question the Good Will in Man might raise evaporates; by seeing conflict everywhere this system negates the significance of conflict.

This same gesture towards homogeneity reveals itself in Wells's systematic elimination of the problem of conflicts of interest in *A Modern Utopia*. The relation between the human and the nonhuman has been a source of deep interest and questioning in the early fictions, but now Wells abruptly erases it. The world of Utopia is free of all nonhuman species with which humans might have any kind of problematic relations. Weena was part human, part pet, but in Utopia there are no pets. And within the human species itself, while allowing there may be racial difference, Wells denies that it matters. And just as Utopia is free from biologically derived classifications, it is free from economic divisions. The planners of this society explicitly reject "the classification of men into labour and capital, the landed interest, the liquor trade, and the like" (p. 235). They consider these categories "accidental."[10] Insofar as "class" denotes groups with different interests, there are no classes in Utopia and therefore no conflicts. The playful, paradoxical theory of "The Rediscovery of the Unique" has turned serious, and Wells now uses it to eliminate all criteria for social classification. He has, thus, created a situation in which no discriminations are possible; there are no oppositions except the absolute and therefore irrelevant opposition of every unique individual with every other.

Yet, after eradicating any significant biological or economic classifications, Wells then sets up in the cleared field his own structure of classification which, because it is "real" rather than "accidental," is supposed not to generate conflict. All Utopians fall into one of four categories: poietic, kinetic, dull, and base. Wells admits that the system is not strictly logical (base, for instance, does not exclude any of the other categories, and there is much ambiguity about where the lines between categories are to be drawn). Also he asserts that the system is applied "loosely," as if that somehow rid it of any taint of unfairness (p. 240).

Why, after so carefully denying classification, should Wells set up this crude, almost childish set of divisions? I suggest it is the very ambiguity about what is being classified that makes it useful for him while the strictly biological, economic, or moral divisions won't do. Wells calls his categories "classes of mind" (p. 235), but it is not at all clear what is being measured as mind or how discriminations between categories are determined. Wells's prose is extraordinarily ambiguous at this point:

> They are not hereditary classes, nor is there any attempt to develop any class by special breeding, simply because the intricate interplay of heredity is untraceable and incalculable. They are classes to which people drift of their own accord. Education is uniform until differentiation becomes unmistakable, and each man (and woman) must establish his position with regard to the lines of this abstract classification by his own quality, choice, and development. (p. 236)

The divisions are somehow biological, but they are not biologically determined. The language here strongly implies that each individual gets to *choose* his or her own class, but they do so on the basis of an "unmistakable" genetic inclination. In place of the "accidental" divisions of class society, the Utopians give us a system of divisions which they call "real," but which is simply the substitution of biological accident for the accident of class. Underlying the Utopian ethics is a ruthless evolutionary discrimination: some people are born better (poietic, kinetic) than others (dull, base), and the former will dominate the latter.

The Problem of the Elite

Although there are no conflicts between species in *A Modern Utopia*, between the different categories of human lurks a strong potential for conflict, and as he works toward imagining a conflict-free situation Wells must now find a way around this division. On the one hand for Wells the exceptional person is the necessary instrument of the world's salvation; on the other hand such superiority often leads to tyranny and overreaching. Griffin's megalomania and Moreau's sadistic divinity are but two of many examples one could find in early Wells of how the gifted person preys on society. Chaffery, after all, attractive as he is, is a scoundrel. Imbalances of any sort lead to what Chaffery celebrates as an evolutionary competition and to an overthrow of ethical controls. If at times Wells abhors this intrusion of evolutionary competition into the social machine, he is also deeply skeptical about the chances of emancipation and progress without the guidance of the gifted. Thus, while without the exceptional person the world seems trapped in its suffering and blundering, society is nevertheless often right in its distrust of such a person.

In "The Country of the Blind" Wells explores the contradictions posed by the exceptional individual in society. Like "Æpyornis Island," this story defines the problem in terms of unmediated oppositions. Nunez, a mountaineer from Bogota, falls into the valley inhabited by a race of humans who have been blind for generations. His first thought is of the adage, "In the country of the blind the one-eyed man is king," and he sets out to claim his throne. He badly misjudges the competence of blind people working together, however, and finally, after almost allowing himself to be blinded so as to be "cured" of the "insanity" of sight, he escapes back into the desolation of the mountains and, perhaps, dies. In the process of the tale Wells explores the promise and the drawbacks of individual superiority and the solace and terror of social cohesiveness.

One set of truths in the story is critical of Nunez and approving of the static civilization of the blind. Why, after all, do the blind need a king at all? They originally came to their valley "fleeing the lust and tyranny of an evil Spanish ruler." What could Nunez offer them that they need? Their valley "had in it all that the heart of man could desire," and they carefully work with nature to achieve something like paradise:

> They led a simple, laborious life, these people with all the elements of virtue and happiness, as these things can be understood by men. They toiled, but not oppressively; they had food and clothing sufficient for their needs; they had days and seasons of rest; they made much of music and singing, and there was love among them, and little children.
>
> It was marvellous with what confidence and precision they went about their ordered world. Everything, you see, had been made to fit their needs.

Nunez's dream of kingship is a selfish fantasy that both ignores the happiness the blind people enjoy and condescends to the adjustment they have made. In the tradition of European imperialism, he aims to exploit a culture he does not appreciate, and Wells takes a certain pleasure in thwarting him. The blind, working together, unawed by a sense which they cannot comprehend, subdue Nunez and force him to conform to their way to life.

The triumph of blind society over Nunez's individual superiority gives rise to a second theme which directly contradicts the first. The blind paradise becomes totalitarian, and Nunez's arrogance becomes imaginative openness and majesty. The blind rulers are not merely defending their idyll against Nunez's sophistication, they are closed-minded and are unable to conceive of the very possibility of a sense of sight. And precisely because they are "scientific" about the world, because they exercise a sane skepticism and doubt about the ancient folklore that tells of a world outside their own, they trust a firm view, an unshakable paradigm, which leaves no room for the exceptional. The story emphasizes the oppressiveness of such scientific narrowness:

> The story of the outer world was faded and changed to a child's story; and they had ceased to concern themselves with anything beyond the rocky slopes above their circling wall. Blind men of genius had arisen among them and questioned the shreds of belief and tradition they had brought with them from their seeing days, and had dismissed all these things as idle fancies and replaced them with new and saner explanations. Much of their imagination had shrivelled with their eyes, and they had made for themselves new imaginations with their ever more sensitive ears and finger tips.

The inadequacy of such an empiricism is most graphically displayed for us by the blind people's incomprehension of birds, which they call angels. Their windowless rock houses, which at one level are symbols of the world to which they have successfully adapted and which baffles Nunez, are also symbols of dwarfed thought. When Nunez is contemplating being blinded—an operation the blind propose to make him a worthy husband for Medina-saroté, his beloved—he laments, "I must come under that roof of rock and stone and darkness, that horrible roof under which your imagination stoops." Even Medina-saroté's understanding of Nunez's claim to vision, though by far the most generous to be found among the blind, treats it as a trivial poetic fancy, and she is offended that he insists on it when he might so easily be "sane."

At the end of the tale Nunez reasserts the grandeur of the unfettered imagination. His ability to see the sun gives his experience a quality altogether different from that of the blind. Early in the tale we see the first of his epiphanies:

Nunez had an eye for all beautiful things, and it seemed to him that the
glow upon the snow fields and glaciers that rose about the valley on every
side was the most beautiful thing he had ever seen. His eyes went from
that inaccessible glory to the village and irrigated fields, fast sinking into
the twilight, and suddenly a wave of emotion took him, and he thanked
God from the bottom of his heart that the power of sight had been given
him.

Near the end Wells's imagery defines the difference in "scale" between
the sighted and blind imaginations:

He had fully meant to go to a lonely place where the meadows were
beautiful with white narcissus, and there remain until the hour of his
sacrifice should come, but as he went he lifted up his eyes and saw the
morning, the morning like an angel in golden armour, marching down
the steeps. . . .

Once again the ability to see the heights as well as the local, domes-
ticated surroundings is a sign of imaginative power, and here, instead
of the birdlike angels of the blind, Nunez can imagine a majestic
Seraph. Inspired by this power of metaphoric vision, his "imagination
soared." He realizes he has a depth of vision that makes the blind
world merely a prison:

He thought how for a day or so one might come down through passes,
drawing ever nearer and nearer to its busy streets and ways. He thought
of the river journey, day by day, from great Bogota to the still vaster world
beyond, through towns and villages, forest and desert places, the rushing
river day by day, until its banks receded and the big streamers came
splashing by, and one had reached the sea—the limitless sea, with its thousand islands, its thousands of islands, and its ships seen dimly far away
in their incessant journeyings round and about that greater world. And
there, unpent by mountains, one saw the sky—the sky, not such a disk as
one saw it here, but an arch of immeasurable blue, a deep of deeps in
which the circling stars were floating. . . .

The expansions of this passage show how Nunez, because he can see,
can imagine more than he can see and can thus transcend the closed
empiricism that restricts the blind imagination. He exists, thanks to
his sight, in a two world system. Though he is in a valley, he can
imagine the vast expanse of the sky on the ocean, and in the blue he

can imagine "a deep of deeps." In order to be true to this imaginative openness he flees the valley of the blind, and we last see him lying "peacefully contented under the cold stars."

The acuteness of the dilemma "The Country of the Blind" poses betrays Wells's sensitiveness to and difficulty with the issue. The alternatives the story offers—the cavelike house of society and the open mountainside of lonely individualism—are antithetical and unmediated. We find here none of the ambiguous structures that in earlier stories and novels allowed the outside and inside to interact. The story acknowledges conflicting imperatives: blind society survives happily by enforcing conformity, but for the sighted (gifted) individual to submit is to deny the integrity of his imagination; society's traditions and scientific expectations are oppressive, but to demand kingly freedoms is selfish and involves a misunderstanding of the adaptive virtues of social organization. Thus, "The Country of the Blind" sets up the conflict between the gifted individual and society and treats it from both sides, and yet it offers no possibility of reconciliation.

In *The Food of the Gods* (1904) Wells again treats this theme, but after dealing with it in a purely ironic way at first, in the last part of the novel he begins to seek out a solution. The novel starts as a comic exemplum of humanity's inability to master its own reform. The inventors of Herakleophorbia ("Boomfood"), the chemical that creates giants by maintaining continuous rather than ordinary staged growth, are duffers who hire even more incompetent people to handle their "experimental farm," with the result that they loose a plague of giant wasps, rats, and various monstrous and unpleasant flora on the neighborhood. But if the first section is a comic allegory of human incompetence much like "The Man Who Could Work Miracles," in the last section the images reverse and the story becomes a utopian allegory of human potential. Gianthood, formerly a monstrosity, now becomes a virtue, and the giant brood, persecuted by normal humans, becomes a symbol, not just of increased size, but of a general moral and intellectual improvement. In the last section normal humanity, as it tries to control the outbreak of gianthood—that is, as it tries to rectify the clear blunders of section one—is seen as murderously narrow-minded.

The spiritual and intellectual superiority of the giants is made clear near the beginning of the third section:

We see over their walls and over their protections; we look inadvertently into their upper windows; we look over their customs; their laws are no more than a net about our feet. . . .

Every time we stumble we hear them shouting; every time we blunder against their limits or stretch out to any spacious act. . . .

Our easy paces are wild flights to them, and all they deem great and wonderful no more than doll's [sic] pyramids to us. Their pettiness of method and appliance and imagination hampers and defeats our powers. There are no machines to the power of our hands, no helps to fit our needs. They hold our greatness in servitude by a thousand invisible bands. We are stronger, man for man, a hundred times, but we are disarmed. Our very greatness makes us debtors; they claim the land we stand upon; they tax our ampler need of food and shelter, and for all these things we must toil with the tools these dwarfs can make us—and to satisfy their dwarfish fancies. (Atlantic Edition, vol. 5, pp. 229–30)

The equation of small size with selfish and petty thought gets reiterated later (p. 300), and the giants themselves are made to stand for generous, bold, utopian imagination.[11] If therefore the allegory of the first comic section warns against tampering with nature, the allegory of the last sees that same attitude as a servile and selfish conservativism and looks optimistically to the intelligent restructuring of the world. This second allegory represents an attitude that by 1904 could be called "typically Wellsian."

In this second allegory *The Food of the Gods* differs importantly from "The Country of the Blind," If Nunez, because of his ethical ideals, is forced to choose between submission with its consequent mutilation and escape with its similarly tortured implications, the giants at the end of *The Food of the Gods* reformulate the issue as one between the survival of them or of normal humans. In other words, they propose the "evolutionary ethics" of survival of the fittest, and they have no doubt (and in this case neither does Wells) who is the fittest.

Along with this simplification of the issue of superiority comes a blindness to the implications of the potential ironies in the novel's imagery. At one point a group of young giants, Cossar's sons, after being told by a lawyer that they can't make a road straight because it would violate private property, begin to meditate on the injustices of the world:

"Lots of them haven't houses fit to live in," said the second boy. "Let's go and build 'em a house close up to London that will hold heaps and heaps of them and be ever so comfortable and nice, and let's make 'em a nice little road to where they all go and do business—a nice straight little road, and make it all as nice as nice. We'll make it all so clean and pretty that they won't any of them be able to live grubby and beastly like most of them do now. Water enough for them to wash with, we'll have—you know they're so dirty now that nine out of ten of their houses haven't even baths in them, the filthy little skunks! You know, the ones that have baths spit insults and call 'em the Great Unwashed.—You know. We'll alter all that. And we'll make electricity light and cook and clean up for them, and all. Fancy! They make their women—women who are going to be mothers—crawl about and scrub floors!

"We could make it all beautifully. We could bank up a valley in that range of hills over there and make a nice reservoir, and we could make a big place here to generate our electricity and have it all simply lovely. Couldn't we, brother? . . . And then perhaps they'd let us do some other things."

"Yes," said the elder brother, "we could do it very nice for them."

"Then let's," said the second brother.

"I don't mind," said the elder brother, and looked about for a handy tool.

And that led to another dreadful bother. (pp. 210–11)

Here is the essence of the utopian imagination, but the style makes it clear that we must consider it childish and naive. By the end of the novel, however, any irony that we may have felt has disappeared, and the giants appear as part of the great "purpose" of nature and their utopian presence as an evolutionary necessity:

"It is not that we would oust the little people from the world," he said, "in order that we, who are no more than one step upwards from their littleness, may hold their world forever. It is the step we fight for and not ourselves. . . . We are here, Brothers, to what end? To serve the spirit and the purpose that has been breathed into our lives. We fight not for ourselves—for we are but the momentary hands and eyes of the Life of the World." (p. 305)

The childish naiveté of the earlier passage has meant nothing; the giants are self-appointed agents of the divine that Wells discovered in *Anticipations*.

The last section of *The Food of the Gods* might be said to depict the utopianist's paranoia, a not uncommon feeling among those who would save the world and find the world reluctant to be saved, even hostile. The elite, necessary in Wells's view for the salvation of the world, are also in conflict with the world. That conflict, as we have seen, has energizing intellectual potential, but as with other aspects of his thought, Wells now seeks to free his imagination of conflict. The solution for him, which has been implicit in his thought for a while, finds its most elaborate embodiment in *A Modern Utopia*. That alternative world is led by the Samurai, an elected corps of sane, intelligent, and unselfish men and women who would guide civilization into a rational, ordered pattern and whose only reward for ruling is the knowledge of service well done. If in *The Food of the Gods* there is a disastrous conflict between racial and democratic homogeniety, in the idea of the Samurai that contradiction is resolved. The resolution is expressed in the phrase Wells picks to depict the corps: a "voluntary nobility" joins the ideas of democratic freedom and of hereditary (biological?) superiority; his later phrase, "the open conspiracy," reconciles separation and union, secrecy and publicity. The Samurai ideal solves the problem of the gifted person's alienation from the general crowd. The Samurai are both gifted and common, both exclusive and democratic; they are unalienated Moreaus working for humanity, and they are super beast men who by an act of will and by a voluntary obedience to a rigorous "rule" lift themselves above themselves.

In the *Experiment in Autobiography* Wells himself draws the connection between the giants at the end of *The Food of the Gods* and the Samurai,[12] but that very connection, if looked at closely, reveals the difficulties that the idea of the Samurai is avoiding. The giants are supermen whose genetic relation to ourselves is ambiguous. On the one hand they have grown more than we have; they are just bigger. On the other hand they are saner, more generous, have a broader personality, and all in all represent a profoundly different nature, a new species. Boomfood has caused an evolutionary change which is also an ethical change (in this way the giants are very unlike the Martians whose evolutionary superiority is not combined with an ethical superiority). Because the Samurai are not racially different from the mass of humanity and have been educated the same way all humans have been, there is no evolutionary component. Where, then, do Samurai come from? What makes one person want to be a Samurai and another not? What makes one person more successful as a person than another? These are not idle questions; they lie at the heart of the problem of how to create a better society. Wells's image of the Samurai seems to solve the problem, but in fact the image only obscures it. Like the fallacy of the first cause, the conflict of evolution and ethics when it seems solved has only been displaced to a deeper level and remains a puzzle. There is no way to avoid it.

The Image of the Engineer

The Samurai represent an attempt to imagine an elite without the problems of the elite. Yet this exercise in finding a realm without conflict of interest leads Wells into a strange paradox: as he gets more politically active, as he becomes a more outspoken socialist, he progressively denies the truly political dimension of this thought. If politics is the art of dealing with conflicts of interest, Wells defends his intensely political position by arguing that there are no true conflicts of interest, that in effect the moral questions that have been the subject of many of his earlier imaginative forays are false issues. In his tracts written for the Fabian Society Wells even suppresses the muted conflicts that might exist between the Samurai and the rest of humanity. Neither *New Worlds for Old* nor "This Misery of Boots" ever mentions anything like the Samurai class. Rulers are not needed; the society is run by social engineers who make no moral choices, who merely perform their jobs of insuring efficient distribution. This engineer in Wells's view is not a political figure; his only task is to make the machine work. Gifted not with genius or moral fervor, but simply with the desire to serve and the intelligence to master a complex system, the class of engineers leads society without ever placing itself outside society or trying to take advantage of it.

In such a future world the engineers are not even mediators because there are no deep conflicts between humans that need to be bridged. I do not think that this idea will bear much examination; Wells has based his ideal of a conflictless society on a fantasy about machines; after all, even the factory manager must, in times of shortage, make decisions as to which machines will benefit and which will be deprived. Wells's engineers, however, do not have to make such political decisions; they are merely efficient, honest bureaucrats. Although Wells later in his life compares his Samurai to Lenin's disciplined communists who volunteer for membership, undergo severe discipline, and are permitted to resign their positions,[13] the comparison is misleading because Wells's vision of the structure of society is completely at odds with the Marxist-Leninist one. In place of the central and inevitable class conflicts working themselves out dialectically, Wells posits a good-natured amelioration:

There may be a concentration of capital and a relative impoverishment of the general working mass of people, for example, and yet a general advance in the world's prosperity and a growing sense of social duty in the owners of capital and land may do much to mask this antagonism of class interests and ameliorate its miseries. Moreover, this antagonism itself may in the end find adequate expression through temperate discussion, and the class war come disguised beyond recognition, with hates mitigated by charity and swords beaten into pens, a mere constructive conference between two classes of fairly well-intentioned albeit perhaps still biassed men and women. (*New Worlds*, p. 226)

While he advocates change, Wells is also able to assure his readers that it need not be revolutionary because there is really no conflict of interests. One cannot escape the conviction that Wells has reached a point at which only by denying conflict altogether can he see a way out of civilization's muddle. This vision of temperate reasonableness is at a deep level a betrayal of the oppositional structure of his imagination, so that in place of balanced conflict we get total imbalances in which one side (reason and order) triumphs over the other (muddle).

"The Land Ironclads," published late in 1903, epitomizes the new shape of Wells's imagination. The story "invents" the military tank, and the very nature of that machine warns us of a change, for Wells here is imagining the possible and practical whereas, as he himself acknowledged, his previous fictional inventions were more "artistic" than realistic: the time machine, Cavorite, invisibility—all allow for abrupt new perspectives, but it is unlikely that any of them will ever actually appear and change our world. And not only is the idea of the land ironclad realistic, but also the patentable quality of the invention was a source of great pride for Wells: years later he would claim credit for the tank when the government tried to bestow the honor elsewhere.[14]

But, while this practical aspect is a sign of the new turn in his concerns, our interest is still in the artistic and logical pattern, in the way Wells imagines opposition and how he treats it. The movement towards practicality that we saw lead to a denial of conflict in *Anticipations* leads to the same quality in "The Land Ironclads." The story is impatient with opposition and balance. It solves issues by the victory of one side and the defeat of the other. In this respect it is totally different from the earlier stories and novels.

"The Land Ironclads" begins in stalemate, an absolute balance in which the two sides exactly mirror each other. A lieutenant looking through his field glasses at the enemy's lines sees field glasses looking back at him. The war has become an entirely static configuration: the "tangle of trenches" suggests a knot no one can untie. Bloch's prophesy of the triumph of defense in warfare has come true.[15] The fact that neither side is given a motive for the war adds to the symmetry of the situation.

This kind of balance may remind us of the two-world system in which the very identity across a line of difference is the source of intellectual pleasure, but in this story Wells at the very beginning suggests that he is now playing with new rules. One side has invaded. We watch the war from the defenders' side. As the defending lieutenant points out, the invaders have "got to win or else they lose. A draw's a win for our side." This rule lays the base for a new relation between opposites. Whereas before, in "The Flying Man" for instance, the "solution" is to bridge the two sides, here the solution is for the invader to defeat the defender. Anything short of victory is defeat.

Though at the start the two sides seem almost identical and their powers exactly equal, soon a set of distinctions is introduced which, minor at the beginning, becomes more significant until at the end the victory of the invaders is seen as the triumph of one set of values over its opposite. The defenders are "country" people while the attackers are "town" people. The defenders are physically superior ("Our boys of fourteen can give their grown men points") and enjoy the heroics of battle; their cavalry has spent three years mastering the charge in which the horsemen shoot from the saddle. The attackers on the other hand are "poor amateurs at war," but intellectual and industrialized. The conflict is between traditional, rural, athletic heroism and innovative, urban, intellectual competence.

The earlier Wells would have been interested in studying the claims of both sides, but the writer of "The Land Ironclads," having set up the balance, is interested in breaking the stalemate by the total victory of one side. The machine, the land ironclad, like the flying man's parachute, is the instrument by which the standoff is transcended; the tanks, however, simply annihilate the opposition. The central part of the story describes how the land ironclads rout first the infantry in the forward trenches, then the artillery, and finally the pride of the defenders' forces, the horse cavalry. One by one the machine demonstrates the inadequacy of each of the defenders' forces, and the final resolution is not a complex equation, but the eradication of one side.

The ambiguities that military victory might give rise to, the kinds of mediation across the boundaries of opposition that make *The Time Machine, The Island of Doctor Moreau,* or *The War of the Worlds* such complicated investigations, are consciously overridden here in "The Land Ironclads." The young engineers who invented the tanks and operate them in battle appear as unquestioned heroes. The War Correspondent tries to generate some irony at their expense by describing the battle as "Mankind versus Ironmongery," but such a position is merely a sentimental expression of antimachine prejudice; his irony recoils on himself, and Wells ends the story with supercilious sarcasm at the War Correspondent's expense:

> And he was much too good a journalist to spoil his contrast by remarking that the half-dozen comparatively slender young men in blue pyjamas who were standing about their victorious land ironclad, drinking coffee and eating biscuits, had also in their eyes and carriage something not altogether degraded below the level of man.

To admit the value of the other side of the opposition would "spoil" the War Correspondent's "contrast," but Wells himself has become too good a "journalist" to allow for such complexity or exchange either. The glimpse we are given of the engineers' own attitude bears out this single-mindedness. Even if these were the defenders rather than the attackers talking, the following passage would sound much like what one imagines an insensitive Martian might have thought; the fact that this whining self-defense is the invaders' makes moral hash of the position. Here is the voice of pure evolutionary competition; technological superiority obviates all ethical considerations:

> For the enemy these young engineers were defeating they felt a certain qualified pity and a quite unqualified contempt. They regarded these big, healthy men they were shooting down precisely as these same big healthy men might regard some inferior kind of nigger. They despised them for making war; despised their bawling patriotisms and their emotionality profoundly; despised them, above all, for the petty cunning and the almost brutish want of imagination their method of fighting displayed. "If they must make war," these young men thought, "why in thunder don't they do it like sensible men?" They resented the assumption that their own

side was too stupid to do anything more than play their enemy's game, that they were going to play this costly folly according to the rules of unimaginative men. They resented being forced to the trouble of making man-killing machinery; resented the alternative of having to massacre these people or endure their truculent yappings; resented the whole unfathomable imbecility of war.[16]

One is reminded of Thurber's parable of the wolves and the rabbits. "Imagination" has lost all ethical dimension here and has been reduced to technological ingenuity. Such a passage would have been subject to ironic modification in earlier Wells; the Artilleryman, for instance, even as he voices ideas not unlike these, is undercut, both by his own inadequacy and by the general structure of *The War of the Worlds* in which all claims to evolutionary superiority and triumph ask for ironic rebuttal.

Given the kind of precise and insistent ironies we are used to, the engineers are treated with a surprising lack of skepticism by Wells. Even the following short passage, which might to the jaundiced eye contain the basis for ironic condemnation, seems uncritical: "Meanwhile, with something of the mechanical precision of a good clerk posting a ledger, the riflemen moved their knobs and pressed their buttons." The language here is like Cavor's describing the Selenite education, but any complex response is denied. It has been explained earlier in the story that this wondrous machine causes every shot to be a hit, but the language of the passage sterilizes the ethical problem of such murderous efficiency. While I find Wells here ethically offensive, my point is not primarily ethical, but logical; here we have a prose that has grown impatient with balance, with seeing wholly; it simplifies in order to champion one side. Like the invaders, Wells has decided that a draw is no good, that unless you win, you lose. He has become the champion of efficiency.

The failure of the image of the land ironclad itself to function symbolically suggests the complete change Wells has worked. The tank is in many respects very much like the Martian war-machines. It isn't just that they are invincible, but they perform the same ingenious operation of creating an indoors outdoors. The cold-hearted efficiency of the operators resembles the Martians'. The history of the battle likewise echoes the early war with the Martians in which the artillery finally injures one war-machine but such a token victory hardly slows the enemy advance. The problem with "the Land Ironclads," however, is not that Wells has switched sides—as we saw, a part of him always sided with the Martians. The problem is that the imagery has ceased to function in any complex imaginative way. Instead of using his images as a way of thinking through a conflict, Wells is engaging in a kind of propaganda for technological efficiency. One side is right, the other is nostalgic and wrong: in order to maintain that simple vision the story has to ignore the imagery's implications.

CHAPTER **7**

Utopian and Anti-utopian Logic

Utopia and Anti-utopia

MY aim in the preceding chapter has been to show how Wells, as he consciously moves towards "directed thought," changes his logical procedures. If, in terms of the occasions that generated the work, this later mode may serve as more effective polemic, nevertheless we can see that it also entails a great sacrifice. On the other hand, not to risk that sacrifice, to remain balanced in the midst of contraries, while it can be position of energizing tension and of broad perspective, may be to render oneself powerless to change the world. Without claiming that it is impossible to do both, we can readily admit that Wells's particular imagination cannot. The dichotomy he poses between directed and undirected thought defines two antithetical modes of his own imagination, and he is unable to yoke them successfully.

If we are to take the aesthetic and intellectual issues of this dichotomy seriously, we need to do more than merely chart the various ways Wells handled them. We need to question the possibilities and failures of the forms themselves. In this final chapter I want to evaluate Wells's accomplishment as described in chapters two through five in terms of the development of a particular genus of literature with a special set of structural characteristics. My purpose here is to understand the intellectual possibilities of certain structures and to sketch how the two forms Wells works in suggest a larger intellectual field of utopian and anti-utopian structures. When later in the chapter I compare Wells's structures to those of other writers, I am interested, not in establishing the debts others owe him, but in tracing a few of the possibilities beyond Wells himself as a way of sketching the larger field.

The frustrations of the situation we observe in "A Story of the Days to Come" force Wells to try new forms. We have tracked some of them. By the first decade of this century he is more often applying his main imaginative energy to developing a fiction that addresses contemporary realistic social issues.[1] During this period when he does attempt the scientific romance, he repeatedly returns to a very special form of it in which he depicts a strange and magical transformation from a corrupt and conflict-ridden world to a purged, sane, and entirely harmonious one. *In the Days of the Comet* (1906) is the first of these, but the form recurs again in *The World Set Free* (1914), *Men Like Gods* (1923), and *The Dream* (1924). These novels have not stood up well; it would be merely diligent to study all of them. But we need to understand the aesthetic issues Wells's imagination is confronting as he pushes his logic towards solution, and for that purpose a glance at the form of *In the Days of the Comet* is in order.

The major alteration in the structure of Wells's logic that has occurred in *In the Days of the Comet* is camouflaged by his use of what looks like the two-world system. The novel juxtaposes two worlds that share personalities and geographies but which are radically different. The old world is ours, an "insane" world of war, class hatred, and murderous jealousy; the new world is that which a rational treatment of society and of human relations might supposedly create, an organized utopia in which all humans are free to realize their whole potential. The agent of juxtaposition is the comet through whose tail earth passes. Our atmosphere is so modified that humanity, while remaining biologically the same as it was, suddenly acts sanely. One sees the possibility for ironic inquiry of the sort we have studied, but the similarity to the structure of earlier works is superficial; the before-after balance conceals a deep imaginative imbalance. The opposition we see so clearly in *In the Days of the Comet* is not a puzzle at all; the two worlds do not exist in any cognitive tension with each other. Instead the new world, nearly faultless, a model of uncomplicated rationality, simply displaces the old. We have no problem; we reject the first. Thus, in its large structure, this novel asks us not to balance ironically but to choose, to eliminate, to simplify.

A small detail near the end of *In the Days of the Comet* tells us much about the different spirit that rules this novel. Leadford, the narrator who has experienced the abrupt transformation, enumerates the absurd, ugly, and cruel artifacts of the old world that are ritually burnt as a way of opening the "new age." Among the "dirty, decayed, and altogether painful ornaments" of the old ways he is amazed to find "even *stuffed dead birds!*" (Atlantic Edition, vol. 10, p. 302, emphasis in original). His enlightened incomprehension of the pleasures of taxidermy is a fine sign of how his whole attitude differs from that of the Wells of ten years earlier who would find in the same image the possibilities of a liberating and joyful irony. The old, drunken taxidermist who created new species out of "the skeletons of a stork and a toucan and a job lot of feathers," who subverted truth in the interest of the "pure joy" of imaginative rearrangement and re-creation, has been replaced by a mind which has little tolerance for such outlaw imaginings unless they conduce in some "directed" way to the shaping of the New Republic. In place of complex, overlapping ironies we now have purification and order.

It is because of the comet that *In the Days of the Comet* is lumped with the earlier scientific romances, whereas in fact neither part of the novel employs the kind of ironic thought we have studied in Wells's early fiction. The realistic part of the novel, while it has attractions, lacks the element of logical fantasy, of organized landscape and plot that distinguishes the authentic scientific romance. I do not intend this as a complaint, only as a distinction. The first part of *In the Days of the Comet* seems to me immensely successful in the tradition of Wells's realism. On the other hand, the utopian solution presents us with a world without conflict. The scientific romance falls in a range between these two broad generic types: it is neither realistic nor utopian. It is what I will call, with careful attention to its precise, stipulated meaning, *anti-utopian*.

The dichotomy in Wells's thought between directed and undirected thought expresses itself in a dichotomy of genera, two forms of imaginative procedure, *utopia* and *anti-utopia*. By these terms I refer not to optimism or pessimism but to the imaginative attempt to put together, to compose and endorse a world, and the opposite attempt to see through, to dismember a world. The familiar terminology here distinguishes not political attitudes but opposed structural principles of thought.[2]

Darko Suvin defines *utopia* as "a verbal construction of a particular quasi-human community where sociopolitical institutions, norms, and individual relationships are organized according to a more perfect principle than in the author's community."[3] Suvin is especially concerned with seeing utopia as a *literary* form. Accepting that, I want here also to stress the importance of *organization, community,* and *principle* in this definition. The utopia is an exercise in thinking through a way things might fit together, might work; it strives for consistency and reconciles conflict. Utopia is, therefore, in the sense I am using the term, a verbal artifact with a distinctive imaginative imperative: it seeks coherence. At its purest, utopia is like a mathematical equation: it achieves imaginative order; it accounts for all doubts; it solves.

Dystopia, in the structural configuration I am here defining, is similar to utopia. Dystopia (the bad place) is for our purposes utopia in which the positive ("more perfect principle") has been replaced by a negative. Though opposites on the surface, utopia and dystopia share a common structure: both are exercises in imagining coherent wholes, in making an idea work, either to lure the reader toward an ideal or to drive the reader back from a nightmare. Both are the expression of a synthetic imagination, a comprehension and expression of the deep principles of happiness or unhappiness.[4]

By *anti-utopia* I propose to refer to a type of skeptical imagining that is opposed to the consistencies of utopia-dystopia. If the utopian-dystopian form tends to construct single, fool-proof structures which solve social dilemmas, the anti-utopian form discovers problems, raises questions, and doubts. Both utopian and anti-utopian modes partake in some way of the "what if?" premise so valued by utopian and SF commentators, and both work by contrast of sorts, by what Suvin calls "cognitive estrangement." And since every utopia is a criticism of the world as it is, all utopian thought has a satiric dimension.[5] But anti-utopia, as I am here defining it, is not simply satiric; it is a mode of relentless inquisition, of restless skeptical exploration of the very articles of faith on which utopias themselves are built. Thus, while there is much anti-utopian satire, it is not an attack on reality but a criticism of human desire and expectation. While the utopia attempts a vision of a coherent preferable world and draws our attention to the way it improves on the world we have, the anti-utopia questions utopian solutions even as it proposes them.[6] It enjoys the construction of imaginary community, but it does not succumb to the satisfactions of solutions. By the same mechanism the anti-utopia can acknowledge virtues in dystopia even while denouncing it.

At the core of the anti-utopia is, not simply an ideal or a nightmare, but an awareness of conflict, of deeply opposed values that pure utopia and dystopia tend to override. If utopia seeks imaginative solutions, anti-utopia goes beyond to return to the powerful and disturbing ambivalences that come from perceiving simultaneous yet conflicting goods. Thus, the Selenites represent an ideal that twists into horror, and a horror that takes on shadings of the ideal. In the passage on physically shaping infants to prepare them for their adult tasks, Wells forces the reader to consider whether it is better to "use" or to "waste" a person. Philosophically this may be a false dichotomy; there are of course other ways than these two of dealing with humans; but rhetorically the passage makes us approve and condemn both our own world and the Selenite solution. By ingeniously posing the issue in terms of a narrow and irresolvable conflict, the passage generates yearning and skepticism, and that conjunction is the essence of anti-utopian thought.

The body of this book has been a defense of the anti-utopian mode. At this point it would be redundant to develop further the virtues of anti-utopianism; my aim is now to explore further the various ways the structural principle based on conflict functions at a level beneath that of explicit theme. In tracing Wells's own progress from anti-utopian imaginings to utopian prophetic ones, we have seen how he changes the way he negotiates contradictions. His earliest period is one of rigorous thought and exploration which, though it flirts with deep pessimism, never falls into simple dystopia. *The Time Machine* is a guide which leads us away from a delusive utopian vision of pastoral simplicity towards a much more complex vision of antithetical balances; guilt and innocence, labor and ease, decline and triumph, change and stasis. This first major work represents anti-utopianism at its purest; it does not condemn utopian imaginings, nor does it despair about the possibility of a planned future (one of the strong messages of *The Time Machine* is that the predatory world of 802,701 is avoidable); it gives aesthetic form to the contradictions existing within our own civilization and its values. The other early works which we examined in chapter two through five together constitute a large anti-utopian project.

When the Sleeper Wakes: The Generic Problem

In an investigation of the difference between anti-utopia and utopia-dystopia, *When the Sleeper Wakes* (1899) assumes a remarkably important position, for it marks the point of intersection of the two genera. As a transitional work this novel serves Wells in ways that are

evident to us only after we understand the contradictions between
the two ways of thought that he espoused. "A Story of the Days to
Come," we saw, while it has signs of frustrations, remains anti-utopian:
at the end Denton and Elizabeth balance at the edge of the monstrous
city and try to "find their place." *When the Sleeper Wakes*, though it
shares the same city and the same technological imagery, cannot
remain content with such meditative perspectives. It reaches towards,
though it does not grasp, the sort of utopian solution we see at the
end of *In the Days of the Comet*. Embedded in the horror of dystopian
servitude are gestures of utopian liberation, and while the novel ends
on an ambiguous note, it is also clear that it has by the end broken
clear of the static conflicts of anti-utopia. If "A Story of the Days to
Come" is a novella that seems to have begun with hopes of becoming
a utopia, slid into dystopia, and finally retreated back to anti-utopia,
When the Sleeper Wakes has started from anti-utopia and thrashed
its way towards utopia-dystopia. Wells himself was unhappy with the
"solutions" the novel offers, but whatever its failures as an individual
work, it marks an important point of possibility that has attracted
many imitators. It is an artistic and intellectual failure, but it is an
extraordinary historical success.

   When the Sleeper Wakes shares with "A Story of the Days to Come"
a deep ambivalence about the liberating possibilities of technology.
We have already seen how in "A Story of the Days to Come" the
imagery of the future, while it seems to promise alternatives and mediation, circles on itself and closes off escape. In *When the Sleeper
Wakes*, by beginning to explore the political-economic structure that
governs that technology, Wells would seem to be pushing the issue
further. In this novel he turns to revolution for his promise of alternative, but then, after setting up what might be fruitful antitheses
between the few and the many, capital and labor, he abandons the
conflict.

   The crucial figure for understanding the dilemma the novel faces
is Ostrog. Early in the novel he opposes the Council, and as long as
he stands for labor against the capitalist Council the opposition seems
meaningful. But, like the transition from Morris to Mwres in "A Story
of the Days to Come," the change from Council rule to Ostrog turns
out to be a change which makes no difference. Graham, the hero, soon
learns that Ostrog, the Boss, stands not for change but merely for an
alternative tyranny and that the revolution still has to be made. So
Graham challenges Ostrog, and we approach again what looks like the

same opposition. But an important change has taken place that deprives this new opposition of real content: the Council stood for an idea of economic structure, privilege, and control, but Ostrog stands for no economic, social, or political idea. He is merely the egoism of the powerful personality.[7] We never know who benefits from his rule or why others follow and obey him. The revolt against Ostrog partakes in part of the economic ideals of the initial revolt against the Council, but now it has become mainly a matter of personalities, of the good man, Graham, against the bad man, Ostrog.[8]

If Ostrog lacks an economic basis, he might nevertheless be seen to represent an oligarchic idea of the necessity of an elite to maintain social order and thus appeal to a theme we have seen Wells examine a number of times. Against this elite stand the rights of "the people," for which Graham vaguely argues. But the novel, just as it gets rid of the economic motive of the council, never sees the people as much more than a source of explosive energy. Graham, their defender and advocate, comes to the realization that to save the world he must rule. The difference between him and Ostrog lies, not in any explicit political ideas about structure and priority, but simply, to use the phrase that Wells later insists on, "good will." Graham, like the Samurai, serves as he rules. He proves he is not like Ostrog by sacrificing himself at the end.

Graham himself works well as a mediating figure of the sort we are used to, but whereas in the more general conflicts of the earlier work such a symbol allows for imaginative movement between opposed truths and goods, in this potentially more specific world such a symbol becomes simply ambiguous. Graham, "The Sleeper," is an outsider in the age, but he is at the center; he is a common man of no special distinction who is also "the Master"; he is economically most powerful, but also most moral; he rules, but he is powerless; he despairs at the beginning and he ends up an optimistic idealist. Graham combines in a single figure the double ideal represented at the end of *In the Days of the Comet* by Leadford and the Prime Minister. These combinations involve familiar issues, but now a more concrete question has been posed: how can we change the social structure so as to prevent the nightmare of the future? In this context the symbolic mediation, while an important element in the preliminary thought on the issue, is obfuscating.

Similarly, the puzzle of the future is nicely figured in the statue of Atlas supporting the world: Atlas is both the Sleeper, who as arch-capitalist supports the world, and the embodiment of suffering labor. He is a figure of entrapped power and of potential for change. But just as Graham's symbolic function heightens our sense of the problem but obscures the political solution, the Atlas statue, while its ambiguity helps us focus on the contradictions of this civilization, frustrates resolution. Wells himself seems impatient with it; he destroys it along with the council hall.

The clearest sign of the emptiness of the political-economic content of the novel is the fact that Graham, much as he objects to Ostrog's policies, is unable to justify revolution on economic grounds. Only when Ostrog employs Negro mercenaries is Graham roused to revolutionary action. A sense of racial outrage displaces and obscures the problem of economic oppression. The racial theme is not entirely a false issue; it has an ethical dimension, for at one point Wells links the black invasion with the idea of justice we saw being explored in *The War of the Worlds*: the Negroes "have been under the rule of the whites for two hundred years. Is it not a race quarrel? The race sinned— the race pays" (pp. 235–36).[9] There is an important element of imperialist guilt here. But this theme is completely at odds with Graham's heroic resistance, and in any case has little to do with the issues of Ostrog's rule. When the mercenaries attack, the conflict between capital and labor is forgotten. As in other racist literature, the racial issue is used as a way of avoiding real political analysis.

We saw in "A Story of the Days to Come" how the circular insufficience of love and suicide defined the closed system Wells's futuristic imagination had generated. Here in *When the Sleeper Wakes* Wells uses these same two motifs to try to break the deadlock. In doing so, however, he has to deprive the gestures of the precision that they had in "A Story of the Days to Come," and he falls back on sentimental romance and heroic martyrdom as solutions.

Thematically, the romantic element is a gesture with powerful hopes behind it but with little thought. It stands in general for a violation of old structures and a revolutionary reinvigoration. Helen is Ostrog's niece, and a number of times it is remarked how extraordinary it is for her to aid the common people when her family connections lead all to expect her to serve her uncle's interests. Her empathy with human suffering becomes a revolutionary re-aligner which overrides tradition, whether genealogical or economic. Graham's love for her solves a problem posed at the very beginning of the novel when Graham, still living in the nineteenth century, confesses to Isbister, "I am a lone wolf, a solitary man, wandering through a world in which I have no part. I am wifeless—childless—who is it speaks of the childless as the dead twigs on the tree of life? I am wifeless, childless—I could find no duty to do. No desire even in my heart" (p. 6). Graham's love for Helen gives him energy and, by inspiring him to initiate ethical reform, duty. While we may approve the gesture, we have to admit that it is unexamined; next to the bitter ironies of the fourth chapter of "A Story of the Days to Come" in which the facts of poverty undermine Denton's and Elizabeth's love, and next to the realistic difficulties of Mr. Lewisham's choice of Ethel, this cursory and undetailed love seems naive and merely conventional.

The suicide motif which we traced in "A Story of the Days to Come" recurs in *When the Sleeper Wakes*, but even more than in the case of love, Wells has stripped it of logical significance and turned it into a romantic gesture. At the beginning of the novel Graham in despair contemplates leaping off a cliff, and at the end he sacrifices himself for victory over Ostrog. Neither suicide is a comment on civilization. Graham's complaint at the beginning is private; overwork has exhausted him; it is implied that most other people, those with wives and children, do not share his malady. At the end, when Graham because of his love for Helen has committed himself to serving civilization, he willingly and heroically uses the tool of civilization, the aeropile, to attack the oppressive machine and bring his own martyrdom. In "A Story of the Days to Come" heroic action is impossible: escape, collaboration, and submersion—all unsatisfactory—are the only responses an overwhelming technological, capitalist civilization permits. In *When the Sleeper Wakes* Wells easily assumes that the technology which so defines oppression can be used against itself.

Students of Wells have remarked on the "diminished intensity" of *When the Sleeper Wakes*.[10] Certainly, the answers here are awfully easy. I would suggest that the problem with the novel lies also in the very nature of Wells's imaginative logic, that the techniques that have been so successful in the earlier fantasies become limitations as Wells tries to become more precise and more utopian. It is because he has taken on the truly difficult issues of his world and has such a lively sense of the areas of conflict that he does a poor job of working out solutions. A writer less attuned to the anti-utopian ironies of the world might succeed better at ignoring them.

In ridding the novel of its disturbing anti-utopianism by melodramatic gestures, Wells is being true to one important dynamic of *When the Sleeper Wakes*: the technological exuberance. The machine-dominated future, so the novel implies, does not have to be a nightmare. The melodrama is an attempt to rescue the utopian intuition that is roused and denied in "A Story of the Days to Come" by the ironic anti-utopianism. In comparison to "A Story of the Days to Come," *When the Sleeper Wakes* is genuinely utopian-dystopian. It rejects the deep ambivalences of anti-utopia. In place of the irresolvable dilemmas of anti-utopia, it prefers the unambiguous horror of dystopia which, it implies, might be transformed to utopia.

When the Sleeper Wakes poses a problem in genre and in thought that Wells never adequately resolved. We have here reached a limit: his anti-utopian meditation seems incapable of change; his utopian-dystopian melodrama leads to unconvincing changes that betray the authentic difficulties posed. Works such as *In the Days of the Comet* are expressions of the desire to leap beyond the dilemma, but as we have seen, the result is only an embarrassing exaggeration of the generic incompatibility.

I suspect that the dilemma Wells is facing lies near the heart of all authentic utopian enterprises. Later writers will pick up the essential situation Wells has posed and develop it in further directions, but the deep structural contradiction cannot be mediated. Either, as in the case of Zamyatin's *We*, we commit ourselves to an infinitely dialectical anti-utopianism, or, as in the case of Orwell's *Nineteen Eighty-Four* or, in a different spirit, Bradbury's *Fahrenheit 451* or Huxley's *Brave New World*, we quash ironic conflict and replace the puzzle with a single-valued structure, either dystopian or utopian. To look at the ways these later writers have handled the problem Wells posed himself tells us much about the structure and limits of the form itself.

Let me note that the following sketch of different resolutions of the logical-aesthetic problem that *When the Sleeper Wakes* presents implies an historical development that is different from that drawn by Mark Hillegas in *The Future as Nightmare: H. G. Wells and the Anti-utopians*. I do not see what I am doing here as a refutation or a contradiction of Hillegas, but simply as the charting of development along a different axis. Hillegas means something different from me by the term "anti-utopian."[11] The Wells that he posits is a more utopian thinker than the one I have been examining, and the later writers whom Hillegas sees as pitting themselves against Wells are reacting to that utopianist, not to the anti-utopianist. I accept Hillegas' historical account. I am here tracing, not the history of attitudes towards Wells's utopian ideals, but the limits and possibilities of a form.[12]

Zamyatin's Anti-utopia

Zamyatin's *We* is useful for our further understanding of anti-utopia for two reasons. First, the fact that *We* shares with the novels of Orwell, Bradbury, and Huxley, which will be discussed later, a loose debt to *When the Sleeper Wakes* allows us to see more neatly than might be otherwise possible the logical differences between utopian and anti-utopian thought. Second, *We* is the most radical variation on the Wellsian mode.

But let us also observe that Zamyatin is not the only anti-utopian developing out of the Wells tradition. Though it would lead us astray from our present purposes to explore their work in any detail, writers such as Karel Čapek, Olaf Stapledon, and Ursula Le Guin deserve mention here. The elegant and pointedly contradictory truths of Čapek's *R.U.R.*, or the shifting satire of his *War with the Newts*, wherein the victimized newts of the beginning become the fascist oppressors of the end, owe much to Wells's early logic.[13] In *Last and First Men* Stapledon transforms the more or less static oppositions of Wells into a serial process of discovery, and his relentlessly dialectical history of the future picks up that mixture of yearning and skepticism that characterizes anti-utopia.[14] Le Guin's *The Dispossessed*, originally subtitled *An Ambiguous Utopia*,[15] uses the two world system of *The First Men in the Moon*; it admires and yet is able to criticise the satellite's utopia. And Le Guin's novel has moments of pure anti-utopianism that rival Wells's descriptions of the Selenite "education" or of the Eloi pastoral. When Shevek, the anarchist protagonist, feels revulsion at the "excremental" excess of the foliage of deciduous trees, or when he is unable to comprehend the achievements made possible by the profit motive, we perceive the deepest issues of the novel struggling against each other: ascetic discipline versus abundant profusion, co-operative survival versus competitive production.[16] Neither is the only possible mode of being; each generates prejudices which blind its adherents to the possibilities of the other.

Such works are important, but they are nevertheless recognizably close to Wells's own practice and therefore essentially familiar to us by now. Zamyatin adds to our understanding of the form of forcing contradiction into outright paradox. *We* is clearly anti-utopian, but it is also very different from Wells's work in the way it generates and negotiates conflict. However intricate the Wellsian logical system may become, it is not confusing; Zamyatin's, even at its most simple, baffles complacent understanding.[17]

We is a novel whose ironic ambiguity is relentless. The reader is made aware of powerful and significant symbols, but every major symbol, besides its primary signification, retains the potential for representing its exact opposite. This quality is acutely, or perhaps obtusely, observed by S-4711 when he reads a line of D-503's praising the Benefactor: "Somewhat ambiguous," he remarks, "Nevertheless . . . Well, continue" (p. 167).[18] S-4711's quick glance has uncovered a quality that marks the language of the novel as subversive, but perhaps at a level different from that usually supposed. In oppressive societies ambiguity serves as camouflage: a statement able to be "misunderstood" will be so comprehended by the proper readers. The ingenious nonsense of the censors, who find subversive meanings in the most innocent-looking statements, is not just stupid: the censors know the level at which covert communication takes place even to the extent to finding communication never intended. The censor is the cryptographer's most sensitive reader. And to that extent S-4711 is D-503's best reader, seeing more, probably, than the author of the memoir himself consciously knows. In this case the ambiguity that S-4711 observes functions as something more than a veil hiding a single subversive meaning. The ambiguous language and symbolism of *We* harbor a set of deep contradictions that do more than simply challenge the repressive One State; they challenge any belief in settled understanding, and throughout the novel Zamyatin keeps alive a self-contradicting tension.

Zamyatin's advocacy of perpetual revolution is well known. It is preached by I-330 in *We*, and, speaking in his own voice, Zamyatin uses some of the same language, argument, and imagery in his 1923 essay, "On Literature, Revolution, Entropy, and Other Matters." It is worth looking at passages from this essay in some detail because Zamyatin's style here tells us more about the radical quality of the anti-utopian heresy he preaches than can any paraphrase of his argument:

> Revolution is everywhere, in everything. It is infinite. There is no final revolution, no final number. The social revolution is only one of an infinite

number of numbers: the law of revolution is not a social law, but an immeasurably greater one. It is a cosmic, universal law—like the laws of the conservation of energy and of the dissipation of energy (entropy). Some day, an exact formula for the law of revolution will be established. And in this formula, nations, classes, stars—and books—will be expressed as numerical quantities.

The law of revolution is red, fiery, deadly; but this death means the birth of new life, a new star. And the law of entropy is cold, ice blue, like the icy interplanetary infinities. The flame turns from red to an even, warm pink, no longer deadly, but comfortable. The sun ages into a planet, convenient for highways, stores, beds, prostitutes, prisons: this is the law. And if the planet is to be kindled into youth again, it must be set on fire, it must be thrown off the smooth highway of evolution: this is the law.

The flame will cool tomorrow, or the day after tomorrow (in the Book of Genesis days are equal to years, ages). But someone must see this already today, and speak heretically today about tomorrow. Heretics are the only (bitter) remedy against the entropy of human thought.[19]

In the first paragraph of this passage Zamyatin alludes to a division close to the one we have seen in early Wells: the difference between social and cosmic law is analogous to that between ethics and evolution. But if the cosmic (evolutionary) principle is invoked as the ultimate law of revolution to counter the lesser laws of social order and development, in the middle of the second paragraph the cosmic process is seen, not as revolutionary, but as entropic. If energy is to be regenerated, the world "must be thrown off the smooth highway of evolution: this is the law." Here Zamyatin in a few lines has come full circle; the principle that will counter evolutionary entropy is not the inevitable cosmic process, but willed heresy, in other words, a form of ethical activity. "Law" at the end of the second paragraph means, not the natural "law" that takes place in spite of any conscious will, but a logical truth which sees the ethical activity of the human heretic as the only bitter remedy to the natural process. Thus, in the act of arguing for the inevitable revolution Zamyatin ends up arguing for inevitable entropy; in place of cosmic process he turns to willed acts. The passage is absolutely contradictory. But in that contradiction lies its true thought-provoking power; the reader is not instructed; he is badgered by hectoring prose which backs him around in a circle. He ends, not believing, but doubting; and that is Zamyatin's real message; that is the endless revolution.

In another passage from this same essay Zamyatin gives a kind of justification for such a procedure:

Organic chemistry has already obliterated the line between living and
dead matter. It is an error to divide people into the living and the dead:
there are people who are dead-alive, and people who are alive-alive. The
dead-alive also write, walk, speak, act. But they make no mistakes; only
machines make no mistakes, and they produce only dead things. The
alive-alive are constantly in error, in search, in questions, in torment.

The same is true of what we write: it walks and it talks, but it can be
dead-alive or alive-alive. What is truly alive stops before nothing and
ceaselessly seeks answers to absurd, "childish" questions. Let the answers
be wrong, let the philosophy be mistaken—errors are more valuable than
truths: truth is of the machine, error is alive; truth reassures, error disturbs.
And if answers be impossible of attainment, all the better! Dealing with
answered questions is the privilege of brains constructed like a cow's
stomach, which, as we know, is built to digest cud.

If there were anything fixed in nature, if there were truths, all of this
would, of course, be wrong. But fortunately, all truths are erroneous. This
is the very essence of the dialectical process: today's truths become errors
tomorrow; there is no final number.[20]

To be alive-alive means to be "in error, in search, in questions, in
torment," and Zamyatin's prose, right at its logical surface, enforces
such a state. There are no "answered questions" here. At best we get
clear paradoxes: "errors are more valuable than truths."

The contradictory process which continually provokes the reader
with inconsistencies and paradoxes is at work at the level of image
as well as explicit logic. In the first passage we looked at, when echoing
I-330's argument that there is no final number, Zamyatin concludes
the paragraph with an image which, given the anti-mechanistic, anti-
mathematical values that seem to dominate *We*, must be confusing:
"Some day an exact formula for the law of revolution will be established. And in this formula, nations, classes, stars—and books—will be
expressed as numerical quantities." This would seem to be, not I-330's
image and argument, but that of the Benefactor. Order of this mathematical sort, order of law, is intrinsically entropic. But then in the
next paragraph the imagery returns to that which fits *We*: the colors,
blue and pink, neatly represent the ordered, enervated One State.
While the reader is invited to find correspondences between the essay
and the novel, at the same time he must understand each image on
its own; to expect symbolic consistency is antithetical to the heretic's
mode.

The logical entanglement the novel performs is most clear when D-

503 manages to become Zamyatin's own mouthpiece and thereby forces us to accept arguments we have already dismissed as sophistry. When D-503 tries to distinguish the evil Inquisition from the benevolent "Operational Section" of the One State which enforces orthodoxy by torture, he uses imagery which implies a clear distinction where in fact none exists:

> About five centuries ago, when the Operational Section was first being developed, there were some fools who compared the Section to the ancient Inquisition, but that is as absurd as equating a surgeon performing a tracheotomy with a highwayman; both may have the same knife in their hands, both do the same thing—cut a living man's throat—yet one is a benefactor, and the other a criminal; one has a + sign, the other a −. (p. 80)

A good reader has an easy enough time side-stepping the implications of this rationalization of oppression. But a little later, in an extraordinary passage, D-503 returns to the subject, and now the same argument and imagery become both more specious *and* more convincing:

> You, Uranians, as austere and dark as the ancient Spaniards who had the wisdom to burn offenders in blazing pyres, you are silent; I think you are on my side. But I hear the pink Venusians muttering something about torture, executions, a return to barbarian times. My dear friends, I pity you: you are incapable of philosophic-mathematical thought.
>
> Human history ascends in circles, like an aero. The circles differ—some are golden, some bloody. But all are equally divided into three hundred and sixty degrees. And the movement is from zero—onward, to ten, twenty, two hundred, three hundred and sixty degrees—back to zero. Yes, we have returned to zero—yes. But to my mathematical mind it is clear that this zero is altogether different, altogether new. We started from zero to the right, we have returned to it from the left. Hence, instead of plus zero, we have minus zero. Do you understand?
>
> I envisage this Zero as an enormous, silent, narrow, knife-sharp crag. In fierce, shaggy darkness, holding our breath, we set out from the black night side of Zero Crag. For ages we, the Columbuses, have sailed and sailed; we have circled the entire earth. And, at long last, hurrah! The burst of a salute, and everyone aloft the masts: before us is a different, hitherto unknown side of Zero Crag, illumined by the northern lights of the One State—a pale blue mass, sparks, rainbows, suns, hundreds of suns, billions of rainbows. . . .
>
> What if we are but a knife's breadth away from the other, the black side of the crag? The knife is the strongest, the most immortal, the most

brilliant of man's creations. The knife has been a guillotine; the knife is
the universal means of solving all knots; along the knife's edge is the road
of paradoxes—the only road worthy of a fearless mind. (pp. 116–17)

Plus and minus zero may be a meaningless opposition, but no sooner
have we dismissed the logic of the infinitesimal difference that makes
all the difference than we are confronted with the argument about
paradox which is too close to Zamyatin's own pronouncements to be
simply rejected. Yet in D-503's mouth the celebration of the "fearless
mind" may be mere nonsense. Here we ourselves must distinguish
between positive and negative versions which are identical, between
plus and minus zero. The act of reading itself engages us in the process
the text describes: in the act of rejecting the argument we affirm it.[21]

This explicit and disconcerting confusion characterizes the symbolic imagery of *We*. The architecture of the One State expresses a
paradoxical state of oppressive innocence much like the state of feeble-
minded peace the Time Traveller envisions when he first sees the far
future. The numbers all live in glass-walled apartments from which
everyone is visible to everyone else. Privacy is unnecessary, it is argued,
because there is no guilt. Of course such openness also exposes guilt,
and the image of emancipation is entangled with that of severe repression. Thus, one of the most shocking images of the revolution for D-
503 is the sight of couples copulating in the open. Similarly, the *In-
tegral*, the glass rocketship which D-503 is in charge of building, is on
the one hand an instrument of totalitarian imperialism by which the
One State will spread its message of obedient uniformity to the whole
solar system, but it is also the key to the revolutionists' plan of escape
and revolt. It is thus a symbol of both a repressive, enforced political
unity without meaningful opposition and of psychic wholeness, the
reintegrated personality that might exist if the numbers could destroy
the repressive state.

The pronouns of the novel work in similarly double ways, The "We"
of the title represents a denial of the individual psyche: D-503, good
citizen, dedicates his diary to the collective:

> I shall merely attempt to record what I see and think, or, to be more
> exact, what we think (precisely so—we, and let this *We* be the title of my
> record). But since this record will be a derivative of our life, of the math-
> ematically perfect life of the One State, will it not be, of itself, and re-
> gardless of my will or skill, a poem? It will. I believe, I know it.

> I write this, and my checks are burning. This must be similar to what
> a woman feels when she first senses within herself the pulse of a new,
> still tiny, still blind little human being. It is I, and at the same time not
> I. (p. 2)

The initial "we" is clearly a pious act of individual negation, a willed
union which exists in conflict with the many "I"s in the passage, and
the reader easily sees the submerged ego abasing itself but wanting
to emerge. But if that first *we* is totalitarian, in the second paragraph
the image of a woman with child poses a more positive idea of "we,"
one which sees generation and creation as enjoying the "not I" and
thereby enforcing a plural even as it is implicitly negated.

Though the pronoun *we* has these suggestions of psychic possibility,
through much of the novel it remains essentially ironic, a self-anni-
hilating expansion of *I*, until near the end of the novel when the
revolutionaries are swarming into the city. To D-503's question, where
is I-330, a revolutionary responds:

> "Here," he cried gaily, drunkenly—strong, yellow teeth . . . "She's here,
> in the city, in action. Oh-Oh—we are acting!"
> Who are we? Who am I? (p. 219)

Having worked throughout the novel to free himself from "we," D-503
finds his liberation in terms of a "we." The deep issue here is how
can there be an "I" without a "we?" The individualism so championed
against the totalitarian state is in itself meaningless; it must place itself
in a social context.

The second person pronoun establishes a less complex ambiguity,
but one that leads directly to the central conflict of the novel. As his
attraction to I-330 deepens and as they get more intimate, she uses
the archaic intimate pronoun which he sees as a gesture of
condescension:

> "Do you like fog?"
> She used the ancient, long-forgotten "thou"—the "thou" of the master
> to the slave. It entered into me slowly, sharply. Yes, I was a slave, and
> this, too, was necessary, was good. (p. 72)

Though D-503, so used to serving others, is probably misunderstanding I-330's linguistic gesture, we should be aware of an ironic truth
here. He has just compared himself to a piece of iron drawn to a

magnet, and the love relationship has a definite aspect of obedience and servitude to it. A little later, in a rapturous fantasy of meeting I-330, D-503 himself uses the intimate pronoun: "I will use the warm, familiar 'thou'—only 'thou'" (p. 87). Here the pronoun suggests intimacy more than servitude, but the gesture remains servile.

The puzzle about love is given mathematical expression somewhat later:

> I am like a machine set at excessive speed; the bearings are overheated; another minute, and molten metal will begin to drip, and everything will turn to naught. Quick—cold water, logic. I pour it by the pailful, but logic hisses on the red-hot bearings and dissipates into the air in whiffs of white elusive steam.
>
> Of course, it's clear: in order to determine the true value of a function it is necessary to take it to its ultimate limit. And it is clear that yesterday's preposterous "dissolution in the universe," brought to its ultimate point means death. For death is precisely the most complete dissolution of self in the universe. Hence, if we designate love as "L" and death as "D," then $L = f(D)$. In other words, love and death . . . (p. 135)

The formula engages both uses of "thou": love is tyrannical bondage, an obliteration of self, and love is an intimate devotion in which one gives up private interests in attending on the other. But the irony does not end there, for the formula also expresses the relation of the good number to the One State: the annihilation of the "I" in the "We" so celebrated by D-503 at the beginning corresponds exactly to the relationship expressed by the formula. I do not mean to suggest that the love for the state and the love for I-330 are in every way identical. Clearly they are not; clearly the love for I-330 is energizing while that for the One State is entropic. The formula turns out to have a further meaning when in "Entry 35" D-503 plans to murder U-, drops the curtains of his room, and realizes that the terrified woman thinks he is sexually aroused. In its comic, grotesque inversion of the central energy of his liberation, this scene suggests both the truth of D-503's bondage to I-330 and the absurdity of it. If we compare this complex ironic exploration of devotion to the simple way Helen inspires Graham, we can see how thoroughly anti-utopian Zamyatin is here.

The structural similarity between D-503's love of the state and his love of I-330 reemerges at the level of plot when it becomes clear that I-330 is using D-503 just as much as the Benefactor is. If the imagery of mechanical order represents one kind of bondage, the imagery erotic mystery represents another. I-330 has awakened psychological depths in D-503 that the well-oiled state machine has put to sleep, but Zamyatin's dialectic will not let us rest with easy platitudes about healthy emotion: the awakening takes its cost; the mechanical, communal state has, after all, some genuine virtues that are lost in the reentry into erotic individualism. At the core of the novel lie two contradictory imperatives. One commands commitment outside oneself; the other demands self and wholeness. Life asks both, but the novel sets them up as opposed, and the process of reading is an act of repeatedly moving across the distinction, of constantly rethinking the issue.

If, in terms of its dystopian reintegration of D-503 back into the One State and the sadistic execution of I-330, *We* has seemed to clarify the heroic ambiguities that muffle the end of *When the Sleeper Wakes*, the texture of the whole novel is nevertheless more thoroughly anti-utopian than anything Wells ever wrote. The history of Zamyatin's reception has perhaps tended to obscure this pervasive anti-utopianism of *We*. Clearly the novel is a satiric attack on Bolshevik totalitarianism, but it does not give easy comfort to the enemies of the One State, either. The novel is "heretical" to the core, and it fights all entropic dogmas, even those which would combat the One State. Unlike Wells's Graham, whose love and heroism remain unquestioned, D-503 is never free to be simply heroic or passionate, for love and heroism themselves are seen as involved in contradictions.

Utopian Logic in Orwell, Bradbury, and Huxley

In *Nineteen Eighty-Four* we see an instance of Wells's and Zamyatin's futures transformed to pure dystopia. Unlike *We*, in which imagery and symbolism remain contradictory, and unlike *When the Sleeper Wakes* in which heroic martyrdom leaves civilization's final destiny ambiguous, *Nineteen Eighty-Four* moves towards a resolution of all puzzles. The cruel reality of power means that experiential reality has no meaning and therefore any contradictions perceived are inconsequential. The pressure of conflict that so energized Wells and Zamyatin appears in Orwell on the thematic level as a naive empiricism. In a logical maneuver somewhat like Wells's absolutizing of the unique individual, Orwell renders everything ambiguous as a way of obliterating the distinguishing importance of ambiguity itself.[22]

Doublethink is D-503's psychological self-denial carried to the point at which thought itself becomes impossible.[23] D-503's distinctions between plus and minus zero and between the dagger and the scalpel have a logical base; as I have argued, the true energy of Zamyatin's insight derives from the fact that D-503's rationalizations of oppression and repression have an element of real truth in them. Doublethink poses even more blatant contradictions, but does so, not as paradox that generates thought, but as an illusion of thought which is non-sense. Contradiction ceases to be meaningful. Two plus two can equal four or five. This is, of course, an obvious thematic truth of the total-itarian state, but it is also structurally true of Orwell's novel.

Orwell begins with a structure that closely echoes Zamyatin's: the totalitarian city is juxtaposed to the natural countryside, and the op-position is mediated by the ancient house, or in Orwell's version, by the antique shop in the prole section. But the opposition is never a real one for Orwell. The countryside turns out to be bugged; real secrecy is possible only in the midst of a crowd. *Nineteen Eighty-four* turns out to expose the naiveté of Zamyatin's hopeful structure. Of course, in *We* there is also a suspicion that the country alternative outside the wall is not a true alternative: D-503 sees the enigmatic S-4711 in the crowd there. But the ambiguity of this connection (it is never clear whose side S-4711 is on, or if he doesn't represent a power above both sides) is, like all the important ambiguities of the novel, unresolved. Therein lies the continuing possibility of thought. In *Nineteen Eighty-four* resolution takes place with nightmarish finality. The Party controls everything—the countryside, the room, Carrington, O'Brien, the past, and the future.

The last part of the novel is ingenious, not for its mediations or its conflicts, but for the skill with which it robs Smith and the reader of any alternatives. The imagery becomes that of total control. Even the room number in the Ministry of Love, 101, while it balances ones, is in its tight symmetry a mirroring trap. And in this room Smith comes to know *The* fear, not a part of a dynamic structure, but the single, totally dominating core image, the rat, before which all reasoning and morality collapses. And here it is that O'Brien explains the real mean-ing of power, not as a political issue, not as a synthesis of competing goods or interests, but simply as a monolithic end in itself which denies the whole issue of freedom and happiness that torments Za-myatin and before him Dostoyevsky. The absolute pessimism implied by the complete triumph of the totalitarian state has upset critics;

some have tried to see a possibility of change in Oceana's shifting foreign relations, but that seems grasping at straws. Orwell has tried to deny change; he has tried to envision the powerlessness of conscious thought and the entropic (in Zamyatin's sense) end of history.

But at the middle of the novel, in the picture of the prole washerwoman singing a trite, machine-made popular song, Orwell suggests, not a revolutionary hope, but a level of being that by its very ignorance of the issues of freedom and happiness, by its unconscious co-optation of the culture-producers' co-optation, transcends the totalitarian state. Here is an alternative, but it is one which, by displacing conflict to a completely different level, makes anti-utopian thought irrelevant. At the moment just before his arrest Winston Smith has a vision of prole endurance which, though he still tries to convert it to a conscious political end, stands as a pure bodily fact, deeper than politics:

> "Do you remember," he said, "the thrush that sang to us, that first day, at the edge of the wood?"
>
> "He wasn't singing to us," said Julia. "He was singing to please himself. Not even that. He was just singing."
>
> The birds sang, the proles sang, the Party did not sing. All round the world, in London and New York, in Africa and Brazil and in the mysterious, forbidden lands beyond the frontiers, in the streets of Paris and Berlin, in the villages of the endless Russian plain, in the bazaars of China and Japan—everywhere stood the same solid unconquerable figure, made monstrous by work and child-bearing, toiling from birth to death and still singing. Out of those mighty loins a race of conscious beings must one day come. You were the dead; theirs was the future. But you could share in that future if you kept alive the mind as they kept alive the body, and passed on the secret doctrine that two plus two make four.
>
> "We are the dead," he said.
>
> "We are the dead," echoed Julia dutifully.
>
> "You are the dead," said an iron voice behind them.[24]

Despite the false note of Smith's political rhetoric ("unconquerable," "Out of those mighty loins a race . . ."), this passage still suggests in simple being an alternative to the Party's rule. In the all-controlling state, consciousness is dead, but life, the singing thrush, the singing woman, persists, not as an ethical social fact, not even as a challenge to the Party's domination, but as simple biology. If there is any hope in *Nineteen Eighty-four*, it lies here in the unreflecting joy of being. We are back at the issue of evolution and ethics, but now the ethical component is seen as impossible and irrelevant. Evolution, not as an historical, social process, but as purely biological survival, is the sole value. Winston Smith's hope of keeping "alive the mind as they kept alive the body" is vain; the mind is always trapped. But the body persists and finds joy even if Oceana succeeds as a thousand-year Reich.

Orwell's imagination, always attuned to suffering, has managed to box itself in; the art of *Nineteen Eighty-four*, its greatness, is in the relentless denial of the possibility of change. If hope is ever raised—as it certainly is by Goldstein's book—it is raised to be dashed. Orwell's pessimism reduces dynamic conflict to a monolithic truth.

To transform such a dystopia into utopia requires discovering a different set of images that will be similarly free from ambiguity and conflict but which will function positively instead of negatively. Positive and negative are deceptive terms here; they imply a symmetry around a neutral middle which is in fact very difficult to achieve. It is a commonplace of modern criticism that there are no authentic heroes, only anti-heroes. Whereas the purely negative image is easily acceded to, the positive is deeply suspect. A single negative connotation, will rob an image of its positive value, while a single positive connotation will not prevent an image from seeming totally negative. To say that a rat is intelligent does not make it any the less powerfully negative; like Satan, "by merit raised/ To that bad eminence," its virtues simply increase its horror. On the other hand positive images can be rendered ineffectual by a simple observation of how powerless they are. Given this imbalance in the present state of values, the utopian image must often depend on what in cinematic terms we would call soft-focus: a blurred vision which never looks closely enough at the image to discover flaws. Wells performs exactly such a shift of lens in the last part of *In the Days of the Comet*, and we see such a blur at the heart of Ray Bradbury's *Fahrenheit 451*.

Montag, the protagonist of Bradbury's novel, like Graham, D-503, and Winston Smith, is a man coming to consciousness and attempting the overthrow or reformation of the closed, totalitarian, futuristic world he valued at the start. As in the other novels we have looked at, here too a woman is the inspiration for the change of mind. As in the other works, the act of seeing beyond the present is at least in part an act of recovery of a lost tradition: Graham is a revolutionary because he retains nineteenth century sentiments of justice which the future world claims to have outgrown; D-503 and Winston Smith find an alternative to the totalitarian state in the antique parts of civilization. And Montag rediscovers books which the future society has banned. Other similarities might be traced, but my point in sketching the by now conventional situation is not to estimate the extent of Bradbury's debt to the tradition, but to establish a broad common background against which we can understand the different way Bradbury's images function logically.

In *Fahrenheit 451* the future is bad because people, denied the rich traditional culture contained in books and imaged by nature, have become unstimulated and unstimulating. The dystopian world is in large part conveyed in terms of the denial of positives. Firechief Beatty's defense of the bookless future is essentially that of the Grand Inquisitor, with the important change that the mass's fear of freedom is seen to be an historical phenomenon, a failure of education. In the past, so the ironic argument goes, people were capable of freedom, but because of technology and the triumph of a debased mass culture they have lost their ability to choose and their joy in freedom. Beatty's argument seems to be that of the author; in Montag's wife we see heavily done exactly the mindlessness, the need for booklessness that Beatty defends. Beatty argues that mass culture is necessarily simple and, therefore, inevitably a decline from our own elite culture based on books, and in much of its satire the novel supports him. Where the novel makes Beatty clearly an ironic spokesman to be refuted is, not in his characterization of the masses and what they want, but in his inadequate appreciation of the sensitive few who are capable of freedom.

The novel expresses this vision of freedom with images of sentimentalized nature (Clarisse rhapsodizes about the smell of leaves, the sight of the man in the moon[25]), the recollection of the small, midwestern town (the front porch and the rocking chair become symbols of freedom), some tag ends of a thirties romanticizing of depression survival, and an unquestioning admiration for books. This cluster poses an absolute pole around which accrues all good and in relation to which all movement away is bad. The dystopian and utopian possibilities in the novel are thus represented by separate clusters of images and ideas that the novel finds unambiguous and leaves unchallenged.

What needs emphasis here is the extent to which Bradbury's novel preserves the dystopian-utopian structure by ignoring the implications of its own imagery. The author advises his audience that they must preserve books to prevent the horror he imagines, but he never questions the values implicit in the books. When the new age is accused of serious flaws—unhappiness, fear, war, and wasted lives—there is no sense that the age of books may have also suffered from such problems. At the end, in his vision of a wandering group of book people, Bradbury invokes an idealized hobo mystique, but with little sense of the limits and tragedy of such a life.

In such a simple system of good and bad values, mediation produces not thought but horror. Nature is good and technology is bad, but the ultimate terror is a mixture of the two, a kind of symbolic miscegenation. When Montag finally makes his break from the technological future he is pursued by a "mechanical hound," a terrifying figure which combines the relentlessness of the bloodhound with the infallibility of technology. In Bradbury's vision the hound is most terrifying for being both alive and not alive.

The threat the hound poses for the imagery system of the novel is put to rest once Montag escapes him and once the clear opposition between technology and nature that Clarisse has preached strongly reasserts itself. Montag hears a whisper, sees "a shape, two eyes" in the forest and is convinced it is the hound, but it turns out to be a deer, not just harmless, but afraid of him (p. 128).[26] Nature is submissive and controllable, while technology is predatory and threatening. This important refuge then leads to a sequence of reversals. Montag sees a fire in the woods and for the first time in his life realizes that fire need not be destructive, that in providing warmth it can be benign (p. 130). And this perception leads to a moment of trance in which Montag resees himself:

> How long he stood he did not know, but there was a foolish and yet delicious sense of knowing himself as an animal come from the forest, drawn by the fire. He was a thing of brush and liquid eye, of fur and muzzle and hoof, he was a thing of horn and blood that would smell like autumn if you bled it out on the ground. (p. 130)

I take it that this reduction of the human to animal parts is somehow consoling and ennobling. Like all the nature images in this novel, the purple rhetoric smudges true perception, but nevertheless the revelation is there and the blurred but central symbolic transformation of the novel is complete: Montag has escaped the urban world of destructive technology and joined the nurturing forest world. By rescuing fire for the good, natural side, he has enabled the novel to convert dystopia into utopia.

The interesting difficulty is where do books fit into this simple opposition? Since Gutenberg the book has been a symbol of technological progress. Bradbury partly counters this meaning of his symbol by reducing his pastoral, not to paper books, but to humans who remember books; thus the replication and general availability that are books' virtues but which the novel has seen as the instruments of the mass culture that has ruined the world, are denied. We have the *idea* of the book without the *fact* of its production. Then, by becoming a general symbol of the past now denied, the book becomes a symbol for all old values. But this symbolism brings up two difficulties. First, whatever good books have propagated, they have also preached the evils that have oppressed the world. The very technology that the novel finds threatening would be impossible without books. Second, books can readily inspire a repressive and tradition-bound pedantry which, while antitechnological, is also against nature.

Through most of *Fahrenheit 451* Bradbury simply ignores these potential problems with his symbol, but in the final pages, in an act of renunciation that is surprising given the values the novel has promulgated, the moral vision retreats from its main symbolism. The memorizers of books are about to move out of the forest to give succor to the cities that have just been bombed, and Granger, the leader of the bookish hoboes, says:

> Hold onto one thought: you're not important. You're not anything. Some day the load we're carrying with us may help someone. But even when we had the books on hand, a long time ago, we didn't use what we got out of them. We went right on insulting the dead. We went right on spitting on the graves of all the poor ones who died before us. We're going to meet a lot of lonely people in the next week and the next month and the next year. And when they ask us what we're doing, you can say, We're remembering. That's where we'll win out in the long run. And some day we'll remember so much that we'll build the biggest steamshovel in history and dig the biggest grave of all time and shove war in and cover it up. (p. 146)

The vagueness, ambiguity, and misdirection of this passage confuse what Granger is saying, but in the technological imagery of the last line and in the attack on the previously sentimentalized past, in the recognition that books have done little to make life better, this paragraph implies a renunciation of the values the novel has been, however naively, building. But perhaps it is also, finally, an awareness of a true opposition, of an irony that gets beyond the simple sentimentalisms of much of the novel. Though one may have doubts as to how to take it, one way would be to see here a titantic revision of values, a deep questioning of the pieties that have inspired Montag and Clarisse. In line with such a reading we might look at the last lines of the novel in which Montag begins to recall *Ecclesiastes*: though he chooses to recite some healing words about time, perhaps we may also recall the Preacher's more famous words against the vanity of life and the vanity of books. But, then, to read it this way would be to suppose that Bradbury is attempting anti-utopian thought, and that seems unlikely.[27]

Bradbury's novel is in the tradition of utopian prose put forth by Wells himself in his later romances. Whatever political differences we might discover between Wells's sane, organized, post-comet societies and Bradbury's nomadic society in nature, we can see that they both depend on an imagery which ignores contradiction. Such utopian thought is, I have been arguing throughout this book, incompatible with the basic logical techniques of Wells's earlier work. It marks an evasion of the pressure of contradiction. It attempts to bring about conviction, not by thought, but by the emotive power of rhythmic prose, the attractiveness of pretty images, the appeal to hope which will treat doubt as merely regretful cynicism. Such utopian images have an honored place, but they belong to a genus quite unlike the anti-utopian investigations that mark Wells's greatest scientific romances.

Bradbury's novel is clearly utopian-dystopian. What may not be so clear is how much a more complicated work, Aldous Huxley's *Brave New World*, shares *Fahrenheit 451*'s rigid values and repeats the same essential logical structure. In the light of the distinctions I am outlining here, *Brave New World*, while it may seem to echo the anti-utopianism of Wells and Zamyatin in a number of ways,[28] is mainly dystopian.

Like Bradbury's novel, *Brave New World* sets up simple plus-minus oppositions. Huxley defends nature against technology, and the individual against society.[29] In the case of the individual-society opposition, the novel echoes the dilemma of "The Country of the Blind," but whereas Wells's story remains poised between the two sources of value, *Brave New World* does not acknowledge society's virtues.

The social is the debased in Huxley's novel, and the recurrent image of the twin multiplied carries that meaning. There are numerous passages which convey satiric thrust simply by rendering in detail "the nightmare of swarming, indistinguishable sameness":

> The menial staff of the Park Lane Hospital for the Dying consisted of one hundred and sixty-two Deltas divided into two Bokanovsky Groups of eighty-four red-headed female and seventy-eight dark dolychocephalic male twins, respectively. At six when their working day was over, the two Groups assembled in the vestibule of the Hospital and were served by the Deputy Sub-Bursar with their *soma* ration. (p. 160)

The numerical exactness, the scientific terminology, and the attention to precise titles here are vehicles of sarcastic scorn. Huxley's point is obvious and much commented on; my aim here is not to criticize it but to observe the way he presents it. There is none of the ambivalence we are used to in Wells; here we know exactly and unambiguously what we are supposed to be scorning.

Against this multiplied sameness, the novel sets up the individual as the only true principle of meaning. In its dignifying of individual suffering and self-sacrifice, *Brave New World* shows itself as much less pessimistic than *Nineteen Eighty-Four*. In Orwell's work the individual has been deprived of meaning, even that of conscious nay-saying, by the unchallengeable power of the party. In Huxley's novel, John, disgusted with the world, can achieve a victory by dying.[30] The motives for John's behavior do not seem to enter the novel's awareness,[31] and the complacent rejection of the whole New World system of test-tube babies, feelies, and soma hardly permits real inquiry. At bottom the novel is a skillful voicing of prejudices in favor of a cultural ideal which it symbolizes by the works of Shakespeare.

It is worth comparing the way this novel treats test-tube methods to the way Wells treats Selenite methods of child-raising.[32] My reading of the Wells passages about conditioning infants suggests that even as he sees the horror, Wells can imagine the virtues. In that tension resides his anti-utopian vigor. Huxley, even as he ironically champions the method, rejects it without reason. Like the reporter in "The Land Ironclads," he is too good a journalist to spoil his contrast by admitting any virtues to that which he attacks. I don't mean to suggest that test-tube methods or multiplied twins are "good," but only that Huxley does not think out why they are not good. An illuminating contrast to his easy rejection would be Ursula Le Guin's short story, "Nine Lives," which explores the virtues and drawbacks of just such identical replication.[33]

In Mustapha Mond's explanation to John of the rationale behind the modern social techniques, we see, not the dialectic of the Grand Inquisitor, but despair. As in Bradbury's novel, the irony of the speech is doubly vicious: the debased mass culture is a horror, and the debased masses deserve it. In the place of the investigation into the freedom-happiness dichotomy that characterizes anti-utopia, this vision denies the possibility of exchange. The logic leads to the conclusion that a free, meaningful society is a contradiction; society is by its very structure valued by the "happiness" it produces, not by the meaning it generates. Thus Mond's horrible paradox: only by debasing life can he perfect it. As Adorno observes. Huxley's "anger at false happiness sacrifices the idea of true happiness as well."[34]

Such dystopian thought depends on secure values and categories. In Bradbury, nature and books, in Huxley, Shakespeare, freedom, and suffering, are undoubted positives against which all social forms look trivial. I suspect that the depressing quality of *Brave New World* is not the result of real pessimism but of this relentless trivialization of all social activity.[35] By contrast, in an anti-utopian form all positives turn upside down, and even the most escapist society has its attractions. In *The Time Machine* the "hateful grindstone of pain and necessity" is both admired and dreaded. In *We* useful books are instruments of oppression; eroticism, while liberating, is captivating; nature is both escape and perhaps betrayal; freedom is an exhilarating illusion.

Such anti-utopian logic is rare; it never becomes the distinguishing mark of a school or movement. Thus, American SF as a whole, from the thirties into the sixties, is generally utopian. In its deep structure Bradbury's dystopia-utopia is typical of the rest. It shares with Heinlein's rhapsodies of powerful, charismatic individuals and Asimov's ironic fables about economic triumph a common assurance that whatever new will occur will not in any deep way disrupt a set of values that conform closely to what might be called "Americanism." There are numerous historical reasons for this cautious utopianism: the perceived threats of Communism on one side and Fascism on the other, the war, the precarious sense that a "positive" attitude was the only way out of economic depression. There are also, of course, lazier reasons: the inertia of popular forms, the use of popular literature for blatant propaganda.

In such a context, the antithesis to the prevailing utopian-dystopian mode is not a genuine anti-utopianism, but an ironic comedy which, far from meditating on the ways opposing truths can be made to co-exist, enjoys debunking all truth. Contradiction here is not enlightening; it simply proves the futility of real thought, the impossibility of discovering or instituting new ideas. The works of such perceptive writers as Tenn, Sheckley, or Vonnegut, outrageous as they can sometimes be, are finally trapped in the dilemma of the prevailing utopianism. Vonnegut's colloquialized Zen ("So it goes") is a resignation to the overwhelming undeniability of the world as it is. The contradictions he perceives merely prove that humans are inconsistent, that society is thoughtlessly cruel, and that, to quote Winnie Verloc, Life does "not stand looking into very much." Such comedy may remind us of some of Wells's ironic tales of incompetence—"The Empire of the Ants," "The Man Who Could Work Miracles," the opening section of *The Food of the Gods*—but it is a far cry from that passionate anti-utopianism of the great romances or even from the exhilarating uto-pianism of Wells's later projects.

Anti-utopia in Wells's *A Modern Utopia*

It is appropriate to close our investigation of Wells's logic by tipping the balance back. Let us look again at Wells's *A Modern Utopia*, for here, in a work which by its title and by the date of its writing we would expect to imitate the utopian style of *In the Days of the Comet*, we find traces of the anti-utopian irony reminiscent of the earlier work.

The narrator of *A Modern Utopia*, what Wells calls "the owner of the Voice," is an ironic device that Wells uses, not as a way of withholding full assent to the ideas he sets forth, but as a way of suggesting the contradictory fullness of human hopes and, therefore, as a way of expressing his anti-utopian awareness of the narrowness of his fervently held utopian ideas even as he declares them. The irony here is not satiric; it is like the wit T. S. Eliot praises in Andrew Marvell: "It involves, probably, a recognition, implicit in the expression of every experience, of other kinds of experience which are possible."[36] Wells's irony allows, perhaps forces, the reader to assume a stance that encompasses a more complex understanding than the speaker is able to render explicitly. The reader sees everything that the author sees *and* he sees those exceptions and flaws which a deep understanding must encompass but which the author cannot acknowledge without undermining the rational force and persuasiveness of his ideas. The irony is, therefore, partly a rhetorical device to absorb criticism at the loose edges of the work, but it is also a logical device that creates a double perspective. Thus, *A Modern Utopia*, like many sophisticated utopias, contains a strong anti-utopian element.

The Botanist who accompanies the Voice throughout *A Modern Utopia* and who dreams of rescuing his childhood sweetheart from "that scoundrel" (her husband) repeatedly draws our attention to the limits of utopia. While the Voice sees the Botanist as an instance of the kind of romantic sublimation that utopia will obviate, the Botanist hates the utopia in which domestic dramas such as the one in which he imagines himself playing the romantic hero will be unnecessary, even impossible. In the midst of rational idealizations we are reminded of the stubborn, self-indulgent irrationality of human nature. The Botanist, for all his foolishness—in some respects he reminds one strongly of the Curate in *The War of the Worlds*—imparts shading to the clear, bright imaginings of the Voice. Yet the Botanist is not simply against utopia. He is, in fact, a warped version of Wells himself; he wants a utopia, but he wants *his* utopia, not the Voice's, and his selfish sentimentalism leads him to be quite unhappy in the Voice's utopia. Wells clearly finds the Botanist comically puerile, but in other novels, such as *The Passionate Friends*, such a man, who secretly and even unconsciously nurses a hidden flame and who at the second chance bursts into full passion, is a sympathetic figure for him. The Botanist, therefore, must be seen not as a trivial negation but as the expression of a reality: the unpredictable individual who cannot conform to the utopianist's neat plan.

We can appreciate the anti-utopian subtlety of this device by observing that Wells gives us, as a foil to the Botanist, a foppish Utopian who declares himself in opposition to all the ideals of Utopia. "The world, he held, was overmanaged and that was the root of all evil" (p. 108). This man is too clearly trivial to be anti-utopian in the sense I am using the term; for Wells himself the root of all evil is the undermanagement of the world, and this silly figure is simply hypocritical and wrong. Like the Artilleryman in *The War of the Worlds*, this man looks to the collapse of civilization as a way of getting back to "nature" and to "human nature." As in the case of the Artilleryman, a deep hypocrisy underlies this stance, for he accepts all the benefits of the wondrous civilization he damns. Unlike the sentimental Botanist, this man, rather than generating any serious questions about the purpose and success of utopia, merely gives criticism of utopia a bad name.

Though the main thrust of *A Modern Utopia* is, as we would expect, utopian, Wells sprinkles an anti-utopian awareness throughout. The Voice's regret about bringing the Botanist along is an acknowledgment that social solutions are easy if we simplify humanity. Sometimes he remarks with a wary sense of self-criticism on how much "discipline and sacrifice" figure in his imaginings (pp. 209, 223). He can in the midst of meditations on social harmony interject an awareness of the serious problems energetic individuals pose: "What will Utopia do with Mr. Roosevelt?" (p. 26). Griffin and Nunez have not been forgotten.

Toward the end of *A Modern Utopia*, when he returns to the horrors of this world, the Voice has a moment when he doubts the value of utopian imaginings altogether. Our own world

> has a glare, it has a tumult and a vigour that shouts one down. It shouts one down, if shouting is to carry it. What good was it to trot along the pavement through this noise and tumult of life, pleading Utopia to that botanist? What good would it be to recommend Utopia in this driver's preoccupied ear?
>
> There are moments in the life of every philosopher and dreamer when he feels himself the flimsiest of absurdities, when the Thing in Being has its way with him, its triumphant way, when it asks in a roar, unanswerably, with a fine solid use of current vernacular, "What Good is all this—Rot about Utopias?" (pp. 324–25)

Here is the anti-utopian structure. Wells's utopia exists in an entirely ironic relation with what is, and if at the center are single-minded imaginings of a sane society, the whole is infiltrated by a pervasive awareness of "insanities."[37]

What we have, then, in *A Modern Utopia*, is a gesture back towards the familiar two-world system of the early scientific romances; this world and utopia are juxtaposed, and Wells delights in tracing the parallels in order to uncover where important difference is possible; the beautiful machine, the efficient hotel room, the election of the ugliest building, the treatment of motherhood as a service to the state— all are discovered as parallels with a difference to our own world. Yet

A Modern Utopia differs from the earlier two-world systems in that the contrast is not balanced; here there is clear choice as to which world is preferable. If the ironies of *The Time Machine* never resolve, here the utopia is pervasively good and "sane," whatever doubts we may continue to entertain, and our world, however much we like it and however much it shouts thought down, is severely undermanaged and "insane."

Once that important difference is granted, however, we can see how the freedoms of the two-world system continue to function in *A Modern Utopia*. They allow for what the Voice praises in Plato: "the experimental inconsistency of an enquiring man" (pp. 186–87). The utopia exists not as a prophecy, not even as a goal, but as an intellectual puzzle which is valuable not for its conclusions but for the exercise of imagination it demands.

In the last chapter Wells says this, and the image he uses is telling:

> For a time I sit restfully enjoying the Botanist's companionable silence, and thinking fragmentarily of those samurai and their Rules. I entertain something of the satisfaction of a man who has *finished building a bridge: I feel that I have joined together things that I had never joined before.* My Utopia seems real to me, very real. I can believe in it, until the metal chair-back gives to my shoulder blades, and Utopian sparrows twitter and hop before my feet. I have a pleasant moment of unhesitating self-satisfaction: I feel a shameless exultation to be there. For a moment I forget the consideration the Botanist demands; *the mere pleasure of completeness, of holding and controlling all the threads*, possesses me. (p. 313, my italics)

In this passage we see both the pure joy in "bridging," reminiscent of the taxidermist's fraudulent art and characteristic of Wells's earliest, anti-utopian work, and the more purely utopian "pleasure of completeness, of holding and controlling all the threads." This latter pleasure, though expressed with some wry irony, is distrustful of the openness and skepticism of irony itself. The passage accepts the structure of early Wells but strives to turn it to a less open yet more assured stance like that characteristic of Wells's later work.

Notes

Preface

1. V. S. Pritchett, "The Scientific Romances," in *The Living Novel* (New York: Reynal & Hitchcock, 1947), p. 122.

2. "'It occurs to me that his stories do not repose on very scientific bases. No, there is no *rapport* between his work and mine. I make use of physics. He invents. I go to the moon in a cannon-ball, discharged from a cannon. Here there is no invention. He goes to Mars in an airship, which he constructs of a metal which does away with the law of gravitation. *Ca c'est tres joli*,' cried Monsieur Verne in an animated way, 'but show me this metal. Let him produce it.'" Quoted in Patrick Parrinder, ed., *H. G. Wells: The Critical Heritage* (London: Routledge & Kegan Paul, 1972), pp. 101–2.

3. *Space Novels by Jules Verne (From the Earth to the Moon; All Around the Moon)*, Edward Roth, tr. (New York: Dover Publications, n.d.). Verne's art, so different from Wells's, has been the subject of much recent study. For a summary see Marc Angenot, "Jules Verne and French Literary Criticism," *Science-Fiction Studies* (1973), 1:33–37.

4. Huntington, "Science Fiction and the Future," in Mark Rose, ed., *Science Fiction: A Collection of Critical Essays* (Englewood Cliffs: Prentice-Hall, 1976), pp. 156–66.

5. Darko Suvin, "Estrangement and Cognition," in *Metamorphoses of Science Fiction* (New Haven: Yale University Press, 1979), pp. 3–15. This important essay was first published in a somewhat different form under the title "On the Poetics of the Science Fiction Genre," *College English* (1972), 34:372–83, and was reprinted in Rose, ed., *Science Fiction: A Collection of Critical Essays*, pp. 57–71.

6. See Paul A. Carter, *The Creation of Tomorrow: Fifty Years of Magazine Science Fiction* (New York: Columbia University Press, 1977).

7. Darko Suvin, "*The Time Machine* versus *Utopia* as Structural Models for SF," in *Metamorphoses of Science Fiction*, pp. 222–42.

8. Harris Wilson, ed., *Arnold Bennett and H. G. Wells: A Record of a Personal and a Literary Friendship* (Urbana: University of Illinois Press, 1960), p. 74.

9. René Wellek, "The Parallelism between Literature and the Arts," *English Institute Annual: 1941* (New York: Columbia University Press, 1942), pp. 29–63.

10. Bernard Bergonzi, *The Early H. G. Wells: A Study of the Scientific Romances* (Manchester: Manchester University Press, 1961); Robert M. Philmus, *Into the Unknown: The Evolution of Science Fiction from Francis Godwin to H. G. Wells* (Berkeley and Los Angeles: University of California Press, 1970); Mark R. Hillegas, *The Future as Nightmare: H. G. Wells and the Anti-utopians* (New York: Oxford University Press, 1967); Patrick Parrinder, *H. G. Wells* (New York: Putnam, 1970). Important essays on Wells have been collected in Bernard Bergonzi, ed., *H. G. Wells: A Collection of Critical Essays* (Englewood Cliffs, N.J.: Prentice-Hall, 1976), and Darko Suvin and Robert Philmus, eds., *H. G. Wells and Modern Science Fiction* (Lewisburg: Bucknell University Press, 1977). The standard biography is Norman and Jeanne MacKenzie, *H. G. Wells* (New York: Simon and Schuster, 1973).

11. Except where otherwise indicated, all quotations from H. G. Wells will be from *The Works of H. G. Wells*, Atlantic Edition, 28 vols. (London: T. Fisher Unwin, 1924-27). Hereafter cited as Atlantic Edition.

Chapter 1. The Logic of Evolution and Ethics

1. For Wells's influence see Mark R. Hillegas, *The Future as Nightmare: H. G. Wells and the Anti-utopians*, and W. Warren Wagar, *H. G. Wells and the World State* (New Haven: Yale University Press, 1961).

2. For instance, in 1915 J. D. Beresford, in a book intended to promote Wells, treats the early scientific romances as interesting for Wells's biography, but unimportant otherwise. "*The Island of Dr. Moreau, The Invisible Man* and *The War of the Worlds* are essays in pure fantasy, and although the first of the three is influenced by biology I class it unhesitatingly among the works of sheer exuberance. Each of these books is, in effect, an answer to some rather whimsical question." *H. G. Wells* (New York: Henry Holt, 1915), p. 25. Such an attitude towards the early fiction was common into the middle fifties. One finds it in Kingsley Amis, *New Maps of Hell* (New York: Harcourt, Brace, 1960), a set of lectures drawing attention to the seriousness of science fiction. It isn't until Bergonzi's *The Early H. G. Wells* that the scientific romances begin to get the critical attention and analysis they deserve.

3. H. G. Wells, *The Work, Wealth and Happiness of Mankind* (Garden City: Doubleday, Doran, 1931). Chapter two of this work is entitled, "How Man has learnt to Think Systematically and gain a Mastery over Force and Matter," pp. 65–131.

4. Ibid., p. 69.

5. The ideal of scientific method that lies behind Wells's distinction has

come under severe critical scrutiny over the last fifty years from two directions. Karl Popper has challenged myths of induction in *The Logic of Scientific Discovery* (first published in German as *Logik der Forschung in* 1934) (1959; rpt, New York: Harper Torchbook, 1968). Thomas Kuhn has criticized the myth from a different direction by arguing that the "normal scientist" is never simply inductive but is solving a puzzle and showing how phenomena "fit" an accepted theory. See Thomas S. Kuhn, *The Structure of Scientific Revolutions*, 2d ed. (Chicago: University of Chicago Press, 1970). See also Imre Lakatos and Alan Musgrave, eds., *Criticism and the Growth of Knowledge: Proceedings of the International Colloquium in the Philosophy of Science, London, 1965, Volume 4* (Cambridge; Cambridge University Press, 1970).

6. Originally published in 1945, this short work has been reprinted in G. P. Wells, ed., *The Last Books of H. G. Wells* (Tiptree, England: Anchor Press, 1968). This confused work has assumed a value for humanists just because it is pessimistic. It is seen as Wells's "Elegiac Stanzas."

Anthony West argues that the pessimism evident here at the end of Wells's life is not a renunciation of his previous optimism, but a reversion "to his originally profoundly-felt beliefs about the realities of the human situation." "H. G. Wells," in *Principles and Persuasions* (London: Eyre Spottiswoode, 1958), p. 6. The issue of Wells's optimism and pessimism used to divide Wellsians. I do not propose to enter the controversy beyond noting that I find West's interpretation of his father convincing. Wells seems a pessimist of the optimistic school described by Ashley Montagu:

> We are living in a time of crisis, and I would suggest that the only philosophically tenable position for even a pessimist in a time of crisis is optimisim—but not the old style optimism which defined the optimist as one who believes that this is the best of all possible worlds and the pessimist as one who is very much afraid that the optimist is right. But rather I think the only practical definition for an optimist in our own time is one who believes that the future is uncertain. It will very definitely be certain if we go on as we have been and do virtually nothing about it.

This is part of Montagu's response to a speech by Loren Eiseley at the "Inter-Century Seminar" at the University of Kansas in 1967. James Gunn, ed., *Man and the Future* (Lawrence, Kansas: University of Kansas Press, 1968), p. 42.

7. H. G. Wells, "The Rediscovery of the Unique," in Robert Philmus and David Y. Hughes, eds., *H. G. Wells: Early Writings in Science and Science Fiction* (Berkeley: University of California Press, 1975), pp. 30–31. Though proposed with a certain playfulness here, radical nominalism will become a serious position for Wells in later work. See "Scepticism of the Instrument" (a paper read to the Oxford Philsophical Society, November 8, 1903) Atlantic Edition, vol. 9.

8. H. G. Wells, "The Discovery of the Future," in *Anticipations and Other Papers* (Atlantic Edition, vol. 4), p. 367.

9. Wells's call for a science of the future has been taken up enthusiastically,

and the science of technological forecasting continues to acknowledge Wells's inspiration. See, for instance, two of the more thoughtful books on the subject: Bertrand de Jouvenel, *The Art of Conjecture*, tr. Nikita Lary (New York: Basic Books, 1967), p. 47, or Wendell Bell and James A Mau, eds., *The Sociology of the Future* (New York: Russell Sage Foundation, 1971), p. 16. For a study of technological forecasting from a literary point of view, see Charles Elkins, "Science Fiction Versus Futurology: Dramatic Versus Rational Models," *Science-Fiction Studies* (1979), 6:20–31.

10. This list of disasters alludes to the themes of a number of Wells's scientific romances. Certainly earlier in his career Wells could contemplate such disaster much more sanguinely. One has only to think of the end of *The Time Machine*.

11. Karl Popper, *The Poverty of Historicism* (New York: Harper Torchbooks, 1961), p. 58 et passim. To my mind Popper's criticism of the *scientific* value of historicism is conclusive, though I would not therefore follow him in his general devaluation of all historicist arguments. And though historicism may be unscientific, its criticism of naturalistic methods of analysis may remain valid.

12. *Early Writings in Science and Science Fiction*, p. 158.

13. Ibid., p. 30. The whole essay is an exercise in nominalist paradox. In their introduction to this collection of Wells's early essays, Philmus and Hughes point to Wells's anticipation of something like the modern scientific idea of *complementarity*, according to which two contradictory truths can be entertained at the same time; p. 6.

14. Ibid., p. 27. Wells again quotes this line of Feste's at the end of *Twelfth Night* near the conclusion of "Zoological Retrogression." Ibid., p. 167.

15. The importance of T. H. Huxley to Wells's education has been much commented upon; see especially Norman and Jeanne Mackenzie, *H. G. Wells*, pp. 53ff. Wells himself throughout his life acknowledged Huxley's influence. In the letter to Arnold Bennett quoted in the Preface he asks Bennett to include a "casual allusion" to Huxley in the article he is writing. Later Wells would declare, "That year I spent in Huxley's class, was beyond all question, the most educational year of my life." H. G. Wells, *Experiment in Autobiography* (New York: Macmillan, 1934), p. 161.

16. In what follows on Darwin and Darwinism I am covering familiar ground. I am, however, particularly indebted to the invaluable collection of selections from Darwin and commentary on him in Philip Appleman, ed., *Darwin* (New York: Norton, 1970).

17. Gertrude Himmelfarb, *Darwin and the Darwinian Revolution* (1959; rpt. New York: Norton, 1968), p. 290. Huxley's own version of the event is in T. H. Huxley, *Life and Letters* (London: Macmillan, 1900), 1:188.

18. Sir Richard Owen, "Darwin on the Origin of Species" [*Edinburgh Review* (1860), 111] in Appleman, ed., *Darwin*, p. 296. Himmelfarb comments on this passage, p. 278.

19. See, for instance, the passage from the Second Notebook (February–July 1838) in Appleman, ed., *Darwin*, p. 79.

20. Charles Darwin, *The Origin of Species* (1859), ed. J. W. Barrow (Harmondsworth: Penguin, 1968), pp. 68–69. Italics added.

21. One can of course argue for domination on other grounds, and one can, though the argument is tricky, argue that even separation does not allow for domination, but by far the easiest and most common argument casually appeals to "their" "otherness" as a release from ethical obligations. Often, to be sure, inferiority is also implied.

22. Owen, "Darwin," p. 298.

23. Ernst Mayr, "Agassiz, Darwin, and Evolution" [*Harvard Library Bulletin*, (1959) 13] in Appleman, ed., *Darwin*, p. 302.

24. *The Origin of Species*, p. 456.

25. Himmelfarb, p. 279. Ernst Mayr, *Populations, Species and Evolution* (Cambridge: Harvard University Press, 1970), p. 12 et passim.

26. Mayr's clear discussion of the "typological," "nominalistic," and "biological" species concepts is very useful: ibid., pp. 10–13. For Darwin's nominalism, see Mayr, "Species Concepts and Definitions," in Mayr, ed., *The Species Problem* (The American Association for the Advancement of Science Publication, 1957), 50:1–22. Morse Peckham makes much of the nominalist direction of Darwin's additions to the fourth chapter of *The Origin of Species* in the 4th edition:"Darwin and Darwinisticism," in Appleman, ed., *Darwin*, pp. 386, 391–92. I find the passages universally more ambiguous than Peckham implies.

27. *The Origin of Species*, p. 455.

28. Quoted in Himmelfarb, p. 269.

29. T. H. Huxley, *Man's Place in Nature* (1863; rpt. Ann Arbor: University of Michigan Press, 1959), p. 130.

30. T. H. Huxley, *Evolution and Ethics and Other Essays* (1896; rpt. New York: AMS Press, 1970), p. 58. Huxley's insistence on the injustice of nature may be partly in response to Peter Kropotkin's *Mutual Aid* which was being published as a series of essays between 1890 and 1896. Kropotkin was challenging the thesis, maintained by both Darwin and Huxley, that competition is the dominant factor in natural selection and was arguing for the importance of cooperation in nature. See Ashley Montagu, *Darwin: Competition and Cooperation* (New York: Henry Schuman, 1952), p. 39. The issues of this debate have recently been revived by E. O. Wilson in *Sociobiology: The New Synthesis* (Cambridge: Harvard University Press, 1975). Short and not entirely representative selections from Darwin, Huxley, and Kropotkin can be found in Arthur L. Caplan, ed., *The Sociobiology Debate: Readings on Ethical and Scientific Issues* (New York: Harper & Row, 1978).

31. Mill's purpose is to criticize philosophies such as those of Montesquieu and Rousseau that attempt to develop an ethical imperative out of a natural fact. Central to his argument is a vision of amoral nature much like that pictured by Huxley: "In sober truth, nearly all the things which men are

hanged or imprisoned for doing to one another are nature's everyday performances." John Stuart Mill, *"Nature" and "Utility of Religion"* (New York: Bobbs-Merrill Library of Liberal Arts, 1958), p. 20.

32. Years later Sir Julian Huxley would make a very similar point in "Evolutionary Ethics" (1943) in Appleman, ed., *Darwin*, p. 406.

33. *Early Writings in Science and Science Fiction*, p. 217.

34. C. K. Ogden, *Opposition: A Linguistic and Psychological Analysis* (1932; rpt. Bloomington: Indiana University Press, 1967), pp. 58–59.

35. See Claude Lévi-Strauss, *The Savage Mind* (Chicago: University of Chicago Press, 1966), p. 9 et passim.

Chapter 2. Thinking by Opposition

1. Lest there be any doubt, Wells showed his skepticism about time travel in a review, which he wrote more than forty years after *The Time Machine*, of J. W. Dunne's *The New Immortality*. Dunne had claimed Wells as an inspiration for his theories about time. Wells demurs, saying that he was merely playing with paradoxes, not a theory of time. "The Immortality of Mr. J. W. Dunne," *The Nineteenth Century and After* (1939), 125:13–17.

2. All references to Wells's stories are from *The Complete Short Stories of H. G. Wells* (London: Ernest Benn, 1927).

3. *The Wonderful Visit*, Atlantic Edition, vol. 1, pp. 181–82.

4. "The Time Traveller was one of those men who are too clever to be believed: you never felt that you saw all round him; you always suspected some subtle reserve, some ingenuity in ambush, behind his lucid frankness." *The Time Machine*, Atlantic Edition, vol. 1, p. 15 (the beginning of chapter 2).

5. *Early Writings in Science and Science Fiction*, p. 217. Discussed in chapter 1, above.

6. Cf. Huxley, *Evolution and Ethics*, p. 55.

7. We can see this figure developed in isolation in another of Wells's earliest stories, "Through a Window."

8. Though a comparatively faceless presence, the scientific manager is structurally much like the bacteriologist in "The Stolen Bacillus": both are opposed to anarchic figures but linked to allies whom they find somewhat antipathetic.

Chapter 3. *The Time Machine*

1. The novella has often been casually lumped with other of Wells's more obviously prophetic novels. The Dover text is entitled, *Three Prophetic Novels of H. G. Wells* and includes along with *The Time Machine*, "A Story of the Days

to Come" and *When the Sleeper Wakes*. The urge to see the novella as a serious exercise in extrapolation of the potentials of the human future persists. On the other hand, Robert Philmus, "The Logic of 'Prophecy' in *The Time Machine*," in Bernard Bergonzi, ed., *H. G. Wells: A Collection of Critical Essays* (Englewood Cliffs, N.J.: Prentice-Hall, 1976), pp. 56–68, despite his title, is not concerned with prediction. What he calls the "dimension of 'prophecy'" (p. 65) is a narrative device common to much fiction.

2. The structure of this decline has been analysed by Darko Suvin in "*The Time Machine* versus *Utopia* as Structural Models for SF," in *Metamorphoses of Science Fiction*, pp. 223–33.

3. The argument of this paragraph owes much to Fredric Jameson's seminal essay, "World Reduction in Le Guin: The Emergence of Utopian Narrative," *Science-Fiction Studies* (1975), 2:221–30.

4. "She always seemed to me, I fancy, more human than she was, perhaps because her affection was so human." *The Time Machine*, p. 82.

5. V. S. Pritchett's distaste for the "Faint squirms of idyllic petting" has found numerous sympathetic readers. See Pritchett's "The Scientific Romances," *The Living Novel*, p. 125.

6. Even when he meets the Eloi, the Time Traveller's first thoughts are violent: "They looked so frail that I could fancy flinging the whole dozen of them about like nine-pins" (p. 30). The obvious but important difference between this "fancy" and his treatment of the Morlocks is that here he is able to resist acting on such fantasies.

7. Mark M. Hennelly, Jr., "*The Time Machine*: A Romance of 'the Human Heart,'" *Extrapolation* (1979), 20:154–67, has observed the Sphinx and the faun as "unification of dual nature" (p. 163).

The Sphinx may have been suggested to Wells by a passage in Huxley: "However shocking to the moral sense this eternal competition of man against man and of nation against nation may be; however revolting may be the accumulation of misery at the negative pole of society, in contrast with that of monstrous wealth at the positive pole; this state of things must abide, and grow continually worse, so long as Istar holds her way unchecked. It is the true riddle of the Sphinx; and every nation which does not solve it will sooner or later be devoured by the monster itself has generated." "The Struggle for Existence in Human Society" (1888), in *Evolution and Ethics and Other Essays*, p. 212.

8. Bergonzi has sketched some basic oppositions: "The opposition of Eloi and Morlocks can be interpreted in terms of the late nineteenth-century class struggle, but it also reflects an opposition between aestheticism and utilitarianism, pastoralism and technology, contemplation and action, and ultimately, and least specifically, between beauty and ugliness, and light and darkness." *The Early H. G. Wells*, p. 61. Contemplation hardly seems appropriate to describe the Eloi.

9. This is a recurrent opposition and puzzle in science fiction of this cen-

tury. See my "From Man to Overmind: Arthur C. Clarke's Myth of Progress," in Joseph D. Olander and Martin Greenberg, eds., *Arthur C. Clarke* (New York: Taplinger, 1977), pp. 211–22.

10. No hint is given by the Time Traveller of the destination of his second voyage into time. Philmus, perhaps influenced by George Pal's film of 1960 (discussed below), twice suggests he returns to 802,701 ("The Logic of 'Prophecy' in *The Time Machine*," pp. 57, 67), but that seems doubtful. Such a return is certainly not one of the possibilities the narrator imagines in the "Epilogue."

11. "The Logic of 'Prophecy' in *The Time Machine*," p. 67.

12. See the last paragraph of "The Rediscovery of the Unique," *Early Writings in Science and Science Fiction*, pp. 30–31, discussed in chapter 1 above.

Chapter 4. The Logical Web

1. In *Out of the Silent Planet* C. S. Lewis makes Wells responsible for our culture's automatic xenophobic reactions. While Lewis may be accurate about how the culture has interpreted Wells, he misses the criticism of xenophobia implicit in Wells's work.

2. Cf. the passage in *Paradise Lost* describing Satan entering the serpent:

> In at his mouth
> The Devil entered, and his brutal sense,
> In heart or head, possessing soon inspired
> With act intelligential.   (IX, 187–190)

The word *brutal* may be read at first as a judgment on Satan, but almost as an afterthought we realize it is a literal characterization of the serpent.

3. For a somewhat different, more thematic and symbolic reading of this imagery in early Wells, see David Y. Hughes, "The Garden in Wells's Early Science Fiction," in Suvin and Philmus, eds., *H. G. Wells and Modern Science Fiction*, pp. 48–69.

4. Bergonzi sees the vulnerability as a flaw in the novel, not as an aspect of a dialectical inquiry into power. *The Early H. G. Wells*, p. 120.

5. Gaston Bachelard, *The Psychoanalysis of Fire*, tr. Alan C. M. Ross (Boston: Beacon Press, 1964), p. 7.

6. The Artilleryman is often taken as Wells's spokesman. See, for instance, Antonia Vallentin, *H. G. Wells: Prophet of Our Day*, tr. Daphne Woodward (New York: John Day, 1950), p. 122, or Bergonzi, *The Early H. G. Wells*, p. 138.

7. Quoted in Norman and Jeanne Mackenzie, *H. G. Wells*, p. 113.

8. Fredric Jameson makes this point as an aside in "Generic Discontinuities in SF: Brian Aldiss' *Starship*," *Science-Fiction Studies* (1973), 1:66. Bergonzi makes a similar point, *The Early H. G. Wells*, p. 134.

Chapter 5. Frustrating Balances

1. C. S. Lewis could say that it was the "best of its sort" that he had ever read (quoted in Hillegas, *The Future as Nightmare*, p. 135), and T. S. Eliot appreciated certain effects, the dawn on the moon in particular (Bergonzi, *The Early H. G. Wells*, p. 159). But the novel's success clearly depends on the reader's expectations, and modern readers tend to ask for a more directed satire. Bergonzi finds the irony insufficiently anchored (ibid., p. 163), and Hughes regrets the lack of "committed satire" ("The Garden in Wells's early Science Fiction," p. 57). These recent reservations point to a special quality of this novel that it will be one of my purposes to explicate.

2. Wells's model here is clearly Swift in Book 2 of *Gulliver's Travels* (Hillegas, *The Future as Nightmare*, p. 54; Hughes, "The Garden in Wells's early Science Fiction," p. 57). The irony possible in the last paragraphs of Wells's novel has not always been perceived, however. Cf. Hillegas.

3. For the significance of the garden, see Hughes, above note. Bergonzi notes a general parallel with *The Time Machine* in that both novels contrast a realistic opening with the "exotic world of the central narrative" (*The Early H. G. Wells*, p. 158).

4. Again I am indebted to Fredric Jameson, "World Reduction in Le Guin: the Emergence of Utopian Narrative," p. 224. Jameson makes the important argument that a world in which "human life is virtually without biological partners" is part of the process of "world-reduction" that shapes Le Guin's utopian method. Wells is here doing the same thing.

5. Hillegas stresses the fact that the division between the "intellectual classes and the workers" persists (*The Future as Nightmare*, p. 53). We need to note, however, that among the Selenites any such division of function does not cause conflict. In the moon there is none of the opposition that dominates *The Time Machine* or human societies.

6. Though I would agree with Hughes (p. 56) that the satire here is "uncommitted," I do not see that as the same kind of failure Hughes does. At this point Wells is working on a moral dilemma, not attacking a clear wrong.

7. In an interesting parallel to this issue, Sartre accuses anyone who studies humans as if they were ants of being an aesthete. Lévi-Strauss counters that ants present a still insurmountable complexity for human reason. *The Savage Mind*, pp., 246–47.

8. E. O. Wilson argues, "to adapt with serious intent, even in broad outline, the social system of a non-primate species would be insanity in the literal sense. Personalities would quickly dissolve, relationships disintegrate, and reproduction cease." *On Human Nature* (Cambridge: Harvard University Press, 1978), pp. 21–22.

9. Robert C. Elliott has argued for the interpenetration of the two modes. *The Shape of Utopia* (Chicago: University of Chicago Press, 1970). I here find them at odds, however. See chapter 7 below for further discussion of the issue.

10. Cf. Hillegas, *The Future as Nightmare*, pp. 49–50.

11. The structure of the chapter is "compound." Cf. "Lord of the Dynamos," discussed in chapter 2, above.

Denton's argument at the end of the chapter is close to that of the Artilleryman in *The War of the Worlds*, but here there is little of the potential for irony we saw in the earlier novel.

12. "A Story of the Days to Come" in *Three Prophetic Novels of H. G. Wells* (New York: Dover, 1960).

Chapter 6. The Dreams of Reason

1. The choice of Ethel has a didactic quality that is perhaps not adequate to the larger experience of the problem. Henry James found himself confused about *Love and Mr. Lewisham*; writing to Wells after receiving a copy of the novel, James said:

> I now *have* read it, and can speak with assurance. I have found in it a great charm and a great deal of the real thing—that is of the note of life, if not *all* of it (as distinguished from the said great deal.) Why I haven't found "all" I will some day try and tell you: it may be more feasible viva voce. Meanwhile be assured of my appreciation of your humour and your pathos—your homely truth and your unquenchable fancy. I am not quite sure that I see your *idea*—I mean your Subject, so to speak, as determined or constituted: but in short the thing is a bloody little chunk of life.

Leon Edel and Gordon N. Ray, eds., *Henry James and H. G. Wells, A Record of their Friendship* (Urbana: University of Illinois Press, 1958), p. 67.

2. Wells spells this out in *Anticipations*: "He will be a father of several children, I think, because his scientific mental basis will incline him to see the whole of life as a struggle to survive; he will recognize that a childless, sterile life, however pleasant, is essentially failure and perversion, and he will conceive his honour involved in the possession of offspring." *Anticipations*, Atlantic Edition, vol. 4, p. 93.

3. Chaffery might be seen here to sketch the beginnings of a sociology of knowledge. He strips truth and honesty of their absolute character and sees them as functions of a particular person in a particular context.

4. We should note that this is a position that a number of characters in early Wells have approximated. One thinks particularly of the tramp in *The Wonderful Visit* and the Artilleryman in *The War of the Worlds*.

5. Wells here is the name of spiritual insight flirts with the crassest materialism. It is against such an attitude that C. S. Lewis years later would direct his science fiction. Lewis attacked what he called the "metabiological heresy," the faith that the imperative of biological survival (i.e., the evolutionary imperative) has precedence over all ethical duties. For Lewis the opposite is true:

the evolutionary is completely trivial in the face of the higher, divinely sanctioned *tao*. See Lewis' *The Abolition of Man* (New York: Macmillan, 1947);
Hillegas, *The Future as Nightmare*, p. 140.

Karl Popper exposes the logical problem of Wells's position as it is rendered
by later evolutionists. See *The Poverty of Historicism*, p. 107.

6. "Human Evolution, an Artificial Process" (1896), discussed in chapter 1
above.

7. *A Modern Utopia*, Atlantic Edition, vol. 9.

8. *New Worlds for Old* (New York: Macmillan, 1908).

9. Wells is fond of this logical trick. We see it early in "The Rediscovery of
the Unique," where by arguing for absolute individualization, even of atoms,
Wells denies all scientific classification. Years later, in *The Open Conspiracy*
(Garden City: Doubleday Doran, 1928), p. 38, Wells will use it to discredit all
the categories of conventional economics.

10. Though Wells here denies a "real" basis to the present categories of
society, elsewhere in his writings of this period he easily falls into the social
Darwinist argument that under British capitalism traits conducive to racial
survival and human progress are selected while others, inimical to the struggle,
are de-selected. In such a view, present class distinctions in general have a
"real" basis in nature; to put it crudely, the rich are rich because they have
proven themselves more competent than the poor. The poor are poor, according to this argument, because they are genetically inferior. The urban
poor, Wells argues in *Anticipations*, is "a recruited class, not a breeding multitude" (p. 70), by which he means that the urban poor are who they are by
reason of individual failures to succeed in society, i.e., by "natural selection,"
not by the accident of having been born to poor parents in a society that
oppresses and stunts poor children. One has only to recall the passage at the
end of *The First Men in the Moon* on the shaping of a young Selenite to be
aware of how much more complexly and sensitively Wells has been thinking.
Wells is less a social Darwinist when it comes to the virtues of the rich
whom he sees as complacent and reactionary in a competitive, progressive
world, and therefore an "accidental" class. He would probably agree with J.
B. S. Haldane's wry insight (made, fittingly, in a Huxley Memorial Lecture) that
the selection that social class performs cannot be compared to the process
the animal breeder performs because among the higher classes in our society
there is no weeding out of the unfit. "Much of the effort of members of a
ruling class is devoted to finding niches within it for those of their children
who do not possess the characters needed to enter it from below. Were it not
for this fact humanity might by now have divided into several subspecies
corresponding to social classes, and aristocracy would be the only possible
form of government." "The Argument from Animals to Men: An Examination
of its Validity for Anthropology," in M. F. Ashley Montagu, ed., *Culture and the
Evolution of Man* (New York: Oxford University Press, 1962), p. 68.

11. The contrast between the way Wells depicts the giants and the way

Swift depicts Gulliver among the Lilliputians in Book 1 of *Gulliver's Travels* is striking. Swift never lets Gulliver be entirely superior to the Lilliputians. His supremacies are always tethered to his human foolishness. Wells sees his giants as offering a new, raw, but energizing vision that is beyond satiric criticism.

12. *Experiment in Autobiography*, p. 558.

13. Ibid., p. 666.

14. The story is recounted in Mackenzie, *H. G. Wells*, p. 432.

15. Wells was much impressed with Bloch's thesis and even as late as 1916 was applying it. See *What is Coming? A European Forecast* (New York: Macmillan, 1916), pp. 29–30.

16. Wells himself can sound very much like his fictional engineers: "Either before or after, but at any rate in the shadow of war, it will become apparent, perhaps even suddenly, that the whole apparatus of power in the country is in the hands of a new class of intelligent and scientifically-educated men. . . . [who will say] 'Suppose instead of our turning [our ingenious and subtle guns] and our valuable selves in a fools quarrel against the ingenious and subtle guns of other men akin to ourselves, we use them in the cause of the higher sanity, and clear that jabbering war tumult out of the streets.'" *Anticipations*, p. 153.

Chapter 7. Utopian and Anti-utopian Logic

1. We here acknowledge another area of Wells's art, immensely interesting, but tangential to our present concerns. We get a glimpse of this other dimension in *Love and Mr. Lewisham*. In the next decade Wells would publish a series of novels (*Kipps*, 1905, *Tono-Bungay*, 1909, *Ann Veronica*, 1909, *The History of Mr. Polly*, 1910, *The New Machiavelli*, 1911, *Marriage*, 1912, *The Passionate Friends*, 1913, *The Wife of Sir Isaac Harman*, 1914, *Boon*, 1915, *The Research Magnificent*, 1915, *Mr. Britling Sees it Through*, 1916) whose concern is not to imagine a future, but to see England as it is.

2. The utopia has been much studied recently, but it is not relevant to the issue I am here developing to worry definitions or history. The essence of *utopia*, as I am using the term here, resides in its presenting us with "a serious vision of society as a single intellectual pattern" (Northrop Frye, *Anatomy of Criticism* [Princeton: Princeton University Press, 1957], p. 310. Cf. Darko Suvin, "Defining the Literary Genre of Utopia: Some Historical Semantics, Some Genology [sic], a Proposal, and a Plea," in *Metamorphoses of Science Fiction*, p. 49). Under *dystopia* I include what Frye elsewhere calls "utopian satire" (Frye, "Varieties of Literary Utopia," in Frank E. Manuel, ed., *Utopias and Utopian Thought* [1965; rpt. Boston: Beacon Press, 1967], p. 19) and what many writers call *anti-utopia* (cf. Hillegas, *The Future as Nightmare*, pp. 3, 4, et passim, and Suvin, "Defining the Literary Genre of Utopia," pp. 61–62). I am reserving the

term *anti-utopia* for a mode of imagining which is critical not of the utopian political structure, but of the way of thought that constructs it. Thus, *anti-utopia*, in this formulation, is a different genre from *utopia*.

3. Suvin, "Defining the Literary Genre of Utopia," p. 49.

4. It is this deep structural identity that leads Lewis Mumford to see all utopian thought as totalitarian (see Lewis Mumford, "Utopia, the City, and the Machine," in Manuel, ed., *Utopias and Utopian Thought*, p. 9). Mumford uses the term *dystopia* in a strange way, however: though at times he seems to mean an oppressive and totalitarian structure such that all utopias are potentially dystopias, at other times he means chaos, "total destruction and extermination," (p. 18) the total rejection of order (p. 23). Such a definition seems too idiosyncratic to be useful. It certainly does not fit what are conventionally called dystopias.

5. Cf. Robert C. Elliott, *The Shape of Utopia: Studies in a Literary Genre*, pp. 22–24; Frye, *Anatomy of Criticism*, p. 310.

6. For example, in the description of the Utopian war policy More may be indulging in what I am calling anti-utopian thought even as he builds one of the great utopias. It may be that pure utopianism is possible only in what I would call naive utopias, that is, in those imaginative constructs such as *Looking Backward* and *Walden Two* which the author has serious hopes of realizing.

7. Though we might see in this charismatic figure a prefiguration of fascism, the charge of obscurity still holds. After all, one of the charges to be made against fascism is that it obfuscates true economic and political relationships by focusing on that leader's personality.

8. The blur here, as Bergonzi observes (*The Early H. G. Wells*, pp. 152–55) results in part at least from Wells's own sympathy with Ostrog's position.

9. In the Atlantic Edition Wells reprinted his later, extensively revised and retitled version of the novel. I have chosen to cite the first published version (1899; rpt. New York: Ace, n.d.).

10. Mackenzie, *H. G. Wells*, p. 150; Bergonzi, *The Early H. G. Wells*, pp. 140–41.

11. See note two above.

12. The importance of *When the Sleeper Wakes* in the history of SF and of utopian literature has been much commented on. My aim in what follows is not to trace a literary history but to define different utopian and anti-utopian modes. For the history, see R. D. Mullen, "H. G. Wells and Victor Rousseau Emanuel: *When the Sleeper Wakes* and *The Messiah of the Cylinder*," *Extrapolation* (1966), 8:31–63.

13. The contraries of *R.U.R.* appear to be quite conscious. Čapek himself describes them: "The General Manager Domin, in the play, proves that technical progress emancipates man from hard manual labour, and he is quite right. The Tolstoyan Alquist, on the contrary, believes that technical progress demoralizes him, and I think he is right, too. Bussman thinks that industrialism alone is capable of supplying modern needs; he is right. Ellen is instinctively

afraid of all this inhuman machinery, and she is profoundly right. Finally, the Robots themselves revolt against all these idealists, and, as it appears, they are right, too." Quoted from "The Meaning of *R.U.R.*" (1923), in Hillegas, *The Future as Nightmare*, p. 96.

14. For Stapledon's dialectic, see Mark Rose, *Alien Encounters* (Cambridge, Mass.: Harvard University Press, 1981), pp. 112–18, and John Huntington, "Olaf Stapledon and the Novel About the Future," *Contemporary Literature* (1981), 22.

15. The subtitle, which appears on the title page of the first edition (New York: Harper & Row, 1974), appears nowhere in the text of paperback edition.

16. *The Dispossessed*, pp. 89, 73.

17. Zamyatin's debt to Wells is great. See Hillegas, *The Future as Nightmare*, pp. 106–7; Patrick Parrinder, "Imagining the Future: Wells and Zamyatin," *Science-Fiction Studies* (1973), 1:17–26 (rpt. in Suvin and Philmus, eds., *H. G. Wells and Modern Science Fiction*, pp. 126–43); Christopher Collins, "Zamyatin, Wells and the Utopian Literary Tradition," *The Slavonic and East European Review* (1966), 44:351–60; Alex M. Shane, *The Life and Works of Evgenij Zamjatin* (Berkeley: University of California Press, 1968), pp. 140, 185. Zamyatin's essay on Wells (1922), which served as the introduction to the Soviet edition of Wells's works, may be found in Mirra Ginsburg, ed. and tr., *A Soviet Heretic: Essays by Yevgeny Zamyatin* (Chicago: University of Chicago Press, 1970), pp. 259–90, and, abridged, tr. Leslie Milne, in Patrick Parrinder, ed., *H. G. Wells: The Critical Heritage*, pp. 258–274.

18. Yevgeny Zamyatin, *We*, tr. Mirra Ginsburg (New York: Bantam, 1972), p. 80.

19. Zamyatin, "On Literature, Revolution, Entropy, and Other Matters," in *A Soviet Heretic*, pp. 107–8. Zamyatin's concept of entropy, though it claims the sanction of scientific metaphor, is antithetical to what physicists mean by the word. For Zamyatin entropy is a deadening order. In physics order takes energy, and entropy entails an increasing disorder.

20. Ibid., p. 110.

21. It might be argued that Wells is generating a similar confusion when he gives Ostrog arguments close to his own ideas, but though the irony has interesting biographical implications, it does not seem intentional. Certainly Wells's novel does not insist on paradox in other ways.

22. See Orwell's review of *We* in Sonia Orwell and Ian Angus, eds., *The Collected Essays, Journalism and Letters of George Orwell*, 4 vols. (New York: Harcourt, Brace & World, 1968), 4:72–75. For Orwell's debt to Wells's *When the Sleeper Wakes*, see Hillegas, *The Future as Nightmare*, p. 125.

23. See Robert Philmus, "The Language of Utopia," *Studies in the Literary Imagination* (1973), 6:76–77.

24. George Orwell, *Nineteen Eighty-Four* (New York: New American Library, 1961), p. 182.

25. Cf. Truffaut's comment about making the film of *Fahrenheit 451*: "I've preferred the character of Linda, conventional but touching, to that of Clarisse,

more heavily conventional because pseudo-poetic." Francois Truffaut, "The Journal of *Fahrenheit 451*," in William Johnson, ed., *Focus on the Science Fiction Film* (Englewood Cliffs, N.J.: Prentice-Hall, 1972), p. 123.

26. Quotations are from *Fahrenheit 451* (New York: Ballantine Books, 1953).

27. It may be foolish to take Bradbury's meanings seriously. Clifton Fadiman in his forward to *The Martian Chronicles* (New York: Bantam, 1951), p. viii, found in Bradbury a deep pessimism about technology, especially space travel, but in recent years Bradbury has been one of the most fervent boosters of the space program. See his fulsome praise of space flight as a religious exercise in "From Stonehenge to Tranquillity Base," *Playboy*, December 1972. Of course the man may have changed his mind, but the style and imagery of his writing remains the same, and I suspect we have here evidence, not of a reversal, but of confused broadmindedness.

28 Huxley disclaimed any knowledge of *We* when writing *Brave New World*, but Hillegas makes the reasonable surmise that as an alert intellectual in the twenties Huxley would know about Zamyatin's novel even if he had not actually read it. *The Future as Nightmare*, p. 186n2.

29. The simplicity of these basic values is somewhat obscured in the novel by being overlayed with a secondary opposition between modern and primitive societies. Huxley himself, in his 1946 "Foreword" to *Brave New World*, focuses on this issue as a Hobson's choice between "insanity" and "lunacy." *Brave New World & Brave New World Revisited* (New York: Harper Torchbooks, 1960), p. xiv. There are some possibilities for anti-utopian thought here, but this anti-utopian puzzle is really a tub distracting us from the novel's championing of a despairing individualism against all forms of social organization.

30. Here, like Kuno and Vashti in Forster's "The Machine Stops" he achieves a "spiritual" escape.

31. "The Savage's outburst against his beloved, then, is not so much the protest of pure human nature against the cold impudence of fashion, as was perhaps intended; rather, poetic justice turns it into the aggression of the neurotic who, as the Freud whom Huxley treats rather shabbily could easily have told him, is motivated in his frantic purity by repressed homosexuality." Theodor W. Adorno, "Aldous Huxley and Utopia," in *Prisms*, trans. Samuel and Shierry Weber (London: Neville Spearman, 1967), p. 106.

32. My comparison agrees essentially with that made briefly by Jerome Meckier, *Aldous Huxley: Satire and Structure* (New York: Barnes and Noble, 1969), p. 187.

33. This much-reprinted story can be found in Le Guin's collection, *The Wind's Twelve Quarters* (New York: Harper & Row, 1975).

34 Adorno, pp. 103–4.

35. Cf. Hillegas, *The Future as Nightmare*, p. 119.

36. T. S. Eliot, "Andrew Marvell," in *Selected Essays: 1917–1932* (New York: Harcourt, Brace, 1932), p. 250.

37. A similar point has been developed by David Y. Hughes, "The Mood of *A Modern Utopia*," *Extrapolation* (1977), 19:56–67.

Index

Adorno, T.W., 166, 185*n*31
"Æpyornis Island," 60–61, 126
Agassiz, Louis, 12
Aliens, xiii, 57–70; species in Darwin, 9, 11, 12; in *The Time Machine*, 43–44, 48, 50, 51; in *The War of the Worlds*, 63; in *The Island of Doctor Moreau*, 67; in *The First Men in the Moon*, 89, 96; dismissed in *Anticipations*, 119; in *A Modern Utopia*, 124
Amis, Kingsley, 172*n*2
Ann Veronica, 182*n*1
Anticipations, xii, 2, 97, 114, 116–19, 120, 131, 134, 180*n*2, 181*n*10, 182*n*16
Anti-utopia defined, xiv, 142–43; and utopia, 139–170
Arnold, Matthew, 113
Asimov, Isaac, 166

Bachelard, Gaston, 76
Bell, Wendel, 173–74*n*9
Bellamy, Edward, *Looking Backward*, 183*n*6
Bennett, Arnold, Wells's letter to, xii, 4, 85, 109, 114, 174*n*15
Beresford, J.D., 172*n*2
Bergonzi, Bernard, xv, 177*n*8, 178*n*4, 178*n*8, 179*n*1, 179*n*3, 183*n*8
Bloch, Jean de, 135
Books: in Pal's *The Time Machine*, 54, 55; in Bradbury's *Fahrenheit 451*, 163
Boon, The Mind of the Race, 182*n*1
Bradbury, Ray: *Fahrenheit 451*, xiv, 148, 149, 160–64, 166; *The Martian Chronicles*, 185*n*27; "From Stonehenge to Tranquillity Base," 185*n*27
Brooks, Cleanth, *The Well Wrought Urn*, xv
Brower, Ruben, xv

Čapek, Karel: *R.U.R.*, 149; *The War with the Newts*, 149; "The Meaning of *R.U.R.*," 183–84*n*13
Categories: in Darwin, 10; in *A Modern Utopia*, 124
Change: problem of in "A Story of the Days to Come," 101, 104–6, 107; Wells's difficulty depicting, 148
Clarke, Arther C., 177–78*n*9
Communism, 166
Complementarity, 174*n*13
Conrad, Joseph, *The Secret Agent*, 167
Contradiction, *see* Opposition
"Country of the Blind, The," 54, 58, 126–29, 130, 164, 169
Creationist theory, 12
"Crystal Egg, The," 22
Cut, as logical device, 17–18, 31, 40, 45, 46

Darkness, in *The Time Machine*, 79–80
Darwin, Charles: *The Origin of Species*, xiii, 8–13, 15, 16; *Notebooks*, 10
"Deal in Ostriches, A," 27–28
"Diamond Maker, The," 28, 88
Directed thought, xii–xiii, 2, 4, 7, 18, 139; *see also* Undirected thought
"Discovery of the Future, The" (The Royal Institution Lecture), xii, 4–6, 7, 8, 114, 115